CW00660223

NOBODY WILL
SHOOT YOU
IF YOU MAKE
THEM LAUGH

Dedication:
To my family and many friends

~⁓~

'Life is to be fortified by many friendships.
To love and to be loved is the greatest
happiness of existence'
Sydney Smith
English Clergyman, 1771–1845

NOBODY WILL SHOOT YOU IF YOU MAKE THEM LAUGH

SIMON MURRAY

ONE MAN'S JOURNEY THROUGH THE
MOUNTAINS AND VALLEYS OF LIFE

UNICORN

This edition first published in the UK by Unicorn
an imprint of the Unicorn Publishing Group LLP, 2021
5 Newburgh Street
London W1F 7RG

www.unicornpublishing.org

10 9 8 7 6 5 4 3 2 1

ISBN 978-1-913491-77-2

Typesetting by Vivian@Bookscribe

Printed in the UK by Jellyfish

CONTENTS

PREFACE

Once, whilst travelling in Africa, I very nearly met my end. And it was not during my time in the Foreign Legion. Four of us were in a jeep driving from South Africa to Botswana. Botswana and South Africa were technically at war with each other at the time. Looking at the map as we set off, I explained to my companions that the drive on the highway was approximately 150 miles but we could take a shortcut through the woods that would reduce the distance by nearly sixty miles. I mentioned possible dangers of going through the woods, such as a breakdown of the car, animals, unfriendly warriors and the rest but we all agreed the woods was the best way. And so to the woods it was.

After travelling across the border into Botswana, we came to a village. A village of some forty-odd mud huts. No concrete buildings. Fires were burning outside all the huts. Clearly it was lunchtime. I stopped the jeep in the middle of the village and as I did so, we were surrounded by aggressive looking locals with sub machine guns.

They made us get out of the jeep..I was showing them our British passports and telling them we were English, not South Africans. It fell on deaf ears. They made us sit on a rock for three hours and raised their guns if one of us even coughed.

Twenty yards away was a tent open on both sides where we could see the chief of the village. He was seated at a small table with his chin in his hands and his elbows on the table, watching us. He did not move in those three hours. Our passports were on the table in front of him and I had the impression he was daring us to make a run for them.

Eventually, very slowly, I stood up. The guns came up and I made gestures to show I wanted to speak to the boss. Slowly, very slowly, I walked towards the tent with the four machine guns two inches behind me and lots of mumblings.

In front of the boss's table was a small stool and I sat down and looked at him. He still did not move.

There was a woman on the floor beside him stirring some sort of gruel.

Very slowly, so that I was hardly moving at all, I took a coin from my pocket and held it in front of the boss in between my forefinger and thumb. He glared at it in silence. I said not a word and I brought my left hand over the coin and then suddenly opened both my hands wide in his face and held them there. The coin was gone.

His face was a mixture of wonder and amazement with a slight trace of fear.

And then the woman on the floor pointed at me and said, 'You… Magician?'

I said 'Yes,' keeping my open palms in place.

And she said, pointing at the boss, 'He, my husband… Can you make him disappear?'

It took all my self-restraint to keep my cool and not dissolve into laughter, but with a straight face I said, 'Yes. But if I make him disappear, very difficult to bring him back.'

And she said 'Good, good, good.'

And *he* said, 'Nor, Nor, Nor, I don't wanna disappear.'

He grabbed the passports and thrust them into my outstretched hands and said, 'Go. Go. Go.'

And we were into the jeep and out of there with a great wave to the boss's wife.

The moral of the story is, when travelling in remote areas always have a trick or joke ready. Jokes don't always work, because sometimes jokes don't cross frontiers, but a trick will always open the gate.

CHAPTER I

THE LEGIONNAIRE

...You smug-faced crowd with glittering eye
Who cheer when soldier-lads march by,
Sneak home and pray you'll never know
The hell where youth and laughter go

Siegfried Sassoon

Sergeant Dornach got to work on the heads with a small, sharp penknife, cutting across the necks. I was numb inside and felt nothing as I watched him hack away, with bloodied hands. It was like something from *Macbeth*. His face was devoid of any expression and he could well have been skinning a rabbit. It took him an hour to remove the three heads.

By this time our company, two miles further down the valley, fearing trouble, had sent men back to look for us. I could hear them calling our names. Dornach put his bloodied finger to his lips for silence. He did not want us to be found by any enemy lurking in the vicinity cutting heads off their compatriots.

The shouts came closer and suddenly I heard my name called from a few yards away and I yelled back in response. Dornach dropped his knife, grabbed his machine gun and pointed it straight at me. He was seething, hissing at me to shut my fucking mouth or he would blow my guts out.

He finished his work and gave me two of the heads to carry in my musette, my punishment for calling out. The third head we left... it was unrecognisable.

Down the valley we trudged, the heads dripping blood in my sack and onto my sleeping bag, over my rations, and down my back. Heads are heavy. It took us another three hours to get back to the camp by which time it was dark and the other legionnaires were cooking their sparse rations over campfires.

An officer from the Deuxième Bureau, the French intelligence service, came over to inspect the heads by the lights of a jeep. He confirmed from photographs in his file that they were Arabs serving in the French regular army, who had deserted after killing their French officers and joined the Fellagha rebels.

Five hours earlier, when we had reached the valley bottom the first time, we had been met by the officer of the Deuxième Bureau, and Dornach had been instructed to go back with two volunteers, (as if anyone would actively volunteer for this grisly task), which ended up being Auriemma and myself. We were to bring back the heads of the three Arabs we had shot earlier in the day for identification purposes. Cameras would have been helpful, but we hadn't thought of that. It was dangerous stuff. If any Fellagha were lurking around and found us cutting heads off their mates, they might turn nasty.

The heads matched the photos in the Deuxième officer's files. Mission accomplished. Revenge complete.

The Arabs serving in the French armed forces were known as Les Harkis. They fought alongside us many times. They were fine soldiers, but as the war dragged on some began to have their doubts as to which side they should be on.

I was told to get rid of the heads, which I did, carrying them by their blood-soaked hair, one in each hand, and tossing them into the bushes. But the day wasn't over yet. Some Spaniards in the Second Section had made a small cauldron of soup by adding water to the dehydrated soup packets in our rations. They had all eaten and there was still soup left over. Unusual!

They hailed a German legionnaire, named Schreiber, and invited him to fill up his tin mug. Just as he was about to put the soup to his lips, one of the Spaniards reached into the cauldron and pulled out by the hair one of the heads that he had found in the bushes. Schreiber, who was much disliked, froze for a second, turned white, and then started shouting for 'Ruth', at the same time giving us a display of his innermost feelings. Everyone laughed, except Schreiber. I laughed too; there are times when I still worry about that laughter.

After finishing our bouff at the campfires, we boarded our trucks and drove back to Medina, our advanced base camp. Exhausted after nearly twenty hours of being on patrol, we just about had the energy to take down the tents. Towards midnight we set off in our GMC trucks for another four-hour drive to our new base camp in the Chelia Mountains. My thoughts turned to Christmas, just days away! Jingle bells all the way!

This extract from my earlier book *Legionnaire* recounts how, when I was nineteen years old I arrived in Algeria and after a week at Sidi Bel Abbès, the Legion headquarters, I was sent to Mascara for basic training. After three months of the toughest physical and mental exercise I had ever done in my life, I was assigned to the 2nd Parachute Regiment, where I did my jumps and got my 'wings'.

Training in any tough outfit is rigorous, whether it's the SAS, Marines or the Parachute Regiment but the Legion is different. Another world entirely. We were not with our own people; we were not in our own country. I was the only Englishman in my regiment of 850 men. About half were German, twenty per cent Italian and the balance spread from across the world. There were fifty-five nationalities in the Legion. No French, legally. It is the *Foreign* legion. The French do serve, but they get in as Swiss or Belgians.

Algeria was like being on the moon. No telephone calls to Mum; no weekends to go home; nobody near you with whom you had anything in common; all speaking different languages, none of which I understood, and all under a reign of terror administered by non-commissioned officers, who were set on teaching us to understand that *La Legion* means 'discipline' above all else.

After the Mascara training, we were sent to our different regiments. I was sent for parachute training for two months and then on to operations in the Aurès Mountains.

There was a routine to our lives from then on. For three months or so we would be out patrolling the Khabylie and Aurès mountains, the huge mountain range in the southern part of the country, flushing out the Fellagha, as the rebel fighters were called.

They were fighting for independence from France. It had been a bloody war with plenty of misdeeds on both sides, where the eyes of the Geneva Convention were not upon us. The drill was always the same: we would

arrive at a particular place, pitch our large tents at what was to be an
'advance' base camp from which we would go into the mountains for
six or seven days at a time, carrying fifty-five-pound backpacks with our
rations and ammunition, half a tent, shovels, hand grenades, a couple of
hundred rounds of ammunition and a machine gun. We would trudge in
the mountains, searching every nook and cranny for the enemy. At night we
would lie in ambush for them in the freezing darkness.

Occasionally we would make contact. An *accrochage*. Bullets and hand
grenades would start flying everywhere. Ten dead Arabs, two wounded
legionnaires. That was the average ratio in any skirmish.

Their rules did not allow them to engage with the Legion because they
would always get the worst of it. They would attack regular army convoys
and French villages, but not the Legion. We had to find them. We had
spotter planes to help us, but the reality was endless patrolling through the
mountains and our best weapon was the element of surprise.

We were good at that. We would rise at 2am, march through the hills
for 15km, board our trucks and drive for 50 more and then march again
for another 20km. By dawn we could be on a hillcrest overlooking a valley
miles away from where we had been the previous evening. They never knew
where we were going to be. But we used to find them, and when we did it
was a surprise... for them.

Periodically we returned to the advance base camp, which itself was
moved every three weeks. Here we would have a day of rest and some
cooked food, and then be on the move again.

We were tireless machines. Day after day, we would march for miles.
Nights were short, interrupted by guard duty. Each day was the same. We
rose at dawn and marched for hours to get into positions for the *fouillage*.
Lined up across the top of a massive valley, where spotter planes had seen
enemy movement and the search for the Fellagha would begin. A second
company would land by helicopter at the bottom of the valley and block
the exit.

A quick cup of coffee and a chunk of cheese and forwards. If there were
Fellagha in the valley, they would know they were trapped with the arrival
of the helicopters and they would make a stand. They had no choice.

They had some advantage. Their guns were cocked, and they could watch us from their positions, in a tree perhaps or a cave as we descended into the valley. Our guns were not cocked. Too dangerous with legionnaires ten yards on either side. One slip, a trigger pulled accidentally and a wounded buddy next to you. The Fellagha often fired first.

But it would be their last shot.

The search down the valley could sometimes take six hours or longer. We were often short of water, our throats parched. There's nothing worse than knowing there would be no water for coffee in the morning when we kipped down at night. But we were as tough as the leather boots we wore. Our bodies were sinewy without a trace of fat. We combined the qualities of the mule and the camel and we could march for miles in the sweltering heat of the day or in the freezing cold of the night, when the rain sometimes fell for hours.

We were immune to the pain in our backs from carrying our sacks. There were no nerves in our feet where the burst blisters suppurated. Sometimes we didn't see our feet for days as it was considered unwise to be without one's boots on at night.

Every three months or so we returned to our main camp at Philippeville on the coast for two weeks of rest and repos: R and R. Most of the time was taken up with kit inspection and guard duty. But we did get some evenings in town. There were bars, bordellos and, sometimes, bad behaviour. Les citoyens de la ville loved and hated us.

They loved us because we kept Algérie Francaise, and they disliked us for our antics. They certainly didn't regard us as potential boyfriends for their daughters.

The discipline was harsh. Standard punishment for being late for roll call or drunk and disorderly behaviour was eight days prison with La Pelote twice a day. This meant one's head was shaved, steel helmet on head, without the inside padding, a sack of rocks on your back with wire shoulder straps, boots without laces and then a run around in a circle for two hours.

A sergeant in the middle of the circle would blow a whistle: one blast forward roll, two blasts march with knees bent (marche canard) and three blasts, crawl. Any slowness in the pace was met with a rope lash on the back.

The 'prison' was a Nissan hut with a concrete floor. Each man was issued with a mat and a blanket. Reveille was at 4:30am. The first chore, cleaning lavatories, was followed by two hours of La Pelote. Breakfast was a chunk of bread and a cup of coffee. Then off to a marble quarry, sledgehammering rocks and loading them on to trucks. Lunch was usually hot soup with chunks of rotten meat eaten out of our *gamelles* (tin plates), plus a chunk of stale bread and a tin of sardines to be eaten while standing to attention in line under the watchful eyes of guards with machine guns.

After 'lunch' which lasted fifteen minutes, it was back to the quarry; rock bashing into the evening, then back to camp for another hour of *La Pelote*.

The finale was a cold shower, then the ceremony of the flag and on into the prison. There were no problems in sleeping on the concrete floor after a day like that.

Never slept better.

I accumulated a total of fifty-eight days in prison while in the Legion. Most of which was on operations, where there was no physical prison and you simply had eight days knocked off your pay. But I had two lots of fifteen days. One for getting into a fight in Algiers with some Arab civilians and another fifteen for supposedly being drunk on guard duty at Philippeville.

After two years' service, I had been granted two weeks' leave at a rest camp in Philippeville. Fantastic. A blast of freedom. You had to check into the camp once a day at any hour, night or day. The rest of the time you were free to roam. On my last day of leave I was told to be back at the main base camp at 6am the following morning and to be ready for guard duty. I never got the message… as they say!

I went out that night, my last day of freedom. Got to bed at 5am and was dragged out of it again at 5am and trucked up to the main base camp. I had an hour to get myself together, iron my uniform and make sure my kepi was whiter than white and be ready to report for guard duty.

The sergeant of the guard, named Reiper, was due to exit the Legion the following day and was in transit from Djibouti, where he had served fifteen years in the 13th Demi Brigade. I did not know him from Adam. He turned out to be a total bastard. It was his last day in the Legion and instead of being relaxed, he was in a mood to demonstrate what a toughie he was.

Periodically a senior officer would come through the main gate and we would have to line up for inspection, present arms and call out name, rank and serial number, one by one. The officer would turn to congratulate Reiper on a good turn-out. For this reason, he did not allow us to sit down the entire day on the pretext that it would spoil the creases in our trousers.

By the end of the day I was really starting to regret the last evening of my leave. I had to do guard duty at 10pm that night and was feeling very weary indeed. I set off to a cliff top overlooking the sea, supposedly to guard an oil depot. On the path to my post I met another legionnaire whom I knew well.

We sat and had a chat at the side of the path, and I told him I was feeling like death. As luck would have it, he was carrying a water bottle full of Mascara wine. After I had consumed half the bottle, I was feeling much better and continued up to my post on the cliff top, where I found a convenient log to rest on.

I must have dozed off because the next thing I knew, Reiper, doing his rounds, had come up behind me, cocked his pistol and pressed it against my head. That is called a 'daymare' as opposed to a nightmare! It occurs when you wake up, not when you go to sleep!

Fifteen days prison… and I probably deserved it. If it had been on operations, I might have been shot. Fifteen days of *La Pelote*, twice a day.

I didn't see Reiper again in the Legion as he left on the morning that I was escorted into the stockade, having completed his fifteen years' service.

There were a couple of things I would have liked to say to Reiper.

At the beginning of 1961 the battlefield changed dramatically in Algeria. The cost to the French of 'occupying' Algeria was running into millions of francs a day. The French had 140,000 troops fighting in the colony and although Algeria was largely under control, maintaining that control was too high a price. This was an uneven battle: about a million people of French descent were holding power over ten million Algerian Muslims.

De Gaulle's early enthusiasm for keeping the country as part of metropolitan France was waning. When he had come to power as President of France in 1958, he claimed that he understood the million *pieds-noirs* – the French citizens born and raised over four generations in Algeria – and he declared Algeria would always remain French.

'*Je vous ai compris*', he had told them in a grand defining speech, '*Algérie Francaise*'.

But De Gaulle was to change his mind after five years of bloody war and a relentless battle of resistance by the Fellagha and the FLN, the Front de Libération Nationale, which kept pushing for independence. A new force had also come into being, the OAS, the notorious 'Organised Secret Army'. This was made up largely of pied noirs and was a private army ready to fight for France's continued control of the country, in case there was any change of plan by the French government.

There was also pressure from America, staunchly against colonialism and very cool toward the French after the fiasco in Vietnam in the Second World War. The Vichy French passively allowed the Japanese to occupy Vietnam, from where they ultimately launched their attacks on the rest of Asia and on Pearl Harbour.

On 8 January 1961, De Gaulle held a referendum in Algeria inviting the Algerians to vote on whether or not they wished to remain part of metropolitan France: Oui ou Non? The answer was an unequivocal non. 70 per cent of the population voted for independence.

But the French army generals had a different viewpoint. They wanted to hold on to Algeria. The generals felt their dead comrades warranted it, particularly after what they saw as a political betrayal in Indochina in 1954. So it was that a military Junta led by four French generals – Raoul Salan, Maurice Challe, Edmond Jouhaud, head of the air force, and André Zeller – plotted and led a coup d'état against de Gaulle, four months after the referendum, on 21 April.

At the head of the coup were the Legion Para Regiments, 1st and 2nd, and the Legion Cavalry Regiment. There were also two regular army units involved. This now put us, The Foreign Legion, in direct confrontation with De Gaulle. Many other regiments of the army sat on the fence to see which way the wind would blow.

France was in a civil war. We Legion paratroop regiments were ordered to take over Algiers, the radio, the telephone network and the airport. We were to be dropped on Paris in the Bois de Boulogne. De Gaulle responded by lining the streets of Paris with tanks and promised to fight to the last.

I was sitting at Algiers airport, with my parachute, my sack and my gun, delirious with excitement, more at the prospects of dinner at Maxim's than the potential exhilaration of being shot at in the air by De Gaulle's men.

But it was not to be.

Jouhaud reneged, saying he had promised to support only a 'bloodless' coup and he now withdrew the air force. Without the air force, there would be no planes, and without aircraft there would be no paras. The coup was over. The generals fled. Many of our officers were arrested and replaced, including the commanding officer of my company, Captain L'Hospitallier. We were shut out of our barracks and bivouacked in the mountains. Pay was stopped and mass desertion began. The First Legion Para Regiment blew up their barracks in Zeralda and deserted en masse. Many joined the mysterious OAS, vowing to keep Algeria French.

These were tough times, filled with uncertainty and rumours. None of us really knew what was going on. At first, we were going to be disbanded. Then stories followed that we would be sold lock, stock and barrel to the Americans. Mixed feelings for me. Prospects of going home. The initial excitement at the idea of being dropped on Paris had dissipated. The whole world had held its breath. But it was over in just six days.

After many months, life got back to normal and our operations continued. No peace treaty had been signed with the FLN; no deal had been done. It was now time to meet and talk with them but no more than that. There followed another year of patrols and skirmishes, before peace was finally signed in March 1962.

Algeria became a new nation. As part of the agreement, the French would be allowed to stay until 1967 to protect their oil and gas interests in the Sahara. My regiment, the 2nd Paras, now known simply as the REP, after the disbandment of the 1st REP, was morphed into an elite shock force ready to go anywhere, any time. The OAS was now the enemy.

Nevertheless, there lingered some doubts in France about the Legion's loyalty. We took the brunt of the blame for the failed coup, although in fact we had been 'used'. We had been the hired help. The Legion was banned from marching down the Champs-Élysées with other elite French troops on Bastille Day for ten years.

Eventually, General Jacques Lefort was assigned to the Legion and it was a great decision. He was going to rebuild us. He had previously commanded the 2nd REP years before and was well liked and respected. We began intensive training in explosives, underwater sabotage, anti-terrorist combat and survival in extreme conditions. We were very much a 'special force' category. I still had two more years to go before *La Quille* – de-mob day. It was the name of the ship that brought prisoners back to France after they had done their time in prison on the dreaded Devil's Island.

We referred to it often.

Many people have asked me why I joined the Foreign Legion and it is not an easy answer. I certainly did not know what was in store; otherwise I might have been deterred. When did I begin to have some doubts about it? After the first ten minutes. But I stayed five long years.

I had read the romantic novel *Beau Geste* by P.C. Wren, as had all young men in those days and been inspired by it and, yes, there was a girl called Jennifer who did not respond to my affection with the same enthusiasm that I had for her… but it was more than that.

I was working in an iron foundry in Manchester on £1 per day. I had read much about the great explorers of the Victorian era. I had a vivid imagination and was rearing to get out of the rut I felt I was in. Someone once said, 'Do not follow where the path may lead, go instead where there is no path and leave a trail.' This was to be my motto. All it needs is a compass. A moral compass which is not operated by reading the Bible but more by listening to one's conscience.

On the path there are forks in the road and decisions to be made. There are mountains to climb and sometimes one is lost in valleys, in the darkness of the night when the rain never ceases and the spirit is low. But there are also sunny days and green fields through which to wander.

At school when I queried God's plan and asked why wars ravaged the planet, the chaplain had said that we could never understand the plan and we should have blind faith, and all would be well. That has not been my experience and I am not good at running blind. For me it's eyes open and straight ahead. Some people call it being impulsive…

Uri Geller said, 'When you come to a fork in the road, take it!'

With a 'no' from the British Army, a 'no' from the girl I loved and a total disinterest in what I was doing, I was at a fork in the road and it was time to get off the path.

I set off for the Foreign Legion. A path many have considered but few have followed.

CHAPTER II

THE GREEKS. THE SCOTS. THE ENGLISH

In the early days of the nineteenth century, two of my forefathers narrowly escaped death and a third had the kind of lucky break that changes not just one life but many.

The first to escape death was Prince Axel Petrocochino. He lived on the Greek Island of Chios. In 1822 the Ottoman Empire was in the final stages of suppressing the Greek bid for independence. In that year, the Turks arrived on this tiny island, just five miles off the Turkish coast, and slaughtered around 100,000 men, women and children. 20,000 were taken away as slaves never to return. 9,000 survived on the island.

The Turks were known for their brutality but what happened on Chios was an unprecedented massacre. Reports of the horrors sent shockwaves across Europe. The islanders were butchered with scimitars, tortured and many were hanged. 25,000 were thrown off a cliff top from 300 feet into a raging sea. A painting by Delacroix in the Louvre entitled *The Massacre at Chios* ensures that this will never be forgotten.

The Petrocochinos were one of the foremost families of Chios, members of what was known as the 'Inner Circle'. Eleven of the family were hanged by the Turks in the town square on the first day of the massacre.

The head of the family, Prince Axel, had made his money by supplying the local mastic gum, which comes from the sap of the chia tree that grows on Chios, to be used as glue for the Ottoman Empire and 'chewing gum' for the Sultan. He had good connections and sensing the approaching disaster, had arranged for his family to escape on a British merchant ship. In the end only three of the family got away, one aged four. His name was Themistocles Petrocochino.

He was my great-great-grandfather.

British ships, carrying the Red Ensign, were not touched by the Turkish fleet. This was only seventeen years after Trafalgar and the British navy was still feared and respected… and not to be messed with.

The Petrocochinos arrived in England with only the clothes they wore.

They left behind their grand villas and their treasures to the invaders. Arriving in Hull, they travelled on to York where they had introductions to business acquaintances. It wasn't long before they were back in business, operating a glue factory and the family's fortunes picked up again. There's money in chewing gum too. The Victorians loved it.

John Petrocochino, the son of Themistocles, didn't have a taste for glue or chewing gum. His father gave him a thousand pounds (around £200,000 today) and sent him to London to buy a partnership in a firm of stockbrokers.

On the train to London, John met Brandon Thomas, an unknown playwright. Thomas had written a new play, which he wanted to stage, and was looking for investors. By the time they had reached London, John had read the play, liked it and had parted with all his money for a half share in it. It was called *Charley's Aunt*. It opened at the Theatre Royal in Bury St Edmunds on 29 February 1892.

An immediate hit in Bury St Edmunds, *Charley's Aunt* transferred to London, opening at the Royalty Theatre on December 21 to rave reviews. It was such a success that it moved to the Globe the following year and played a record-breaking run of 1,466 consecutive performances. D'Oyly Carte set it to music and it had another run for twenty-five years on Broadway in the United States, before going on to tour internationally. It was the longest running musical ever on Broadway until *My Fair Lady* arrived.

That chance meeting with Brandon Thomas had made John Petrocochino wealthy. He bought his partnership in a firm of London stockbrokers and became an active and shrewd investor.

On a visit to Germany in 1934, he met Hitler and realised immediately that the German leader was a man preparing for war. Hitler had just ordered the entire output of German steel production to be committed to the manufacture of weapons of war: artillery, tanks, rifles and machine guns. Back in Britain, Petrocochino bought shares in American steel stocks, which shot up in value as Germany built up its inventory of armaments.

In 1895, John Petrocochino, now known as Jack Petro, had married Alice Mather. Alice was the eldest of the five daughters of Sir William and Emma Mather. The marriage brought together two wealthy families. The couple gave birth to a daughter and named her Violet because of the colour of her eyes.

Violet was my grandmother.

Another of my ancestors who came close to an early death, was Charles Murray, who fought in the appalling conditions of the Crimean war.

In 1854, Great Britain had joined the French and the Ottoman Empire to fight the Russians, who were pushing a little too fast into the Danube regions, occupied by the Turks. The British army was caught up in fierce fighting in the Crimea where Major Charles Murray was second-in-command of his regiment, the 42nd (Royal Highland) Regiment of Foot (The Black Watch).

In the final days of the war, the senior commander of the regiment was killed and Murray took command as 'honorary' colonel. Despite the dreadful conditions, he managed to get his regiment through safely and they survived. When the war was over the British government declared there was no money to bring the men home. They would either have to find their own way back – or wait until funds were available.

Imagine their horror. Murray was incensed. He funded the Regiment's return, nearly bankrupting himself in the process. The government honoured his sacrifice and heroic action with a knighthood. He retired to Dumfriesshire and lived at Murraythwaite, an elegant house set in 3,000 acres, which today belongs to my older brother, Anthony.

Charles Murray had two sons, Hugh, my great grandfather and his brother Charles (junior). Hugh joined the Foreign Service and became head of the Forestry Commission in India, living in an elegant house in Delhi.

In those days, civil servants would get a year's home leave every four years, and when Hugh's turn came, he suggested to his brother Charles (junior), that he might like to stay in his house during his absence.

Charles accepted. He enjoyed polo and croquet and spent his time playing them on alternate days and passed a pleasant year in Hugh's house pursuing his favourite sports. A happy life.

Meanwhile Hugh's name came up for a knighthood, as it does if you remain long enough in the service of the realm. Before a knighthood is bestowed, however, the recipient is approached to ensure that if it is offered it will be accepted, so there can be no embarrassment if the honour is declined.

The government envoy arrived at the house in Delhi and spoke to the Mr Murray in residence and asked him if he would accept a knighthood for services to the country. Charles said he would be delighted, not realising that the envoy thought he was talking to Mr H. Murray and not Mr C. Murray. Charles simply assumed that his service to croquet, at which he was becoming quite adept, was finally being recognised.

Thus, Charles was knighted.

There was a huge row, lots of correspondence, mumblings and grumblings, but it is impossible to take back a knighthood once it has been awarded, even if by mistake. A year later they awarded another knighthood, this time to the correct Mr Murray.

Sir Hugh, as he now was, with his very own knighthood, had produced a son, whom he named George, around the turn of the century. His wife Gwendoline died a few years later and he eventually married his second wife, Dorothy Mather, who was another daughter of Sir William Mather, and a sister to Alice.

The Petrocochinos, the Mathers and the Murrays were now linked: three very prosperous families: Dorothy brought wealth to the Murray clan.

They were all my ancestors and with a line up of three families like this, it was impossible for things to go wrong.

But they did.

The world was about to take a one eighty-degree turn for the worse. A war was coming which would see the death of some seventeen million people and reverse the fortunes of many more.

CHAPTER III
ROOTS

Violet, my grandmother, the daughter of Alice and Jack Petro, was a wild lady with strikingly beautiful eyes. As an heiress, in part, to the Mather fortune through her mother, and also that of the Petrocochino family, she was a London 'belle', much in demand at all the high-society functions and *soirées* which were not dissimilar to those imagined by Scott Fitzgerald for Gatsby. But she stunned her own family by falling deeply in love with a young man called George Murray, Hugh Murray's son by his first wife. George was to become my grandfather. There were concerns, but ultimately the relationship was deemed to be of paper and not blood and it survived some gossip.

The newlyweds, my grandparents, had scarcely time to give birth to a son, Patrick, my father-to-be, before the sounds of war came blowing from across the water.

The Great War began in 1914 following the assassination of an Austrian Archduke and his wife, by a Serb, in Bosnia, a country that most Englishmen had never heard of. It was a war that engulfed half the world. More people were to be killed in this war over the next four years than had died in all the battles fought over the previous thousand years. It was a war of artillery. Heavy guns.

One of the young men who signed up to fight for his country was Violet's new husband, George Murray. He joined the Royal Engineers and was killed in Cambrai in France on 4 October 1918, thirty-eight days before the end of the war and the Armistice which would have saved him. He was twenty-six years old. He was one of the many thousands of young men to die in this terrible conflict. One in five Englishmen between the age of eighteen and twenty-six never came home.

Violet, at home with her five-year-old son, received a telegram from the War Office giving her the news of her husband's death.

Deeply regret Lieutenant G.A. Murray, RE Divisional Company, killed in action October 4th — The Army Council expresses sympathy.

His outstanding pay of four shillings and sixpence together with his personal effects may be collected at the address given below.

Somewhat different to the way it is done today and the telegram has a brevity to it which tightens the heart strings. But they were sending out such telegrams in the thousands and time was something of which they didn't have much.

Violet was devastated: distraught with grief, alcohol became her refuge.

She and her son Patrick went to live with her mother, Alice, now ensconced at Claridge's, after a separation from her husband, Jack Petro, although they remained married. Divorce was frowned upon in those days in spite of Henry VIII's track record.

Violet drank hard and she partied hard too. Every night. The parties were called 'bridge parties' but that was a cover for champagne-fuelled binges.

Often leaving her son with nannies, she went wild; she drove racing cars at Brooklands and travelled through Europe, staying at all the finest hotels, including six months at Raffles in Singapore. These were the roaring twenties; war was behind them. Occasionally her young son joined her on these excursions.

Jack Petro, who had taken up residence at the Westbury Hotel and was by now trading stocks successfully in the City of London, financed both Alice and Violet in their glamorous lifestyle.

Not everyone felt happy with their high spending.

Alice's father, Sir William Mather, used to a more austere and hard-working existence, disapproved of his son-in-law and indeed his own daughter's extravagance. He cut Alice out of his will. It read: 'To my eldest daughter, Alice, I leave nothing as she is well-cared for.'

Quite blunt.

Violet, still only in her late twenties, was by now a total alcoholic and was declared unfit to bring up my father, Patrick. Alice, his grandmother, became his legal custodian. They continued to live at Claridge's.

Violet went on to marry a fellow alcoholic, having two more children by him. When she became pregnant for the third time, she sought assistance from an illegal back-street abortionist. She died shortly afterwards of a virulent disease caused by blood poisoning.

She was thirty-seven years old.

In my living memory, no one in my family ever spoke about her. Quite simply, she was airbrushed from the archives.

Yet my father, Patrick, was still very much part of the Mather family. He was close to them through his grandmother, Alice, and his step-grandmother Dorothy Mather.

He often visited Myddleton, a large house in Roehampton set in eight acres of gardens, belonging to Loris Mather, who was his godfather as well as being his great uncle. Loris's daughter, Gay, became friends with Patrick. In her diaries, she writes of him:

He was of a sunny disposition with a great deal of charm. He was musical and intellectually credible. He followed his father George up to Harrow and on to Oxford, where he lasted but one year... but with all his charm, living at Claridge's, driving fast cars (his mother's influence), he was inevitably spoilt... literally to death!

On the first occasion that we met at Claridge's, Patrick was delighted to meet a contemporary cousin. We shared the spacious bath together and splashed about with our toys. He was very generous and offered me several of his, including a bear named Polar!

Aunt Alice was a well-corseted lady. She wore glittering jewels pinned to her bosom and she carried a little black cane with a silver handle and would clip the ankles of the hotel staff to hurry them along. She was strict with Patrick on manners and deportment, but at the same time he had anything he wanted.

After lunch sometimes we would go to Hamley's toy shop, the best in London. Aunt Alice allowed us to choose whatever we liked. Patrick was always collecting things for his train set which was spread all over the nursery floor. As he got older he wore beautiful little suits, tailor made for him in Jermyn Street. Each one had a waistcoat, so he always looked very smart.

The days went by and Patrick would appear at Myddleton always immaculate in a tweed suit. My elder brother Bill, who was three years older than Patrick, often ragged him and would challenge him to do dangerous things. Patrick wanted to copy Bill in everything he did to show his bravery and determination.

This diary entry is one of the few portraits of my father. Gay Mather was right about him being spoilt. He toured between his grandparents in their respective hotels, Claridge's and the Westbury, receiving pocket money from both, out of which he paid his own school fees at Harrow. He went on to travel the world, never doing a stroke of work in his life.

One Sunday morning in 1937, he was lunching in the bar at the Berkeley Hotel when he caught sight of an attractive brunette and her friend at a nearby table. He sent over some champagne. They raised their glasses in acknowledgement which was sufficient incentive for him to join them. He secured the name and address of the brunette before she left: she was Maxine King, originally from Worksop in Nottinghamshire. Her father owned a pub called the Bell Inn and among other things, her favourite flowers were gladioli. She lived at 25 Hamilton Gardens, and she worked in the perfumery department at Harvey Nichols.

The following day three taxis arrived at Hamilton Gardens laden with gladioli. Maxine was bowled over and the romance began. Six months later they were married. Patrick's grandfather, Jack Petro, gave them a wedding present of £450,000 (worth about £15 million today). The newlyweds went to live in Paris for a year and then moved to Jersey, where my brother, Anthony, was born a year later.

By the middle of 1939 it was clear that Germany was ready for war and there began what an American journalist termed the 'phoney war'. It was time for the Murrays to move back to England and get out of harm's way. They moved again and arrived in Leicester, where I was born three months later. They had managed to work through much of the money given to them on their wedding day and had left behind half of their belongings each time they moved.

I was born on 25 March 1940 and named Simon after the 5th Earl of Leicester, Simon de Montfort. My mother had read a book about this Frenchman and he was the only thing she knew about Leicester.

Jack Petro had died in 1938 and although he left money to Alice, she and Violet had carved their way through most of it with their huge extravagance, with my father giving them a helping hand. By 1941, Alice was broke. She sold her jewellery to pay outstanding bills at Claridge's, which she had to leave for a one-bedroom flat in Hans Crescent. Her younger brother, Loris, helped her out. She died a year later in the middle of a war which had destroyed London. She was seventy-eight. She had had a good run.

As soon as Maxine had delivered me in Leicester, she and Patrick moved to Marlborough and rented an old post office which had been converted into a private house. Money was now seriously short. They were at loggerheads. Six months after I was born my father declared himself bankrupt and joined the army as a private soldier. He left my mother penniless. She moved with her two infant children to a one-room attic flat in London, lent to her by an old friend. The phoney war was about to end, and reality was about to set in.

The German Luftwaffe bombed London continuously from September 1940 through to the end of May 1941, including seventy-three consecutive nights. The 'Blitz' was ferocious: 43,000 civilians were killed and over a million homes destroyed. London was smashed to pieces.

Apart from a tiny trust fund that my father had set up before he went bankrupt, there was nothing left. The Petrocochino inheritance that had seemed so plentiful in Paris had been blown away. My mother committed my brother Anthony and I to what was effectively an orphanage. It was a nurse's training school outside Tunbridge Wells, which took in children in desperate circumstances even if we were not all strictly orphans.

My first memory is the sound of bombs. Coming ever closer like the thumping footsteps of a great giant, mingling with the wailing sound of sirens shattering the night and the screams of terrified children. I can remember the dormitory still. It is night time. In my mind's eye I can clearly see the nurse who is lifting me out of my cot as she carries me down into the darkness to what must have been an air-raid shelter. I am looking up at her face in the light of the yellow bulbs hanging like oranges on long flexes from the roof. She is out of her mind with fear which is transferred to me. Her tears are falling on my face, mingling with mine. This is the stuff of real nightmares, never to be forgotten. The entire building is shaking as we descend into the darkness. In the cellar, we are packed like sardines, lying side by side. Everybody is howling as the earthquake above our heads wreaks havoc and destruction and the endless bombs crack in the darkness.

The world is ending. But for me this was the beginning, not the end, as it was for so many. This was my entry onto planet earth.

My mother was now on the poverty line. That perhaps explains why she left us in a home. I often wondered about it and why and how she was able to leave her two tiny children in an orphanage in the middle of a war.

She obviously thought it was the safest place for us to be. She was just thirty years old, abandoned by her husband and alone in a bomb-shattered London, with no money.

Sometime in late 1942, Anthony and I were sent away to Wales with half the children of London, as far from Hitler and his bombs as was possible. England prepared for invasion.

I have a clear vision of us standing on the station platform with labels around our necks: hundreds of children being sent, courtesy of the Post Office, to the western shores of Britain; tearful goodbyes flooding the ground around us as children were sometimes torn from their frantic mothers. Terrible screams from hundreds of children cramming the windows inside the train as it began to move, watching their desperate mothers running along the platform beside the train, crying their hearts out and yelling the names of their babies: a scene of total despair, almost impossible to imagine. And then we were gone.

We spent the next two years in a kindergarten in Montgomeryshire called Rorington Lodge, managed by a disciplinarian, who had lost his arm in the First World War. We called him 'Uncle'. He was anything but. Those years are a blur to me but again I have a few flash memories. There was one visit from my mother that I do remember; I was so excited. The day was warm, and the sun shone. We went for a picnic. An unforgettable day, but I can't remember her leaving when it was over.

The war finally ended in 1945 and my mother brought us back to her parents' house in Nottinghamshire. They lived in the slums of a small town called Worksop. My mother's brother, Billy, worked in a coal mine. He used to come back in the evening on his bicycle covered in black coal dust. He was great fun for Anthony and me.

The lavatory was outside in the yard at the back of the house and in the front, on the other side of a laterite public path, there was a vegetable plot. Each house in the row had a small vegetable plot. At the end of the path the trains roared past every forty minutes. Once a week a tin bath was filled with water from a boiled kettle. Bath night. We thought it was wonderful but my mother must have yearned for the life she had lived before the war with my father. She was dying to escape back to London.

She finally did. I never saw my grandparents again. I have no memory of what they looked like, although I have a blurred vision of my grandfather sitting in a chair with his head pressed against the radio every time we came downstairs for breakfast. He never spoke to us, except to shout at us to be quiet. My mother kept no photographs of them.

In 1945 at the end of the war, we moved down to London to a tiny basement flat in Robert Adam Street. Maxine had finally left Worksop and its poverty behind. She had spent the war years as a volunteer in the fire brigade. It must have been a nightmare being separated from her children. She was flat broke, but now she got her job back at Harvey Nichols.

The war blew many families apart over the long five years it lasted. Husbands separated from wives, boyfriends from girlfriends, fiancés from prospective brides, never to be reunited. Death, absence and hopelessness severed the links. Hope is a great source of energy and once lost, so are the bonds that pull us along the trails of life. And so it was with Maxine and Patrick. Hope was gone. Their marriage was built on a very easy way of life and inherited wealth. It did not have the structural foundation to survive their separation, nor the fact that Patrick was broke.

They were divorced in 1940. They never saw each other again. I was six months old. At first Maxine did not have the courage to go to her ex-husband's family for help, fearing rejection. She was not of their blood. Eventually, desperation won over fear and my mother went to see her ex-husband's godfather, the brother of her children's great-grandmother, my great-great-uncle, Loris Mather. His daughter, Gay Mather, was at Myddleton when my mother arrived and records the visit in her diary:

Maxine turned up at Myddleton begging for help. She was thin, dirty and destitute. Her boys were in an orphanage. Dr Barnardo's home. She had brought Anthony, the eldest, with her. He stood on a rock and recited 'You are old Father William'. Mother was enchanted. Maxine hoped that father and Aunt Dorothy would create a trust fund that would send her boys to school. At first, they demurred but under pressure from mother, they agreed and the boys were sent to prep school.

My first six years on the planet were not that great but all that was now behind me and I was ready to move forward with a song in my heart.

CHAPTER IV
LEARNING CURVE

Our new boarding school was Belmont, near Dorking. I was six years old and the first day was terrifying. I was crying. My mother took us to the school accompanied by her sister, June, who was only twelve years older than me. I can remember them leaving, waving goodbye and calling out, 'Don't worry Sime – you'll be all right!' I felt numb with fear. Anthony tried to cheer me up repeating what they had said: 'Don't worry Sime, it'll be all right.' But he didn't look particularly stalwart either.

Belmont School was different from the places we had been before. It was much larger and when my mother left us in the courtyard and disappeared behind the huge gates, I was scared. Although I had been left many times before and been away from home for most of my life, this felt different.

Boys were everywhere, yelling and rushing about. Some were playing with conkers, others with cigarette cards and they all seemed to know each other. None of them spoke to Anthony or me. We were completely isolated. Unsure of what to do, we wandered into the orchard nearby and I picked an apple. Somebody came rushing up and started yelling at us to get out of the orchard; it was out of bounds and we would be reported.

We were reported.

Eventually we were in our beds in a dormitory. I thought it was the coldest place in the world.

The next day I was caned by the headmaster, a Mr Anderson, for stealing an apple. The pain from that single stroke has stayed with me for the whole of my life. What kind of bastard would lash a six-year-old boy with a bamboo rod for picking an apple off a tree, on his first day at school?

But it was symptomatic of what I could expect there. Belmont was an institution out of a Dickensian novel and there were to be regular beatings from a perverted headmaster.

On rare occasions my mother would visit and take us out to tea at the Watermill Restaurant. They were heaven-sent days, unforgettable teas with endless supplies of muffins and scones laden with honey and huge slices of chocolate cake, followed by the misery of having to return to school.

Our holidays back home in Robert Adam Street were brighter. We played in the rubble of the bombed-out streets of London. We ate food from brown-coloured tins: black-market army rations. We had a dog called Lassie. I cannot remember a single Christmas before the age of eleven. Aunt June told me years later over lunch one day that I had never been there at Christmas time.

'You were always sent away to stay on farms during the holidays – there wasn't enough room for you in the basement flat!'

Not surprising that I remembered so little.

However, I do remember one incident clearly. One day Anthony had suddenly produced a packet of cigarettes, 'Craven A', my mother's favourite brand, and a box of matches and presented them to her – it was for her birthday and she was all over him with hugs and thanks. The little sod hadn't told me it was Mum's birthday, grabbing all the glory himself.

Frantic at the prospect of being left out, I ran to my tin money box and turned it upside down to get the contents. Three pennies fell out. With this princely sum I ran up the stairs and out on to the pavement and there was my saving grace – a man selling newspapers. I asked him for one and opened my hand with the three pennies. He took one of the pennies and gave me a newspaper in return – I did not know what it was at the time, but it was the Evening News.

Looking at the remaining two pennies, I thought I could go further, particularly given the huge gift that Anthony had provided, so I asked for another. The man took another penny and gave me another copy of the Evening News. I rushed home with my gifts, two identical copies of the paper. My mother laughed until she had tears streaming down her face – but she hugged me and could not stop thanking me. I was happy – if a little confused.

When I was nine, I left the ghastly Belmont School for Bedford, where Anthony was already ensconced, one year ahead of me. I liked Bedford School. Most of the masters were of the Mr Chips variety: dedicated, loving what they did, whether teaching English or coaching rugby. My favourite subjects were History and English. As a sixth former, my form master,

Michael Barlan, would give me books to read and send me to the library for a week, at the end of which he would expect twenty-eight pages of foolscap on a given subject. I seldom read a book recommended to me unless the first line was good.

My own choice of reading was much more entertaining.

I loved historical novels by writers such as Dennis Wheatley, who gave a more thrilling version of the French Revolution than Voltaire. My books included tales by Alan Moorhead who wrote about the explorers Burton, Speake, Livingstone and Stanley as they searched for the source of the Nile and scoured the countries of Africa. Joseph Conrad showed me the Congo and its darkness; Cecil Woodham-Smith took me through the terrible Crimean War in which my ancestors had fought.

Night Runners of Bengal and *Bugles and a Tiger* by John Masters gave me a clearer portrait of India than the prescribed reading on the school list, and Masters introduced me to the wonderful Gurkhas who fought so bravely with the British in the world wars.

My poets were Coleridge, Wordsworth, Dylan Thomas, Macaulay, and Walter de la Mare and I could recite them by heart as well as half of Shakespeare. What could inspire a young boy more than Macaulay's poem of *Horatius at the Bridge* overlooking the Tiber, roaring at her banks: 'And how could man die better/Than facing fearful odds/For the ashes of his fathers/And the temples of his Gods.'

Other authors that I devoured with enthusiasm and delight were John Steinbeck who told me about America's Great Depression in *The Grapes of Wrath*. I loved Scott Fitzgerald's *The Great Gatsby* and Lawrence Durrell's *The Alexandria Quartet* as well as Dostoyevsky and Hemingway.

We had no television in those days and reading fired our imagination. The map of the world was pink, and pink was the British Empire – from Australia to Canada, from Fiji to Mauritius, from India to Egypt. The largest empire the world has ever known, created by a little island called Great Britain and we were proud of it and its history. My heroes were Livingstone, Wellington, Nelson, Pitt, Scott, T.E. Lawrence and Sherlock Holmes.

I had read *Beau Geste*, the fascinating book about a strange army called the French Foreign Legion that operated in the desert in pursuit of wild Tuareg tribesmen. I wanted to travel the world. My essays were full of 'flare and fiction', according to my form master Michael Barlan. Barlan used to give me 'ten for narrative' and 'zero for facts' and often written across my essays when they were returned to me, were the words, 'Murray, where did you get this information? You must quote sources!' and on one occasion, having written an essay on the relationship between Henry VIII and the Pope, 'How do you know this, Murray? You are the only person on the planet that thinks Henry VIII was a homosexual!' Well he had endless wives and kept chopping their heads off – so he was pretty strange, wasn't he?

Bedford was a great school and although I was flogged many times, often for crimes of which I was innocent and dubious causes such as 'attitude', I made good friends and with a few exceptions the teaching staff were terrific and I have fond memories.

There were exceptions. One was my housemaster when I arrived at the school in 1949, a man named Noel Sutcliffe. I boarded at his house for three years during which he gave me thirty-nine strokes of the cane. Never less than three or four at a time. The cane was a bamboo rod and he flayed it on my backside with all the force he could muster. The causes ranged from talking during prep and after lights out, to being late for chapel. I suppose God's messengers come in all forms.

Sutcliffe thrashed me without a referee, which was against the rules. The only person to do so. In his study he had a drawer full of bamboo rods, all different widths and some with tape around the end where the bamboo had shredded. I could see the canes when he opened the drawer and he would select with care the one he was going to use on each occasion. Hallmark of a total sadist. Corporal punishment was banned in schools in 1987, but in the fifties, it was routine.

I was capped for rugger and I played cricket for the school and received trophies for gymnastics. So I enjoyed some moments of heroism, spurred on by our coach Murray Fletcher who was also my English teacher. Another Mr Chips.

My favourite extra-curricular activity was Miss Harding's dancing classes, held every Saturday afternoon at 4:30pm. Dancing class was the only opportunity of any sort to make contact with the opposite sex – to meet girls as well as to hold them. The girls came from Bedford High School and they seemed as enthusiastic as us to learn the quickstep!

Like all good things, dancing classes came with problems which had to be navigated. The timing clashed with my rugger and the boys scrambling to get into Miss Harding's dancing classes outnumbered the girls four to one. This meant that not only did I arrive late – usually covered in mud under my clothes because I had not had time to shower after the game in my haste to get to the dance floor – but there was also the problem of finding a partner that was not a boy. I had spotted that Miss Harding would select good dancers for demonstration purposes and if you were good at a particular dance, this could be the fast track to a female partner.

I focused on the waltz, practising until I made Fred Astaire look like a novice. It was not long before Miss Harding was calling out, 'Now Simon, you pick a partner and come out here where we can see you and show us what you can do with the waltz'. My foxtrot was pretty mean as well.

My mother married again when I was eleven. He was a Dutchman called Leo, seven years younger than her but he loved her well and we adored him. He had a battered old 1934 MG sports car, in which we sat up on the back as he drove at great speed down country lanes.

We went to live in Holland in a small but friendly house in the countryside near Breda. Our situation took a substantial step up in the right direction. We received pocket money for the first time and Christmas presents. Maxine and Leo produced a baby girl, my half-sister Caroline.

We were happy and I had my own bedroom – we sometimes flew in airplanes, rare in those days. People did not travel and there were no cheap airfares. Less than 20 per cent of the population of England had passports.

Food was still rationed: sweets, butter, meat, coffee – England after two world wars had gone from being the richest per capita nation in the world to being, in practical terms, broke. We were up to our necks in debt owed mainly to the Americans, which was going to take half a century to repay.

They were good days in Holland but by the time I was sixteen, my relationship with my mother was what she might have described as 'difficult'. Even as a young child I felt she always favoured Anthony. She gave him more pocket money than me when we took the boat back to school from the Hook of Holland. She would hug and kiss him but shake me by the hand. She said my problem was that I had a chip on my shoulder.

'Simon is argumentative, quarrels with Anthony and answers back', I once overheard her say to a friend and that I was 'prone to sulking if I did not get my way'.

She had a distant relationship with her own mother – I had only seen my grandmother twice in my life. I think my mother had tried to cut herself from her roots when she married Patrick. She never talked about her parents. Ever. Although she did say to me one day that when I was born, her father had held me in his hands high above his head and said to her, 'Look after this one Max, one day you'll be very proud of him.'

Alas, I don't think that day ever came as she died when I was forty.

Anthony and I were in our teens when she told us that our father had not died in the war but had deserted us as babies. She never spoke about him again and nor did any other people in the wider family.

CHAPTER V
A FORK IN THE ROAD

With no real home base, a non-existent father and twelve years of boarding school behind me, it's perhaps no surprise that I started feeling restless when I was around eighteen; I was tired of school, full of energy and needed to take a run at the world.

The greater part of my life had been spent in institutions, punctuated later by holidays in Holland. There was nowhere that I thought of as home. I preferred to go caving in the Mendip Hills or spend time in London rather than pass boring holidays in the Dutch countryside.

At any moment I could have been blown off course by the winds that blow from the windmills of the gods... and I was.

One day in Rotterdam a fork in the road!

I had two weeks to go before my return to Bedford for the summer term at the end of which I would take my A-level exams. I had already secured a place at Cambridge subject to passing two A-levels.

I was walking through the port of Rotterdam and saw a queue of rough-looking individuals. I asked someone what they were queuing for and was told they were hoping to get jobs on cargo boats. I joined the queue: as one does. It was an action replay of the film On the Waterfront and I was in Marlon Brando mode. Eventually I was at the front and was asked for my 'seaman's book'. Lots of laughter as I declared I didn't have one, and I was brusquely shoved out of the way. Dreams of travel came to an end.

The next day I was strolling down the street with my hands in my pockets when I saw someone approaching whom I recognised as the man signing people for work on ships in the port the previous day. He recognised me too and came up to me and asked, 'Are you the boy who wants to go to sea?' I said, 'Yes' and he went on, 'Do you care where you go?' I didn't.

He said, 'What about South America?'

South America! Just the thought of such an exotic place set my heart pounding.

'There is a ship leaving tomorrow and the galley boy has gone sick. Do you want to go in his place?' he asked.

He gave me an address on a piece of paper and told me to present myself there that afternoon.

I did, signing on as galley boy on a 7,000-ton tramp steamer called the St Arvans, a vessel in the fleet of the South American Saint Line. My job would be peeling potatoes and scrubbing the galley floor. Pay was to be eight shillings and six pence a week. No minimum wage in those days. He gave me a seaman's book and asked me if I wanted to join the union for ten guilders.

I didn't see the necessity, but he said if I was a member of the union and fell overboard, they would pull me back on board.

And if not?

I joined the union and signed up for a round trip from Rotterdam to Rotterdam. The duration of the trip was uncertain because the captain would get his orders for his next port when he arrived in each place and picked up his new cargo with instructions on where to deliver it. My journey would end only when we got back to Rotterdam. He told me I would be the only Englishman in the crew and funnily enough the galley boy who had gone off sick was also an Englishman by the name of Martin Fisher.

The St Arvans was a floating piece of junk and she would be sailing initially to Buenos Aires via various ports, up the River Plate and then on to Brazil and around the Caribbean before eventually returning to Rotterdam where I could 'sign-off', as they say! She was a tramp and would go where the winds of trade directed. A liner goes to given ports on a routine schedule. A tramp goes wherever there is a cargo and carries it to wherever it is destined, where it hopes to pick up another cargo and deliver that to where the gods have willed.

That evening I explained to my mother that I had found myself a job on a luxury yacht sailing to the Canary Islands, and I would be gone for a couple of weeks. As most mothers would have reacted, she was aghast at the prospect that I would not be back in time for my last term at school and I would miss taking my A-levels and lose any chance at going to university. I assured her there would be no problem.

Leo, my Dutch stepfather, had no understanding of the English school system and thought it was barbaric that we were at a boarding school anyway, so volunteered no resistance. My mother was hesitant but was finally persuaded.

The next day I took the first steps of my journey through life and set sail for South America. Leo came to the docks with my mother to see me off and both were clearly astonished at my 'luxury yacht'.

I stood in the stern with a great lump in my throat as I watched them become two tiny specks on the quayside until the horizon was finally flat. I would not return for the best part of a year.

I had signed up to sail, unwittingly, halfway around the world but incongruously the first stop after leaving Rotterdam was the port of Felixstowe, England.

Little did I know that thirty years later I would return and 'buy' this port from P&O, but this time round it was to deposit a small cargo of bicycles and to pick up some steel girders. We were there for half a day and then sailed on south.

Our next stop was the Cape Verde islands. We didn't get ashore and were only refuelling. Cruise ships wallowed at anchor in the soft warm waters. Guests on board the luxury liners watched from the railings as they threw bars of soap into the clear blue water and little boys from canoes dived in to retrieve them, braving the sharks that lurked in the depths below. Nobody was eaten and gradually the bored guests wandered back to their gin and tonics in the saloons below.

On board the St. *Arvans*, I peeled 300 potatoes a day, scrubbed the galley floor three times a day and washed out the huge tubs in which hot food was served. They weighed a ton and I carried the leftovers in these urns to the stern and chucked them overboard. Good shark food. It was backbreaking work, and the worst part of my day.

I became the ship's barber: somebody had to do it! I charged two packets of cigarettes per head. It was a short career. I nicked someone's ear with the scissors one day and it drew a lot of blood from a tiny cut. He made a big deal out of it. Four of the crew held me down and shaved me as bald as an egg. My career as an *haute coiffeur* was over.

The crew on board was a motley crowd of varied origins. The captain was a small man from Monmouthshire with a big mouth. The boatswain was a toughie from Belgium and he taught me to tie different knots for different purposes, rig this and lash that, climb the mast in rough seas and he did his best to shape me into his definition of an 'able-seaman'. He also taught me how to use the signal lamp and send messages by Morse code. The majority of the crew were Spanish and I set about picking up the language. I found I had a good ear for languages – and this would stand me in good stead later when I joined the Foreign Legion.

By the time we got halfway to Buenos Aires, I had stopped feeling seasick.

I had a bad mark from the captain one day when I threw one of the tubs of wet garbage over the windward side and it blew straight back across the deck, creating a terrible mess. Unfortunately, he was on the bridge and witnessed the whole thing. He was furious and promised me that when we got to Buenos Aires, as punishment I would be banned from going ashore on the first day along with everybody else.

We arrived in Buenos Aires, where the city was in total chaos with rioting on the streets and explosions going off every five minutes. This was 1958 and Argentina had just gone bust. A sovereign default of spectacular proportions.

On the first night, most of the crew and officers went ashore. The captain informed me that I was to remain aboard and would be in charge of the ship. He told me to get dressed in white trousers and a white shirt. No hat needed.

One or two of the oldies also stayed on board and I arranged a cinema show on deck. The ship had an old projector and a few movies.

Everything was ready to roll when I noticed a very fancy yacht in the middle of the harbour. I decided to signal to them that we were having a film show and they would be welcome to join. I got a flashing signal back and the next thing I saw was a small motorboat emerging from the stern of the yacht with a bloke and three women on board steaming towards us.

I went down the gangplank to welcome three lovely ladies and a young man, who explained they had got the message and would be delighted to watch the movie. They added that the yacht belonged to the Playboy Club and they were in Buenos Aires for a short stay.

I took them up to the captain's cabin and served them vodka tonics and tried to create the impression that I was the officer left in charge of our ship (which technically I was) and the rest had gone ashore, except for the few guys on the deck waiting for the movie to start.

It was all going well, and then halfway through the movie, which was Rock Hudson and Doris Day in Pillow Talk, a bus arrived at the bottom of the gangplank and a group of young kids jumped out with a priest shouting out that they had got the message about the movie and were so thrilled to have been invited.

It turned out that their boat was on the other side of the U-shaped harbour and they had seen the signal and thought the invitation was for them, failing to realise it was for the yacht in between us and their boat.

What could I do? I sat them down on the deck with the old boys and we all watched the film. Doris Day was terrific.

At the end, there was great appreciation from the Playboy group and then the priest said on leaving that he would like to come and preach a sermon with the children on our boat the following day, a Sunday. I said it really would not be necessary although it was a lovely idea and virtually threw them off the boat in order to get them out of the way before the captain returned. Huge relief when they had all gone: a close one.

At 2am the crew began to return in dribs and drabs, all completely plastered. The boatswain arrived out of his mind and went to sleep on the deck in the stern of the boat. At 3am, as I was preparing for bed, he was still lying there with his arm through the railings. He was out cold. After I had completely failed to get him to stand up, I decided I would tie his arms to the railings in case he woke up. This, I reasoned, would prevent him from falling overboard.

The only rope available was curled up in the stern and I cut two short pieces off and tied the boatswain's wrists, not too tightly, to the railings.

At least he was safe.

He woke early the next morning and started screaming his head off, demanding to know who had tied him up. He soon learned it was the galley boy and came charging down to our cabin threatening to chuck me overboard. The banging and shouting brought the captain to the scene and eventually the boatswain was becalmed with half the crew hanging onto him and my life was saved.

But there was more to come.

Around noon the following day, a bus arrived at the gangplank and a bunch of children piled out with the priest at the front. I simply could not believe it and rushed forward to tell the priest that everybody was asleep.

The captain was on the bridge and yelled down to me, 'Murray, what the hell is going on down there for God's sake?' I resisted shouting back that it *was* for God's sake and yelled back that it was a priest who wanted to preach a sermon. He went ballistic and called me to the bridge. When I got there he said, 'Murray you can sit and take the sermon. Nobody else will and as soon as it's over, get him and his kids off my fucking boat.'

I told the priest to make it very quick and I sat on the deck with the kids while he gave us a short talk about God. I shovelled them off the boat at the end, all the while expressing thanks to him for his kindness in coming over.

'God loves you', were his parting words. I'm still waiting for confirmation on that from the Man himself!

We stayed a week in Buenos Aires.

I saw my first dead body.

Chucking a bucket of potato peel over the side one morning, I noticed a carcass floating upside down in the water just below me. It was a star-shaped corpse with a knife in the back. Not a good way to start the day.

I reported it to the boatswain, who did not seem very excited – routine stuff for him. The cops came and dragged the body out of the water, blue and black and bloated. They threw it in the back of a truck and drove off. We heard nothing more about it.

At the end of the Second World War, Argentina was one of the richest countries on the planet. They had fed all sides during the war with beef and wheat at the end of which in 1945, the world owed them US$4 billion. Big dough in those days.

In 1951, they forgave the debt and became the most loved and admired country on earth. The Perons, Eva and husband, were heroes. Statues of them were being erected everywhere; Argentina was booming.

Eva and her husband died that year. Heroes of the country.

By 1956, just four years later, Argentina had inflation running at 1,000 per cent and two years after that, they were broke. Not even enough money to pay Thomas de la Rue for the paper on which to print their banknotes. Top to bottom in just five years. Hence the old term 'life can turn on a sixpence'.

My father knew something about that.

We had arrived in the middle of the collapse: total chaos. Riots, fireworks, screaming sirens and gunshots. Welcome to South America. Land of the free.

My voyage on the St Arvans lasted for about nine months. It was rough and tough, and I was miles off my normal path, but I felt free and devoid of responsibility. I could do anything; go anywhere. No strings, no ties, carefree shipmates except for the ship's captain, who made Bligh of HMS Bounty look like a Benedictine monk.

I must have peeled about 50,000 potatoes on that trip. I pulled ropes and tied down hatches as we sailed across big seas. The Atlantic rollers were enormous and sometimes they splashed across the whole ship.

There were good times too, ashore: bars, booze, girls, beer, lots of laughs and numerous headaches.

There was one more incident, which nearly brought about my having to 'walk the plank!'

Every so often when we were on the high seas there would be a practice alarm. The bell would ring, the engines roar into reverse gear and the captain would start yelling through a megaphone, 'Man overboard! Man overboard! Starboard side! Starboard side! All hands on deck! Engines reverse! Engines reverse!'

We all knew what to do. We would run on to the deck to our known positions for this emergency. We had done it many times. An officer would throw overboard a heavy rubber floating body from the bow of the ship and we would grab long rods with hooks and try to catch it as it floated by. Sometimes we caught it and hoisted it back on board, simulating that we had indeed rescued the man who had fallen overboard, but frequently we missed it and on it drifted past the stern of the ship.

Then the captain would yell 'Boatswain to the stern!'

The boatswain would then run to the stern, pick up a small anchor attached to a rope, swing it a couple of times around his head and fling it to the floating rubber body. He never missed, and he would then haul it back on board.

Cheers for the boatswain from all the crew.

After we left Montevideo and were sailing up the east coast of South America towards Brazil, we had the man-overboard drill. We missed the rubber body as usual and the boatswain rushed to the stern, everybody watching the big throw.

Imagine the horror, followed by hysterical laughter, when the anchor kept on flying and disappeared into the sea.

Gaping faces. Somebody had cut the rope. The suspense lasted a full minute before it dawned on the boatswain. The galley boy had cut the rope to tie him up that first night when he had arrived back on board after his night out in Buenos Aires. He gave a roar – 'Galley!' – that a bear would have been proud of and started running.

I had realised what had happened a minute before everybody else and had started running as well – for the cabin – and locked the door.

The captain ultimately put me in the 'cooler' for the day as a punishment.

By the time I came out, even the boatswain thought it was funny, and I was a bit of a hero.

On this great voyage across the high seas, I had also learned that when you buy cigarettes on board at duty free prices and crew discounts, you can sell them to stevedores at a higher rate when the ship arrives in port and make a profit. This was not big business because there was a lack of capital to invest in the product. There was nevertheless a profit margin and no overheads, since, paradoxically, storage in the bulkhead of the ship was free of charge.

There was a risk factor because the penalty for smuggling cigarettes at that time in Argentina was seven years in jail. About which we had been warned.

We sailed up the River Plate to Rosario and then on to Montevideo, up to Brazil, Santos, Recife, around the Caribbean and finally back across the Atlantic to arrive at Bremen in Germany.

In Bremen, I reported to the captain and told him I would be leaving the ship. He was furious and reminded me that I had signed on for a 'round trip' from Rotterdam to Rotterdam.

When I pointed out that Rotterdam was only sixty miles away, he replied, 'That is Rotterdam. This is Bremen!'

When I queried our arrival date in Rotterdam, I was not prepared for his answer.

'I don't know,' he said, very slowly and with careful articulation. 'We are going to Bombay in the morning!'

That was my first and very valuable lesson in contract law.

Within an hour I was gone.

Down the gangplank and into the darkness of Bremen. I am probably still on a missing list somewhere in their archives.

Penalty for 'jumping ship': seven lashes with the cat o'nine tails.

I caught a train back to Rotterdam. It was the end of my career in the Merchant Navy. No regrets.

⌒⌒

Four years later in my second year in the Foreign Legion, I was on town patrol in Philippeville, a small port in Algeria, where the Parachute Regiment had its base camp. The role of the town patrol was like that of the military police. There were about eight of us on the back of a truck with a sergeant in charge in the cabin with the driver.

We toured around the bars and bordellos, ready to put out fights and arrest drunken behaviour. The form was, when we arrived at a bar, the sergeant would go in and have a few drinks and we would wait to be called in if there was trouble. If not, when the sergeant was ready, we would roll on to the next bar.

On this occasion, a legionnaire came out of a bar and shouted to me, 'Hey, Johnny', (I was always called Johnny in the Legion as my fellow legionnaires believed it to be an 'English' name) 'there's an *Englander* in the bar!'

I told him to go back in and bring him out. I hadn't seen an Englishman for two years.

Out came the Brit, and I told him to go back inside and get a couple of bottles of red and he could join me on the back of the truck, and I would tell him the story of my life. When he came back and we had refreshed ourselves with the red, I asked him what the hell he was doing in Philippeville. It was the arsehole of the world. He said he was the radio officer on a Greek ship. I queried why a Greek ship and he said in the Merchant Navy one could go on *any* ship if one had a seaman's certificate. I then told him that I was once in the Merchant Navy and had got a job on a ship in Rotterdam going to South America, because the galley boy had gone sick.

He said, 'Oh! That must have been the St *Arvans*, a few years ago.'

I was blown away. I said, 'How the hell do you know that? Yes, it was the St *Arvans*.'

He said, 'My name's Martin Fisher. I was the galley boy you replaced.'

Back to the bar, for two more reds!

CHAPTER VI
MATHER AND PLATT

My great-great-grandfather, Sir William Mather, an engineer by training, had started out with a small iron foundry in Salford, making pumps with a partner called Platt.

Their timing was at the forefront of the Industrial Revolution. Mather and Platt, as the company was called, went on to supply electric motors to London's first underground railways and installed the pumps that drove the mighty fountains of Trafalgar Square.

By 1920, they had turned the business into one of the largest engineering companies in Britain.

Sir William was a generous philanthropist with a particular interest in education. He founded engineering schools in places as far away as Khartoum. He had connections with Princeton in the USA and gave the university generous bursaries. He was also a member of Privy Council and introduced the sixty hour working week.

In 1921, he presented Princeton with an exact replica of the Turnbull sundial built at Corpus Christi College Oxford in 1551; it still stands today in the McCosh courtyard at Princeton. The sundial has twenty-four different dials and was given to represent the close relationship between Oxford and Princeton. Woodrow Wilson, the American President, presided over the inauguration ceremony together with James Bryce, the British Ambassador, in front of a crowd of 2,000.

On one of his trips to the United States, Sir William met a fellow engineer, Frederick Grinnell. Grinnell had patented a new invention to fight fires: a 'water sprinkler' with a small glass vial containing a chemical that expanded when heated. The glass exploded at a certain temperature, which released water from a connected pressurised water system. Sprinklers were soon to be installed in the bulkheads of ships and in the ceilings of buildings.

Sir William saw the potential of the sprinkler immediately and negotiated the worldwide rights with Grinnell for the rest of the world excluding

America, on the spot. It was the luckiest meeting of his life and made him a fortune.

Mather and Platt grew fast, supplying the machinery for many of the world's textile mills and employed thousands of people in its offices and factories around the globe, in countries as dispersed as India, Japan, Australia and Russia.

Sir William was a man of grand statements. At the end of the world's first EXPO, the Great Exhibition of Paris in 1889 (*L'Exposition Universelle*), timed to coincide with the 100th anniversary of the French Revolution, he bought the steel-framed buildings that had housed the exhibition (built by Monsieur Eiffel) from the French government and had them erected at Newton Heath, in Manchester.

The buildings had covered two square kilometres of Paris and they fitted perfectly into his sixty-five acres of land at Newton Heath.

Many years later his great-great-grandson, me, was to participate in the acquisition of the leftovers of another Expo site. This time in Vancouver in 1987, several of us bought the land on which the Expo had displayed the grandness of Canada.

~~~

Six months after I had disembarked from the St *Arvans*, I joined Mather and Platt, the 'family firm', as a 'special' apprentice. I was the great-great-grandson of the founder but there were no special privileges. My pay was £7 per week (That's £1 a day, just in case anybody didn't catch that, or £365 per annum, less contributions to national insurance, net £300). My digs cost me £4 a week and travel on the bus cost me £1. Food cost £3.10. I was broke before I had started. Losing £1.10 per week. Negative cash flow. Bad news. Bad start.

My day began at 7am with a bus ride to M and P, through the gloomy smog of Manchester. Manchester in 1958 was a dreary place with evidence of the war everywhere in the form of bombed-out ruins. The smog was so thick sometimes that they had to light fires at crossroads. People often drove cars at three miles an hour with a man walking in front swinging a lantern.

I initially worked on the shop floor on a lathe, and then was transferred to the iron foundry. It was gruesome work: dust and constant noise.

The days were spent crafting moulds for pumps and then in the evening it was the moment for the big pour of molten iron from massive furnaces that had been roaring throughout the day.

I loathed it. The only relief was the 'snuff' supplied by Cartwright, the foreman, who thought I was a 'good lud' because one day I had introduced him to Earl Grey tea instead of the foul black stuff his wife brewed.

Peter Paulson, a cousin, worked in the company as well. We became close friends.

The only good thing about Mather and Platt as far as I was concerned was the chairman's granddaughter, Jennifer, known as Jeffa. She was effectively my second cousin once removed, but we lived on different planets. We had first met at a children's outing at London Zoo. We were on an elephant. I was on the trunk and she was on its back with a bunch of other kids. We were eleven years old. The romance was on.

The one person who seemed to take an interest in me was Loris Mather, the chairman, who one day gave me a cheque for £60, which brought much relief.

Uncle Loris was the nearest to what having a father must be like and always appeared to be there for me at the right times. He realised I was having a problem making ends meet on the salary I was paid (good observation). He had arranged for me to meet the manager of the Midland Bank at their headquarters at 100 King Street, to open an account with my new cheque.

In 1958 the Midland Bank was the largest bank in the world. It was interesting that the largest bank in the world was in Manchester not London – perhaps an indication of the economic benefits that are derived from manufacturing rather than the service industry. Certainly in those days.

Midland Bank was also the largest company in the world by market capitalisation – eat your heart out Henry Ford and all the rest of them!

There I was at the HQ of the Midland Bank being ushered into a small private room, clutching my cheque, and feeling like Howard Hughes. The manager arrived, all smiles and queries about Loris Mather's health, and how wonderful it was to have a member of the family opening an account at the Midland. 'Uncle' Loris had done good prep work.

He failed to conceal a slight trace of disappointment when he saw the amount on the cheque, but bravely soldiered on explaining how the system worked. He finally gave me a cheque book. The cheque book was somewhat thinner than the rather fat accompanying book I was given for registering my deposits. He then muttered something about the perils of an 'overdraft' – I didn't know what he was talking about – and thought somebody must have left the window open. I left feeling good. The wheel was spinning. I had cash in the bank for the first time. Nothing like it.

After the First World War there was a huge deficit of engineers in England and most of the large corporations took on apprentices to ensure future supplies. At Mather and Platt they were known as 'special' apprentices. We worked on the shop floor with the 'trade' apprentices but ultimately, we would be selected for management roles. My future was assured... if I stuck it out.

When I arrived, the rising star at Mather and Platt and identified successor was coincidentally, Uncle Loris's son, Bill. He was Jeffa's father.

Bill Mather lived with his family in a very impressive residence in Cheshire called Whirley Hall, standing in 200 acres of lush countryside. I was the impoverished relative working in a boiler suit on the shop floor of the iron foundry and living in a one-room bedsit earning £7 a week.

I once asked Bill why most of the 'special' apprentices who were at universities doing a 'sandwich' course at Mathers (a year of practical experience during their three years at university) never came back to work at Mather and Platt when they had finished their degrees. His reply was, 'It doesn't matter, Simon, because they make good ambassadors for M and P, in the companies in which they eventually become senior executives.'

A good lesson. Allow people to leave feeling good about their time spent with you. They will always remember and want to repay.

From time to time, I would receive an invitation to stay at Whirley for the weekend and for even longer sometimes over Easter or Christmas. The Mathers were kind to my brother and I and we mixed well with their four children, the elder of which were two girls, Jeffa and Gillian. They were studying art in London and would arrive for weekends with their London friends, looking affluent in fleets of cars. There's that 'chip on the shoulder' again.

Negative cash flow from working at Mather's necessitated me taking an evening job as a waiter at the Pack Horse Hotel in Bolton. This helped bolster my income and enabled me to finance an occasional visit to the cinema.

Despite the gaping financial gap, Jeffa and I were slowly drawn to each other. I was her friend. She liked me but was not in love with me. Whereas I was in love with her and it grew each time I saw her.

One day, I got around to asking her out to dinner and a movie. The film was called *Gigi* featuring the lovely Leslie Caron and I bought the tickets before going to dinner, just in case I ran short. I had decided to take her to dinner at the Midland Hotel, where I had never been, but hoped it would impress her.

She arrived in her father's Jaguar and it was me that was impressed!

When we entered this enormous railway-station hotel, a man came up and asked, 'The Grill or the Pierrot, sir?' I said, without a fraction of hesitation, as if this was where I regularly dined, 'I think the Grill this evening.'

The Grill was slightly larger than the railway station itself, with about 500 tables, and it was empty. Impossible to imagine anything more romantic, except possibly Dartmoor prison.

I ordered two glasses of champagne and was presented with a menu.

One glance at it told be me this was going to be a close-run thing and I gave thanks to the Lord for giving me the presence of mind to buy the cinema tickets in advance.

I put the thought in Jeffa's mind that to be sure of getting to the cinema on time, we should perhaps just do a main course and skip the starter, and I even suggested that 'as life was uncertain,' we should perhaps go straight to the dessert.

I also told her I was on a diet. Anything to get out alive without being flung into a debtor's prison.

We finally got to the bill and I made it with three pennies to spare.

The movie was wonderful and when we emerged from the cinema and were walking towards the car park, we passed a bar with a policeman standing outside, and Jeffa said, 'Why don't I buy you a night-cap?'

We went in and had a nice drink, with a rather noisy band playing, but it was great fun. When we came out, I asked the policeman, 'Who are those people playing in there?'

He replied, 'It's a group wot calls themselves the Rolling Stones.'

It sounded like it.

Then Jeffa offered to drive me home. My digs were in a grotty part of

Bolton and I felt terribly ashamed of them. I said my car was around the corner and 'no problem'. A kiss on both cheeks and she was gone in the Jag.

It started to rain.

I walked down to the main road leading to Bolton and started thumbing a lift. Many cars went by, but none stopped. Finally, at about 2am a truck stopped, and I clambered in. By this time, I looked as though I had just climbed out of a swimming pool and it provided the answer as to why no cars had stopped for me.

We drove for about forty minutes when the driver asked me what part of Wigan I was heading for. I replied that I was going to Bolton. He looked at me in amazement. 'You're going the wrong way, mate. Bolton's in the opposite direction!'

Forty minutes in the wrong direction at two in the morning. Nothing for it but to disembark, turn around and start thumbing again. I got to Bolton and my digs at 4:30am. How romantic is that.

My landlady had a rule that the front door was locked at midnight. My room was on the first floor and next to it was a box room where we kept our trunks and boxes. She never rented out the box room – or so I thought! There was a drainpipe running down from the box room and up I went. The window was slightly open. I had pushed it halfway open when suddenly there was a great shout from within and the next thing I knew, somebody had me by the throat and was trying to push me out. I managed to cling on to the drainpipe and at the same time get across to a complete maniac that I lived in the next-door room. I was finally in bed and will always remember what had begun as a romantic evening had ended with a very unromantic morning.

But despite the attraction to Jeffa, Manchester was not for me. It was a massive bombed-out slum. The war had finished thirteen years before, but there was no money to rebuild. The factories belched out from their 'dark satanic mills' a yellow putrid waste through which the sun could never shine. I had no money. I was up at 6:30 every morning to catch the bus to the foundry. Boiler suit on. Clock in. All day in the scum of it and at six in the evening, clocking out. Sometimes a beer in the pub and then back to my digs. A quick shower and off to the Pack Horse to wait on tables every night. A robotic existence that would have depressed a hyena.

On occasions there were debutante dances in London and Jeffa would invite me to join her as her 'deb's delight'. This meant hiring a dinner jacket and travelling for four hours, often without a seat, in a crowded train to London. I would stay in London with Peter Paulson, my cousin who had moved there, and then, slightly ashamedly, take the midnight train back to Manchester in order to be at Mather's to clock in at the foundry at 8am. This journey would find me, more often than not, sleeping in the corridor of the train on the floor, doing what is known today as a 'Corbyn'.

This was my first real introduction to the gap between the haves and the have-nots. And all because my father had thrown it all away – or perhaps his mother had done so, or maybe his grandmother had been the root of the woodworm in the Murray family.

There are those who make money, those that use money, those that lose money and those that waste it: in my family we had them all.

At the top of our family tree were the Petrocochinos, the Mathers and the Murrays: a firm and well-established trio of families with deep roots. Wealth travelled down the treeline initially evenly, but the big waster, the branch that broke the cash flow, was undoubtedly my father. He was the crack in the floor. The fortunes of those that make them with axe and lever often trickle through the softer fingers of their descendants. I did not take it personally, but it was irritating.

Having said that, starting with nothing sows the seeds of incentive and I had already been halfway around the world, which was much further than many of those around me had travelled.

Jealousy did not gnaw at my insides and I had many laughs and remember them as good times, but there was a slight question of 'why me?' We were all in this together – all branches from the same tree. My brother and I were the only ones in the flock to have ended up with nothing. It wasn't a curse, but it was a bore – and I felt I had to break out or it would always be around me if I stayed on this path.

It was time to take the fork in the road.

The Murray family had a long history of military service. My brother Anthony was an officer in the Scots Greys. I had a father, grandfather, great-grandfather and a great-great-grandfather who had all served in regiments such as the Black Watch in the Crimea, at Waterloo and in the Boer War as well as the First and Second World Wars. There were not many countries on the planet that the British Army had not invaded, and the Murrays had done their stuff.

I decided to join the British Army.

CHAPTER VII

W.O.S.B.

It was time for a chat with Uncle Loris. I told him I wanted to join the army. He understood. He wasn't angry and I think he felt I was doing the right thing. He said, Bill, his son, had a few contacts and could help. Bill had been Montgomery's ADC in the North African campaign in the Second World War and he knew a Gurkha officer who could offer guidance. I wanted to join a Gurkha regiment.

Two weeks later an interview was arranged with General Pugh, the commander of the 2nd Gurkha Rifles. I liked him immediately and perhaps more importantly, he liked me. His ADC, Lieutenant Brian Skinner, was enthusiastic, but before going any further I had to do a medical.

Two months later I discovered I was 'green and red' colour-blind. Apparently, one in five men are colour blind. Women never are. I received a letter from the War Office informing me I could not join a Gurkha regiment because of my eyesight, but all other regiments would be open to me as an officer, if I first submitted myself to a War Office Selection Board (WOSB). But for me it was Gurkhas or nothing.

Lt Skinner was in touch with me within minutes, with instructions to turn up at Westminster Hospital for another eye test by a brigadier who would come to a different conclusion about my eyesight than the sergeant in the ophthalmic corps. Unfortunately, he didn't.

This is when I had my first thoughts about the French Foreign Legion. I contacted the French Embassy in London and was given the information that they had a recruitment office in Paris, together with the address. But Brian Skinner came back with commendable persistence and told me that General Pugh wanted me in the regiment and didn't give a damn about my eyesight. Clearly a perceptive man! I would still have to do the WOSB.

Three weeks later the War Office were back in touch with instructions to appear before a WOSB in Hampshire. Skinner gave me advice on how the interview process worked.

'There will be a team of three, a captain, a major and a colonel. It's a piece of cake. You can't fail. The captain does the physical stuff. He'll have you jumping through hoops, climbing ropes, crossing rivers with sacks of cement on your back and he'll be looking for leadership qualities in group exercises. You'll have to start by writing an essay and probably be asked to give a ten-minute talk. The major will then ask you about current affairs. Tell him you read *The Times* and for God's sake don't say you read *Hank Jansen* or smoke black cheroots. They don't like that stuff... And by the way, for the last six months he's been asking for the name of the premier of the Sudan.'

He told me that nobody had provided the answer, '... So if you can find that out, it will be a "coup", if he asks you. The colonel will check you for attitude and your religious inclinations. You'll have a ball. See you when you get back. Good luck.'

I did my homework and was ready for WOSB. I arrived at the Royal Artillery Barracks in Hampshire, slightly surprised to find I was the only civilian. The other twenty-odd candidates had all been in the army for six months or more. We kicked off with an essay. Choice of subjects ran from 'Relationships with the Kremlin', and 'Views on the Italian Campaign in the Second World War', to 'An Adventure,' for the non-intellectuals. I opted for the latter and wrote three pages on my boat trip to South America. I was pleased with what I had written.

But I was getting ahead of myself!

I gave a talk on Hindu fire-walking, which seemed to go down well with the captain. On the physical side, I jumped through all the hoops and climbed the ropes. Bedford School gymnastics came in handy. This was easy.

The major probed me on my reading habits, and I responded with *The Times*. He then asked me for the name of the premier of the Sudan, and I answered 'General Aboud'. I thought he was going to drop dead. He simply couldn't believe it.

He said, 'I've been asking that for six months and finally someone with the answer – how on earth do you know that?'

I told him that I knew he'd been asking it for six months and so I took the trouble to find out. His disappointment was apparent but then he laughed and said, 'Ten for honesty.'

Everything seemed to be looking good and there was only the colonel left. He was a quiet, subdued man who looked more like a priest than someone in the military.

'Do sit down,' he began, and then looked at me in silence for a few moments. He flicked through some papers and said, 'You have done rather well so far. There's a good report from the captain. You're obviously very fit and the major told me you delivered on General Aboud.'

There was a long silence.

'I was very interested in your essay on your trip to South America', he said, adding, 'Did you enjoy that?'

I answered briefly and added that I thought that overall, it was a good experience. He then said quietly, 'Tell me about the cigarette smuggling – why did you do that?'

I paused, sensing a bear trap.

I guessed that 'because everybody else was doing it' might not be the right answer. Similarly, I was wary of the 'honest' response, which was that it was a good way to make some money.

I told him that the cigarette smuggling had been on a very small scale and provided some extra centimes on top of our miniscule weekly income. Then he asked, 'But did you think this was a very good thing to be doing?'

I replied carefully, but maybe not carefully enough, 'I didn't really think too much about it in the context of whether it was a good thing to be doing or not.'

'But did you think it was a *morally good* thing to be doing?' he then asked.

Even more carefully this time, I said I had not considered it in moral terms, and that anyway the scale of it was so small as not to be relevant.

I added for good measure that I thought a man's morals were governed by his conscience, and that over this issue my conscience was not causing me any trouble.

Mistake… Big mistake!

From nowhere I was suddenly in quicksand. I knew immediately I was doomed.

Two hours later we were assembled to hear the results. The colonel explained that he would pass down the line and hand each one of us a piece of paper. The paper would state 'Pass, Fail or Deferred Watch'. Deferred

Watch meant we had failed but we could try again in six months. If we had any queries, we could go to his office afterwards and he would do his best to answer them.

I opened my hand: 'Deferred Watch'. It was like receiving a death sentence.

The captain told me how sorry he was and that he and the major had fought hard to get me through, but the colonel was adamant. The colonel's view was that I was too young and not ready, and that I could try again in six months' time.

I returned by train to London where I was due to dine with Uncle Loris at his house with my brother Anthony, who was still in the Scots Greys, and Francis Widdrington, Loris's son-in-law (ex-Welsh Guards). All were waiting to congratulate me, thinking I couldn't fail. They tried hard to make up for my embarrassment by naming great officers who had failed WOSB the first time, but I was feeling very sorry for myself. My first big failure and it was like lead upon my shoulders.

I returned to work in Manchester with my tail between my legs, depressed as hell. All I could think about was that I must get out of this rut. I remember telling one of the men in the foundry that I was going to join the Foreign Legion; he laughed out loud and told me I was mad. A few days later, Brian Skinner called me at my digs and told me that General Pugh had intervened and that I would be doing another WOSB in two weeks' time at a different place with a different colonel.

'… and not too much about cigarette smuggling this time,' he laughed.

But the Gurkhas were already a thing of the past in my mind. There had been recent reports in newspapers that the French Foreign Legion was fighting in Algeria against rebel forces who were seeking independence from France. Leaping into the unknown was not unknown to me and it didn't worry me. I flipped a coin. Heads to France, tails I stay.

It was heads.

I took the ferry from Dover to France the next day.

I had told Skinner that it was too late and that I was going to join the Legion. 'For God's sake Simon,' he said. 'Don't be a bloody fool. That's an absolute nightmare. You'll be dead in a week. Relax. Everything's going to be fine. Give it one more go… For heaven's sake man. The general wants you in the regiment.'

I told him that the Legion medical was apparently very tough so I'd probably be back, and I would see him in a week's time.

'Let's hope so,' he said.

But I wasn't to see him again for fourteen years.

I also telephoned Jeffa. We had become very close friends but although I was madly in love with her, she was still not yet at my level of enthusiasm. I had asked her to marry me about twenty times. We were dancing to Frank Sinatra once in the Blue Angel nightclub and he was singing a song about the French Foreign Legion and I had told her that I would run away to join if she didn't marry me. All very jokey then, but here I was, ready to go. Reality. She pleaded with me not to go. But my mind was made up.

A day later I found myself at eight o'clock in the morning in the Paris Metro heading for the Old Fort in Vincennes, the recruitment centre of the Foreign Legion. On the doors of the massive gates was a simple message:

'*Bureau d'Engagement Légion Étrangère* – *Ouvert Jour et Nuit 24 Heures.*'

I was one of forty volunteers that day. After some serious medical tests and interviews, they took seven of us. They also had the colour-blind test. Lots of multi-coloured dots on a page in which you are supposed to see a number or a figure if you are not colour-blind, but nothing if you are. On the page I could see nothing behind the dots. When the sergeant doing the medical thought I had a language problem and started making a clucking noise, I said '*poulet*'. Roars of applause. Then he made a 'meow' for the next one and I said '*chat*'.

'Bravo' came the response and I was through.

Bedford School French lessons finally paying off.

That evening I signed a contract to serve in the Foreign Legion for five years. There was a clause that said they could fire me after three months if I was not up to their standards. This seemed reasonable. We spent two weeks in an old fort in Marseilles doing chores and then I was on a troop ship called the S.S. *Sidi Bel Abbès*, sailing to Algeria. One thing I did learn in the Legion, is that five years is a long time and time does not fly as fast as some people are so fond of telling us.

CHAPTER VIII

A BREAK

After four and a half years' service in Algeria, I could go on leave to France for the first time: generous. It was June 1964. I hadn't seen my mother since I had left England and she and Leo together with my little half-sister Caroline flew to join me in Paris. The reunion did not go well; my mother had aged, was drinking far too much and gave me a drubbing for having joined the Legion.

I needed a passport to go to England. The Legion still had mine. I went to the British Embassy and explained the situation. They put me in a room with an MI6 guy who said I could have a passport in return for answering some questions. I was then grilled on all aspects of the Legion, where they were stationed, in what countries, what type of armaments did they use, how many troops in total and so on. No great secrets were divulged because I didn't have any! They gave me a temporary passport and I took the ferry boat on which I had travelled to Calais so many years earlier, now going in the opposite direction, with great enthusiasm.

I arrived in London and stayed with an old school friend, Ian McCullum, but phoned Jeffa to see if we could meet perhaps for a drink. She said she was due to go to Spain the next day but agreed to go out to a nightclub with me there and then. She had written to me all the time I had been away and, I think, fallen in love with the romantic image of a legionnaire.

A couple of years earlier, I had saved enough money to buy her a watch in a little town on the Moroccan frontier called Oujda. The watch had cost me six months' pay and I had asked the Arab shopkeeper to post it for me. I regretted this later, fearing that the shopkeeper wouldn't send it and had cursed myself many times for being such an idiot for being so trusting.

Wrong. He did post it. My parcel to Jeffa crossed with a letter from her to me telling me she was engaged to be married. Somehow or other the watch and the letters crossed with perfect timing. I was distraught on hearing about her engagement and she was distraught when she received the watch.

But that watch from the man in Oujda worked magic, and she broke off her engagement. In reality it was for other reasons, not needed here.

Having persuaded her to come out, we went to the Revolution nightclub – next door to what is now Bellamy's restaurant - where we danced all night. I started off by being very blasé and off-hand, as though I didn't really give a damn, and then later as we danced to the soft night music and I held her closely in my arms, I told her how much I still loved her and always would. To my astonishment, she confessed that she loved me too.

I was the happiest I had been all my life and I went back to the Legion the luckiest man on earth. She wrote to me constantly for the next six months.

Time rushed by. At the end of 1964, my five years in the Legion were about to end and it was time to return home.

I left Algeria for Marseille on 18 December 1964, wondering if I might perhaps return to Algeria one day in more peaceful times. I did, but that's another story.

Six weeks later it was my final assembly in my new Legion demob suit on the parade ground in Aubagne, southern France. This was now the Legion headquarters, replacing Sidi Bel Abbès, which had been the Legion's nerve centre for a century and a half in Algeria.

Churchill died during my last week. I listened to the radio all day. The French obituaries were fantastic. They didn't let up for a single second during the day in singing his praises, paying tribute and showering him with honours. It was very moving.

On 12 February 1965, those leaving gathered for the final parade at 7am. Colonel Vadot, the commanding officer at the Legion headquarters, presented us with a certificate of 'Bonne Conduit,' which stated that we had served for five years with 'honneur et fidélité.'

I was very proud.

There were eight of us leaving – none of them among the six that had joined with me five years earlier. I wondered what had happened to them. Of the forty enthusiasts who were ready to sign on in Paris so many years ago, only one seemed to have made it through to the finishing post… Me!

We went to the Deuxième Bureau at Fort Saint Nicholas to collect our belongings. I was given a small brown envelope which had my old British passport in it and my address book that had been confiscated when I arrived.

It was an emotional moment, like meeting all my friends again. I scanned the address book and so many names brought faces to mind that I had not seen for so long or thought about in years.

Good times coming.

I walked out of the fort gates, saluted the sentry and saluted the Foreign Legion flag and then raced for the train to Paris. Jeffa was in Paris to meet me off the train. It was wonderful to see her again now both of us were up to our eyeballs in love.

CHAPTER IX

RETURN OF THE PRODIGAL

The cocktail party was swinging when I arrived. The room was a beehive in full buzz. Mostly people I did not know. Then suddenly I saw my cousin Peter Paulson, whom I had last seen five years earlier. He came jostling towards me through the crowd, a huge grin on his face, holding high in his hand a brown paper package, calling my name above the noise, 'Simon! Simon!'

People stopped screaming at each other and turned to find the focus of his calls. I felt very conspicuous. My head was shaved (unusual in those days) and I probably looked a little rough in my Foreign Legion demob suit of a speckled grey colour, two sizes too big and crafted a long way from Saville Row! Peter's arms were around me in a fraternal hug with much back-slapping.

'It's Simon!' he yelled, to one and all who now stood gaping. 'He's back from the Legion – five years, for God's sake, and he's back!'

'Look what I've got for you,' he said, handing me the brown paper parcel. 'I've been keeping it for you for five years and here you are!'

I opened the parcel. Everybody was watching in anticipation.

'Your laundry' he shouted. 'I've been holding it for you.'

And there indeed was my laundry – a shirt, a pair of underpants, a handkerchief and a pair of socks, as familiar to me as old friends.

'Fabulous,' I stuttered. 'Apart from what I'm wearing, this is all I've got in the world.'

I stood there with my laundry in my hands and received a modest, if confused round of applause. Then a tall man standing next to me introduced himself.

'Hello, I'm Charles Letts,' he said, in a gravelly voice, the cause of which I learned later was a rifle butt being slammed into his oesophagus by a guard in a Japanese prisoner of war camp some years earlier. I also discovered later from Godfrey Paulson, Peter's father and a great friend of Letts, that

Letts was a 'spook'. Godfrey Paulson was in the Foreign Office, and more pertinently, in MI5. He was known in 'the firm' as 'Paul'.

Charles Letts was an unpaid 'friend' of 'the firm'. He was also the managing director of Jardine Matheson's operations in South East Asia, principally in Singapore, Malaysia and Thailand.

Jardine Matheson was the great trading company based in Hong Kong, known locally simply as 'the Princely Hong', later christened *The Noble House* in the eponymous book by James Clavell. It was said in days of yore that Hong Kong was run by the Governor, the Jockey Club and Jardine's... But not necessarily in that order!

Letts asked me what I was doing. I said I was looking for a job. He told me that Jardine's recruited five graduates a year exclusively from Oxford and Cambridge, who formed a training cadre. He had long felt that they should broaden this recruitment base and if I could get myself to Singapore, he might have something for me. He gave me his card and we shook hands. For an unemployed ex-legionnaire, aged twenty-five, with no idea about what to do next, this was a ray of light. I started thinking about Singapore. But I still had to find a job, now.

I answered an advert in the *Daily Telegraph* looking for 'a man seeking a sales career in Europe'. I applied and was thrilled when I was invited for an interview with a man called Clive Morris. Morris had an office slightly larger than a tennis court in a modern building in Cheam. As I walked into his office, he said from behind a fortress desk at the other end of the room, 'We are looking for someone who is expecting to make at least £5,000 a year in commissions: is this you?' This was supposed to knock me off my feet. And it nearly did. It was huge bucks. I walked towards him. Given the distance I had to cover, I had plenty of time to think. I resisted a smart answer and simply said, 'It depends on what I have to do.'

This got me as far as the chair in front of his desk. But I was still in the room. He liked the fact that I spoke French and German, and was slightly stunned that I had been in the Legion and asked me why I had not put this on my CV. I said I thought it might have put him off.

'On the contrary, I think it's terrific,' he said.

Morris was a sales agent in Scandinavia and elsewhere in Europe for British manufacturers who had no distribution outside the UK. In 1965 there were many. His products ranged from carbon paper, typewriter ribbons, scotch tape - which he claimed to have invented - and by way of diversification, fold-away beds and chemicals for delousing sheep. The employment terms were accommodation, a car and a commission on anything I sold, but no salary. I would start in Denmark and be trained by his best salesman, Max Brook.

Fine by me.

I left for Copenhagen two days later, after promising Jeffa that we would be married as soon as I had made some money. I was met at the airport in Copenhagen by Max Brook and taught the art of selling carbon paper. Max sold truckloads of carbon paper, which he referred to as reprint sheets. When he demonstrated its qualities, he made it look like rare silk impregnated with gold. He sold it to the chairmen of huge companies. Fairly soon, I was selling masses of the stuff too.

Slowly I made a little money selling Morris's products. I had a few problems with the chemical for cleaning the sheep. It was poured into a sump through which the sheep were driven, and they were then theoretically free of lice. On one occasion a farmer had not read the instructions properly, which clearly stated that the chemical had to be diluted with five parts water to one part of the chemical. He had filled the sump with 100 per cent of the chemical, which is the exact percentage of his sheep that he lost. He took it out on me, and Morris's lawyers saved a bad situation.

Evenings were cheery affairs in the bars of Copenhagen and at weekends Jeffa would fly out to join me. I was getting ready to officially ask her to marry me but wanted to be certain I had a proper job and could look after her.

One day 'Paul' Paulson asked me if I would like to consider something in the Foreign Office. He arranged for me to meet Maurice Oldfield – 'C' – in a splendid office overlooking the Thames.

'C' was positive and arranged a follow-up meeting at 4 Carlton Gardens, where an immaculately dressed young man greeted me. He ushered me into a waiting room, at the end of which was an enormous door, rather like one might find at the entrance of a cathedral.

After half an hour the door opened. I walked through into a large room in which there was a semi-circular table with seven people around it. In front, bang in the middle, facing the team, was a chair and a side table with a glass of water and a packet of cigarettes on it. Benson and Hedges, no less.

The man in the centre said in a very friendly, rather smooth voice, 'Good morning. My name is John Briance. Do feel free to smoke if you wish,' and waved with his hand to the fags on the table. 'This is a general board covering several departments, so that we can all get a chance to take a look at you and of course it will be in your interests as it will provide a broader opportunity for us to find something that suits you.'

By way of casual conversation and knowing my Legion connection, and probably to help me relax, he told me that 4 Carlton Gardens had been the headquarters of Charles de Gaulle during the war, from where he commanded the Free French forces: primarily the 13th Demi-Brigade of the Foreign Legion. I thought of our putsch against de Gaulle in 1961, but decided not to mention it.

He then went around the table. Each man had a bundle of papers in front of him and they took it in turns to interrogate me. Their questions ranged from my school days, (notably the absence of any A-levels), to the Foreign Legion experience and one asked me what I thought of 'our policy East of Suez'. I said I didn't know we *had* a policy East of Suez.

Wrong answer, but it raised a laugh.

During the next couple of hours, they all took their turn at grilling me. I was then let free for an hour. Finally, they summoned me again and told me that two of them would like to have further discussions.

President Sukarno was running Indonesia at that time and steering the country towards communism. The British Army was active in combating communism in Malaysia, and the Americans were gearing up for the same thing in Vietnam.

The Americans had a theory about Asia, known as the 'Domino Theory,' which held the view that the communists would topple all the countries in South East Asia one by one, unless stopped by force. The deal on offer was for me to work in the jungles of Indonesia and corral dissident groups to fight against Sukarno and stop the drift to communism. I would be paid £3,000 tax-free, plus expenses. We discussed it for some time, particularly the subject of expenses in the jungle. I was enthusiastic.

I went to seek advice from an old friend of mine, who was one of the many surrogate fathers I had in my life: Peter Clapham, an MI5 man. He had been Douglas Bader's navigator during the war and had lost a leg in the process of flying Spitfires against the Luftwaffe. A wonderful man and one of my life's heroes. He was enthusiastic about the work but warned there were 'spiders and flies' in this business and I was being recruited as a fly. I was not sure I liked that idea.

Jeffa's uncle, Carol Mather, had also been in 'intelligence' and agreed to have breakfast with me at the Queen's Hotel in Sloane Square to talk over the proposition. He bombarded me with questions. 'Whom had I seen? What did they look like? How much was 'the firm' offering?' He spoke to me the whole time in a subdued whisper. Every time a waiter came to the table, Carol would lean back and say something like, 'So, are you going to Ascot this year?'

He told me to read a book called *The Spy Who Came in from the Cold* by John Le Carré and not to be carried away by any notion that this was James Bond stuff. Le Carré's book was perhaps more realistic about 'the firm' than that portrayed by Sean Connery in a film Jeffa and I had seen when we were in Paris, called *Goldfinger*.

Eventually, I told the men at the Foreign Office that I would like to reflect for a while and that I was going to do a little bit of work in the commercial world first and would get back to them shortly.

I continued to flog Morris's carbon paper around Europe and was becoming quite adept at it.

The Scandinavians held high opinions of the Brits, probably as a direct result of the war, which was not a too-distant memory. I was always well received and ushered into the boss's office. I think they trusted me more than the product I was selling and certainly had a greater interest. This sowed in me the importance of trust and reputation in business over all other matters. Anybody can sell something once!

Jeffa sent me letters almost every day and they were forwarded on to me wherever I went, through the good services of *poste restante*.

One day, I received a letter which had been following me for months with an envelope covered in addresses, with 'Please Forward' stamps all over it. Inside there was no letter, just tickets for the Malta State Lottery. My first reaction was intense jubilation as I thought I had won the lottery. A closer study of the envelope revealed this was not in fact the case and the original addressee was:

> *P.A.G. Murray*
> *c/o Warren Murton Foster & Swan*
> *45 Bloomsbury Square,*
> *London WC1.*

The letter was for my father, whom I was unaware still existed and it had found its way to me by mistake. I sent the tickets back to Warren Murton (lawyers), explaining what had happened and enclosed a letter to be forwarded on to my father.

My letter to him read simply:

> *Dear Father,*
> *We have never met but I am returning these lottery tickets sent to me in error.*
> *If you win, I get 50 per cent.*
> *Your youngest son*
> *Simon*

A month later I received a reply similar in its brevity:

> *We lost. You get nothing. If you are ever in England, come and see me at the above address.*

I made a note to do so.

After a few months with Morris, I had saved enough money for a return trip to Singapore and told him that I wanted to take a couple of weeks off. I sent a telegram to Charles Letts to say I was on my way. Another step off the path, this time eastwards to Asia.

CHAPTER X

EASTWARD BOUND

I arrived in Singapore after a twenty-hour flight, including stops in Rome, Dubai, Delhi and Bangkok. I was travelling light: £250 and a rucksack. I didn't have a credit card in 1965.

At Changi airport I went to the hotel counter and requested something cheap and cheerful, as you do when you have little money. The girl behind the counter said, 'How about the Ritz?' I thought she was kidding but then she said it was only ten Singapore dollars a night. I could hardly believe it. 'I'm in', I said, and she rang the hotel. They had a room and I ran to the taxi rank.

We drove through Singapore city and I noticed that as we did so, the surroundings were becoming more and more squalid. We arrived at the Ritz: what a disappointment. A dingy three-storey building with red lights outside, located in the pits of Singapore. I entered, to be confronted by a bar teeming with American GIs obviously enjoying R&R from Vietnam, and hundreds of Chinese girls wearing very tight cheongsams. I stood for a moment taking in the scene when the barman spotted me. He waved his hand and he yelled across the crowd, 'Mr Murray?' A nod from me.

'The airport telephoned. You are on the third floor... only one room. Number 301. It's for you.'

I went upstairs. Yes, it was the Ritz, but not as imagined. The room was large, with a metal bed (memories of boarding school), a wash basin against the wall and a Victorian clothes cupboard. I showered and changed my clothes and went down to the bar. I needed a drink. I had to fight my way through the throng to get to the bar, where I was finally able to order a beer. There was a Chinese girl pressed against me. 'You buy me drink?' she asked.

'Yes' I said. 'What would you like?'

'I like cognac.'

It was a come-to-Jesus moment, but I kept cool.

'Barman, a cognac for the lady,' with heavy emphasis on the word 'lady'.
We struck up a conversation.

'You come today?' she asked.

'Yes,' I replied

'How long you stay?'

'I don't know. Maybe a week.'

She reached forward and squeezed my biceps.

'You welly stwong man,' she said. 'Most people come, stay one hour!'

I stayed a week, because the following day Lett's secretary told me that
he was away in Afghanistan and wouldn't be back for a week. Six days later
he called.

'Simon, Charles Letts here… What the hell are you doing in the Ritz? It's
a whorehouse.'

I said, 'How do you know?' which had him guffawing down the phone.

'My car will pick you up in twenty minutes,' he said. 'Bring all your kit,
you're staying with me'.

Letts lived in a grand mansion in Tanglin Hill, a fashionable quarter of
Singapore. He had two acres of garden to go with it, flush with tropical
trees and flower beds and an army of gardeners and servants to attend his
every need. He entertained at home or in restaurants every night. He knew
everybody, whether in government or commerce. His friends were mostly
Singaporeans, but he covered all the ambassadors from every nation and all
senior ex-pats from all major companies.

He was tireless. He never went to bed before 1am. He loved the bars at
the end of an evening and could drink brandy the way most people drink
milkshakes. He was up with the dawn and was gone to the office long
before I had surfaced each morning. He introduced me to everybody, took
me to all his dinners, and was simply fantastic to this young man he hardly
knew, because of his friendship with 'Paul'. They do not breed them like
Letts anymore.

He told me all the ins and outs of Jardine Matheson: who were the guys
to watch, the good ones and the ones of whom I should be wary. He told me
the history of the firm. How they had made money in the mid-nineteenth
century, shipping opium from India to China, and how they had been the
company at the forefront of the development of Hong Kong after 1949. He

told me Matheson's was the heavy end of the group, based in London. This was where the real strategic decisions were made. This was the real gateway to Jardine Matheson and I would need to go back and prove myself to them in London if I was to secure a job with the group.

In Singapore, Jardine's had acquired a 35 per cent interest in Waugh and Co, which itself had been a German-owned company before the Second World War, trading mainly in German products: cars (Mercedes Benz), printing machines, beer, textile machinery, rubber, palm oil, and tea, to which Jardine's had subsequently added aircraft from the UK and a host of other goods from around the world. It was now called Jardine Waugh.

Jardine Matheson had a controlling interest although Jardine Waugh was a public company. Letts was on the main board of Jardine's in Hong Kong but was responsible for Jardine Waugh.

By the time I had spent a week with Charles, we were friends for life, and I had another surrogate father. His plan for me was a brief visit to the company in Bangkok and then on to Hong Kong, where I could meet the 'heavies', before then going on to London for formal interviews. I knew he would give me a good 'ticket,' which would obviously enhance my prospects. He was keen for me to join Jardine Matheson, the head company, and he said if I got through the gate, he would make sure that I was posted to Jardine Waugh in Thailand for my first tour.

I set off to Thailand, backed by a tremendous push from Letts, draped in a feeling of well-being and the self confidence that came from his encouragement. I felt that I was on the threshold of a great journey. If ever I owed somebody something, it was and will always be to the late Charles Letts. For me, he will forever be Kipling's 'The Thousandth Man'. He had given all the right messages to the manager of Jardine Waugh in Bangkok, an Australian, Douglas Massey, so the path had been cleared for me.

I received a warm welcome and was given lodgings with Robin Hackman, the Jardine man responsible for the sale of Gillette products. Hackman was going through a tough time because his warehouse, which he presumed was packed with boxes containing razor blades, had been emptied by thieves who had cleverly left the front row of boxes in place and stolen the rest through the rear door. When the sliding doors at the front were opened, Hackman was confronted by a wall of boxes from floor to ceiling all displaying the great Gillette name. Alas, behind the first row of boxes, contrary to assumptions, was an empty warehouse. Hackman had discovered this when leaning on it one morning and the whole thing collapsed. Grand theft and a great surprise. The fury of his boss, Massey, rained down on the shoulders of the wretched Hackman, together with all the boxes. He was consoling himself with brandy when I arrived, and I gave him a helping hand.

Jardine's Bangkok headquarters were housed in an old Thai mansion. There was lots of teakwood everywhere. The rooms were dark and dingy with people seated at metal desks. The place was full of paper box files and Underwood typewriters. Wicker-work chairs and large fans hanging from high ceilings do have a certain charm to be sure. There was a distinct 1920s feel, even though this was 1965. The expatriates dressed casually and there was an informality that was attractive. There was an absence of any arrogance or hierarchy. Everybody was down to earth, friendly and full of good advice.

The Thais were charming, wonderfully polite, bowing as they passed you without being obsequious at all. It was their culture. They are lovely people, very humorous sometimes with cheeky smiles on their faces but a soft, self-effacing humility without subservence. Totally different from any people I had previously encountered.

Bangkok was a hot, steamy, slow-moving city with people on scooters and 'tuk-tuk' taxis (scooters with a box attached that would hold two passengers). It was over-crowded, noisy and dirty but like no other place I had seen and without any of the taller buildings evident in Singapore. There was nothing remotely modern.

The Thais wore sarongs, both men and women. They were colourful and elegant. Everybody was moving but nobody seemed to be going anywhere. One of those places where one should not confuse motion with action. People drifted. Some sat on the grass under palm trees doing absolutely nothing, seemingly waiting for the coconuts to fall.

In the middle of the town was the main Silom Road that went down to the massive but sluggish Chao Phya river. There was the old beautiful Oriental Hotel, a romantic place which came straight out of a Somerset Maugham novel.

The centre of life for the expatriates was the British Club. They lunched there, followed by a siesta on the sofas in the club for the senior members and then dined there again in the evening. It was a rustic building, very similar to the Jardine Waugh office. Once a prince's palace, it was now surrounded by lawns, tennis courts and a swimming pool.

The British Club, like everything else, was laid back. There was a bar with wicker-work chairs. Everybody who drank there was friendly, welcoming and interested in me, the new arrival. There was an immediate acceptance at face value. It reminded me of Alexandria between the wars, portrayed by Lawrence Durrell in his *Alexandria Quartet*. I loved it. It still stands there today. An elegant reminder of something English at its very best.

I was given a good tour of Jardine's Thai operations over the next four days. Douglas Massey was kind to me, showed me around, and explained what they did. They were a trading house, handling agents and distributors covering everything from consumer goods to heavy engineering equipment. After a few days in steamy Bangkok, I flew to Hong Kong to meet the big boys, the *Taipans*, at Jardine Matheson.

Kai Tak airport was rated among the most dangerous in the world. As we turned into finals, the runway beneath us looked far too short as it jutted out straight into the Hong Kong harbour. We were going too fast and yet the pilot still increased the pitch. At last we levelled off and were skimming the rooftops of the twelve-storey resettlement blocks, housing two million refugees who had come pouring in from Mao Zedong's China three years earlier. China's Cultural Revolution was about to begin in earnest.

In six months, Hong Kong had become the most densely populated place on the planet, and the Hong Kong government the world's largest landlord. As the plane descended, we could see the television sets in the apartments blasting away and practically smell the noodles steaming in the woks ready for the evening meal. Pilots took the landing at Kai Tak very seriously. One error and they could overshoot the end of the runway and be in the harbour. We landed with a firm thud followed by a serious application of brakes.

Hong Kong could not have been more different to Bangkok. This was a great modern fast-moving metropolis. It bustled with bankers, dark-suited businessmen and tall buildings – many with fourteen storeys. This was New York in Asia. In contrast were the locals with their rickshaws offering rides.

Hundreds of Chinese with big straw hats ran along the streets at lunchtime with horizontal bamboo rods across their shoulders, from which dangled lunch baskets full of dim-sum. The women wore colourful and attractive cheongsams. The great peak of Hong Kong was covered with a shanty town of mud huts with corrugated tin roofs.

The description of Hong Kong in Collier's magazine dated 1941 summed up my own first impression quite well: 'To newcomers, Hong Kong seems like a combination of Times Square on New Year's Eve, the subway at five-thirty in the afternoon, a three AM fire alarm and a public auction at a county fair.'

60 per cent of Hong Kong lived on a dollar a day. And yet Hong Kong is about money. Money is king and all things are subservient to it. The Jockey Club owed its position in the hierarchy to that fact and that alone. More money is wagered on one race, the Hong Kong Derby, at Happy Valley, than on all races combined during the entire season in the United Kingdom.

Jardine Matheson traded in everything, everywhere. They sold aircraft, ships, tea, cosmetics, food, toothpicks, lavatories, steel, lifts, textiles, toys, air conditioning, bull's semen, whiskey, brandy, champagne, helicopters, insurance, real estate, railway sleepers and condoms. It was joked that the motto of the company founded by thrifty, hardworking, sea-faring Scottish Presbyterians was: 'At Jardine's, we work six days a week and on the seventh we keep the sabbath... And anything else we can get our hands on!'

The Keswick family controlled the Jardine Matheson Empire through a shareholding of 8 per cent. Jardine's controlled the largest property company in Hong Kong, the Hong Kong Land Company, albeit with a mere 3 per cent stake, but enough to give them in perpetuity the chairmanship and the right, through the company's articles of association, to appoint all the directors.

Jardine's appointees sat on the boards – again by virtue of their articles of association – of the electricity company, the telephone company, the airport authority, the wharf company (which controlled the island's ferry services) and a host of other companies including, of course, the Legislative Council, through all of which they wielded an influence unequalled in the colony. There was no pie in which they did not have their fingers.

When you landed at Kai Tak airport, Jardine's ground staff were there to see you through immigration. They helped you across the harbour in their ferryboats. You checked into the Mandarin Hotel, which they owned, through Hong Kong Land. When you turned on the lights you were boosting their profits and when you called home to England to say you had arrived, they were appreciative.

The history of the firm had a lot to do with a perhaps romantic, but not so glamorous involvement in the opium trade. To be fair to them, they claimed to be shippers of the 'foreign mud', as opium was known to the Chinese, rather than producers, which was the province of the East India Company. But they were accessories in the trade and they certainly benefitted from it. They were the barons of Hong Kong.

The Jardine big boss was known as the *Taipan* and they ruled a certain world, still a British colony, which gave them distinct advantages over local companies. This advantage would be eroded over time. Nevertheless in 1965, Jardine's was still known as the 'Princely Hong' and they were the house that young men in Britain aspired to join if they wished to take the Eastern route.

From the airport, I drove to a little hotel in Kowloon called the August Moon. Absolutely charming. Certainly better than the Ritz in Singapore. From there I crossed the 'fragrant' harbour on a ferryboat. There was no tunnel in those days, and I presented myself at a fourteen-storey skyscraper at the bottom of Pedder Street. This was the headquarters of the mighty Hong. Today all that has gone. Jardine's headquarters is on the top of a sixty-four-storey building; Hong Kong has 'out-sky-scrapered' New York.

I was to report to the Jardine directors. I had had a suit made in Singapore in one day that had set me back £30, and I was looking smart. It was just as well, as this was a smart sort of place.

Two Jardine directors, Messrs Landale and Shoppe, took me for a drink at Maxime's Restaurant and although they were full of enthusiasm about Jardine Matheson, they were far more interested in my time with the French Foreign Legion.

Trevor Shoppe was the trading director of Jardine's in Hong Kong, and David Landale was the aviation director with oversight on human resources. They confirmed to me that Jardine's recruited five university graduates a year, who were then dispersed throughout the business and were regarded as a 'cadre' for the first year, when they would be given a business department with a profit and loss account to manage. Their first 'tour' would be three years followed by six months' leave.

Landale and Shoppe were friendly and positive, recognised that I was not standard cadre material, but explained that I would be an exception because I had Charles Letts' backing and he had sent a glowing report. They had prepared the path to Lombard Street, in London, where I would be interviewed by the real 'heavies,' and my visit to Asia would, they said, be a great plus in that interview. Ah, the virtues of experience! I was beginning to feel like an old Asian hand.

It was going to take me fifty years to become one. But first I had to be accepted by this company with a long history of tradition, one of which was to employ only young men who had attended Oxford or Cambridge or who were founders' kin.

I did not qualify.

CHAPTER XI
THE HEAVIES

Matheson and Co Ltd, 3 Lombard Street, the beating heart of the Jardine Matheson empire, was diagonally opposite the mighty Bank of England.

Entering Matheson's was like going into a London club. The doorman was dressed in what looked like a French *chef de gare* outfit: lots of brass buttons on his tunic representing authority. The lights in the entrance were sombre and the surrounds were wood panelling with portraits of ancestors long gone and George Chinnery paintings of Chinese gentlemen in flowing robes, sitting cross-legged in dark brown leather armchairs.

My first encounter was with David Middleditch. He was softly spoken, with a subtle but clear sense of humour. He told me that having no degree and no A-levels was not a fact that would be in my favour. However, he did like the Foreign Legion stuff and said I would certainly be the first to be recruited from the Legion, if I were to be taken on. I asked him if he knew of any cases of the reverse having taken place. He doubted it. He said he was not sure where I might employ my sabotage and explosives skills in Jardine's, but one never knew.

He obviously knew Charles Letts well and said his patronage would be positive. He briefed me more about the firm and said I was scheduled for three interviews with the men who ran Jardine's – Tony Keswick, John Keswick and Henry Keswick and that it was important that I jumped all the fences. They had already interviewed over a hundred candidates and had a short list of ten. He reminded me again that they only needed five.

The first interview was with Tony Keswick. The chairman. I walked into his office as he was patting himself all over, ostensibly looking for a match for the cigarette that was dangling from his mouth. He said as I entered, 'I say, you don't have a match by any chance do you?' I shook my head, and he carried straight on and said, 'So, how much do you want to get paid?' I started mumbling something about money not being the most important thing in my life and he interrupted and said, 'Wrong answer... the correct answer is "*as much* as I can get".' That evoked a laugh from me and I said, 'I'll remember that.' The interview was short and straight-forward and lasted five minutes with him doing most of the talking.

Then it was Henry, Tony's son, who took the trouble to tell me a lot about the firm over the course of an hour and finally it was John Keswick, Tony's brother. He started reading my file and then suddenly jumped up before saying anything and rushed out of the room muttering 'excuse me,' in a rather alarmed voice.

Middleditch told me later that John Keswick had not been properly briefed before my arrival because he had come in late and he had come rushing into his office with his eyes popping out saying, 'There's a Foreign Legionnaire in my office!' to which Middleditch had replied with a nonchalant air, 'I know… Letts wants him.'

Two weeks went by and I received a letter from Middleditch, expressing in gentle terms his real sorrow that it was not to be on this occasion and if it was of interest to me, I had done very well and was in sixth place, but had just missed the final cut. His letter covered two pages in his own hand, beautifully penned, to say how much he had enjoyed meeting me, and how he wished it had gone the other way. He was one of nature's real gents. Never to be forgotten.

Dreams of Hong Kong were over… for now.

Disappointed, I turned back to the boys at MI6 to request another meeting. A rendezvous was arranged at a flat in Chelsea Cloisters at noon on 13 October 1965. I was there on the dot. The door opened to reveal a man whom I had never seen before wearing a scruffy beige suit that might have been tailored in Shepherd's Bush. He ushered me in and offered me a pre-lunch gin and tonic. It was quiet and relaxed and just slightly spooky. Essentially the deal was still the same. Indonesia.

I asked if they could up the ante, as I thought £3,000 per annum, even with expenses (in the jungle), was a little light. My short time with Jardine's had already taught me the art of negotiation. Tony Keswick's words of wisdom were paying off. The MI6 man said he would investigate and come back to me. The meeting was over.

A week later, out of the heavens, came a letter from Middleditch, saying one of the candidates had fallen out and if I was still keen, Jardine's had a place. I was on fire with enthusiasm and delight. Huge uplift of the soul. I rang Middleditch. He was as thrilled as I was. I accepted. Starting date July 1966. Salary £800 per annum plus accommodation. Double my salary at Mather and Platt and just enough time to get married!

Before I could write to MI6, they wrote to me confirming a new salary of £5,000 plus expenses. I felt awful and wrote a grovelling apology, to which I received a charming reply along the lines 'That if I ever changed my mind about working in warmer climes, the door would always be open and they would keep in touch.'

They did!

CHAPTER XII

BRUSSELS. THE MANNEKEN PIS

I had a job. I asked Jeffa to marry me. She said 'Yes please' or words to that effect. Ten days later I took a trip to her parents' residence, Whirley Hall, with a planned arrival two hours before Jeffa got there, to give me adequate time to submit a request to her father for the hand of his daughter. Jeffa of course had already primed him weeks before and the champagne was already in the ice bucket when I arrived. He seemed very excited by the whole thing and had already fixed the date for an engagement party for 1 January 1966 (getting slightly ahead of himself). He had actually started sending out invitations.

This created a problem for me because I had a long-standing engagement that same day at the statue of the Manneken Pis in Brussels, agreed many years go in the Algerian mountains with Soto and Vignaga. Soto and Vignaga were my closest buddies in the Foreign Legion and we had decided over a mug of coffee early one morning in years gone by, sitting deep in the jungle, that when we were out of that hellhole, we would meet up in a neutral country and sup our wine, tell tales of old battles and laugh at all we had been through together. We were brothers in arms. The best.

A rendezvous had been fixed for New Year's Eve, when all three of us would have left the Legion, at the Manneken Pis in Brussels. Having made the pact, we never spoke of it again. And after the Legion, we had never seen each other or spoken a single word. That day was about to dawn and clashed with the very day my future father-in-law had selected to invite 200 guests to celebrate his daughter's engagement. Over the next four hours, including dinner, I tried to explain the problem.

I had a rendezvous with two legionnaires in Belgium, signed and sealed with a word and a handshake in the Khabylie mountains at 2am in the early hours of a morning some years before. This went down like a lead balloon and was followed by a vigorous interrogation with a thousand questions: 'When was this agreed? When did you last see them? How do you know they will be there? Why don't you ring them now and cancel? Surely this is absurd to think they will turn up after so long without a word? How do you know they are still alive?'

In short, there was total disbelief that I was doing this. I stood my ground. I did not want to spend the rest of my life wondering whether or not Soto and Vignaga had made it, and I had not. But of course, if I was having doubts after all these years, perhaps they were too. It was an agreement made years before in a completely different world and it had not been referred to since. I had not seen or spoken to Vignaga for years. He was still in the Legion when I left. In fact he was doing time for knocking a sergeant's teeth out. Soto had left the Legion a year before me and I had not seen or heard from him either. But I was going and that was that, and Jeffa said she would come with me. My first black mark from my new father-in-law to be, and my prospective mother-in-law was not looking too pleased either.

I had purchased a second-hand Morgan sports car from my friend Allister Hall for £210. He had moved up to a second-hand Rolls Royce. On 31 December 1965, Jeffa and I drove to Belgium. It hosed with rain the whole way and for the record, convertible second-hand Morgans are not waterproof. We found a small hotel in the early evening and then set off in a taxi to La Grande Place in the centre of Brussels.

Off La Place there is a narrow cobblestone side street down which we walked until we reached the Manneken Pis. It turned out to be a tiny statue of a boy pissing, built by a father who had lost his son and proclaimed that if he ever found him again he would build a statue of whatever the boy was doing at that moment. He found him pissing into a canal!

The statue, in a corner of the street surrounded by railings, was a bit of a disappointment, given its fame. The tiny street itself was dimly lit and without significance of any sort. There was a small bistro opposite the statue, open for business but empty, with six little tables covered with check tablecloths.

Despite the lack of a New Year's Eve atmosphere, we were soon enjoying a bottle of wine and some good Belgian food, but with just the two of us in the restaurant, we found ourselves talking very quietly. The conversation was restricted to things like wondering whether her father might have been right, and this could turn out to be a face-losing experience. The hands on the clock turned slowly but finally reached the vertical. The bells of Brussels chimed and we could hear fireworks. All very jolly, but in the bistro things remained subdued.

We kissed and drank champagne. It was a lovely moment. We were engaged to be married.

I got up to look at the statue across the street. The rain continued to pour down. No sign of anybody. No other restaurants open; just a dank little street. No glamour or sign of any festivities. Back inside the bistro, more champagne and we waited and we waited and we waited.

At 1:30am I realised that it was not going to happen. They were not coming. Jeffa's father had been right and I had been wrong. I sort of half grovelled but professed nevertheless that I had been right to come, otherwise I would never have known and for the rest of my life I would have wondered. Jeffa was sympathetic and full of understanding at my disappointment. I wrote on a paper napkin, '*Je suis venue et je suis à la Novotel… Johnny 1:30am.*' I went outside and ran across the street into the rain and pinned the napkin on the railing surrounding the statue. It was washed away immediately and I turned and belted back to the bistro with my jacket over my head. As I did so, suddenly from out of the night and the pouring rain a voice rang out: 'JOHNNY!'

Coming down the dark cobbled street was a figure carrying an umbrella, not clearly visible in the dim lights: it was Soto. He had walked from Barcelona, hitching rides when he could.

Jeffa was staggered. She had been expecting a toughie with scars all over his face, but Soto was a gent. Immaculately dressed, particularly considering his journey. He could have been a banker.

He had joined the Legion in a hurry in 1958. He was anti-Franco, the Spanish dictator, and with a small group of students he had blown up the metro at 3am one morning. Because of a 'leak' he had to leave Spain in a hurry. The Legion gave him asylum.

We drank another bottle of wine or three. Jeffa eventually retired and we put her in a taxi and waited for Vignaga. We battled sleep until 4am and then accepted that Vignaga was not going to make it.

The next day we said goodbye to Soto. He told us he was going to lose his job, because he had been told by his boss not to go to Brussels. He said he would get a job in Paris. He eventually started a window-cleaning business using cheap Algerian labour. It was a success. We kept in touch and every year I would go to Paris and we would meet up, get a few sausages and a couple of bottles of red, go to the Bois de Boulogne, have a picnic and sing a few of the old songs.

And then in 1970 he disappeared. No answer to telephone calls. At his digs his landlady said he had left a few months earlier. No word since. No faxes in those days. No mobile phones. Only telegrams and the postal services. Soto was gone – but not forever.

CHAPTER XIII
WEDDING BELLS

Our wedding was a warm and wonderful day. Jeffa's grandmother on her American side rang me from the States and said, 'Remember, Simon, successful marriages are not made in heaven.' That has stayed with me for over half a century. 250 people came to be with us and I knew at least 50 of them. Leo and Maxine made it and it was good to see them happy. They were probably relieved to see Simon settled at last.

My best man, Allister Hall, ran off the rails a bit and failed to put a bottle of champagne in the back of the car as planned. When we left, Jeffa's father came to the rescue. As we drove off in the Roller, he threw a bottle through the window. Unfortunately, it hit me in the face and practically laid me out and I started to bleed profusely. I yelled frantically to the driver, Walter, to get going and held a handkerchief to my face in a vain effort to prevent the cheering crowd from seeing the damage.

We stayed the night in a small hotel called the Haut Boy, on the south coast. They knew we were just married and had laid on a most romantic dinner in a quiet corner of the dining room with cake and candles and all the right things. When we left the next morning, my face was swollen and blue and it looked as though I had just done a couple of rounds with Mike Tyson. The porter loading our cases in the car looked at my face in amazement and then went up to Jeffa and squeezed her bicep and said 'Cor!' in a voice full of admiration, muttering something about 'Black Beauty'.

Our honeymoon was in a villa in the north of Italy, loaned to us as a wedding present by Allister Hall's family. Unbeatable: sunshine every day, even when it was raining and then ready for the very big step and the new life in the East.

Three days before we left for Hong Kong, I decided to go and meet my father. Jeffa came with me.

We found him in a small house in a village in Hertfordshire. Outside the house was an antique XK140 Jaguar sports car. He was still clinging to old habits. He had remarried somebody called Alice. Jeffa stayed with Alice and my father took me to the local pub for lunch.

Any emotion on my part had been smothered by curiosity. He was a stranger. For his part he was much more emotional. He told everyone who was interested, in the pub, that I was his long-lost son, as though it might have been me that had run away, and this was a 'prodigal' moment.

He gave me his life story with lots of anecdotes about the family: the Mathers, Petros and the Murrays, most of whom were long dead. He himself was fifty-six years old, very plump and filling himself with gin and tonic as though anticipating a world shortage. It was interesting to hear all the stories. Some of them not so good. Sadly, it left me empty, with no inclination to linger any longer than necessary. We left after lunch.

One of the sad moments on leaving England was the need to say goodbye to my lovely Morgan that Allister had sold to me. I put an ad in the paper and got a response from a young man who was clearly an enthusiast. His enthusiasm was spurred on by the fact that his dad was paying.

I discovered that I had missed my métier. I should have been a second-hand car salesman. I took the young man for a spin around Wimbledon, tearing round corners on two wheels, accelerating and braking and generally scaring the hell out of him. I told him he should be very careful when taking it out of second gear because the car was a dangerous animal and could accelerate out of his hands and go wild. He was terrified but dying to buy it. I let him have it for £410. On a visit to London three years later, I saw him driving it. He was still in second gear!

CHAPTER XIV
'GO EAST YOUNG MAN'

We arrived at Hong Kong's Kai Tak airport at 2am after a long and typically delayed flight from London. British Airways in those days was called BOAC (British Overseas Airways Corporation) but referred to by many of its passengers as 'Better On A Camel'. Not much has changed.

Despite the hour, in the Hong Kong immigration hall there was an immediate sensation of pace. Energy was everywhere. Voices were high pitched, people were rushing in all directions; gates clanged, the clock was ticking, and everybody was in a hurry. We were quickly through customs formalities in spite of the crowds. In the mid-sixties there were no security gates or metal detectors. No 'belts off, shoes off, watches off, mobile phones out, laptops out'. You arrived at an airport, showed your passport and wandered into the departure or arrival lounge.

That all changed after the attack on the Israeli team at the Munich Olympics in 1972. Eleven members of the Israeli team were kidnapped by the Black September terrorist group and later all were killed when an attempted rescue operation failed. The Israelis retaliated and organised a revenge operation code-named 'Wrath of God' which was primarily the formation of a secret squad, the sole purpose of which was the assassination of senior Palestinians.

The Israelis and Palestinians have been at each other's throats ever since. When I was in Israel in 1982, a wise Israeli to whom I asked the question how long would it take to solve the problem with Palestine, replied, 'Simon, it will take at least fifty years.' At that time the peace talks were about to be concluded when Yasser Arafat changed his mind. Airport security worldwide went into overdrive and it has been continuously intensifying ever since – even shaving lotion is banned.

But in 1966 there were no security gates at any international airports, which is why I was able to walk into Hong Kong with a 9mm P.K. Walther pistol, picked up from a dead Arab in the Legion, tucked down the front of my trousers, supported by a piece of string around my waist. No problems at all.

Jeffa and I were met by a driver who escorted us to a small flat in Stewart Terrace, our home for the duration of my short induction to the company. A letter welcomed us and informed me that I had a series of meetings with directors the following morning at 8:30 sharp.

Over the next two weeks our cadre of five new recruits was shown the Jardine empire and we drifted through all the different departments getting a broad impression of things, confirming with certainty that Jardine Matheson owned the town. As if we didn't already know.

After ten days of the Jardine Matheson exposé, I was summoned to the office of David Landale to be informed that I was to be sent on my first assignment to Jardine Waugh in Thailand and I was given an air ticket. Charles Letts had made good on his promise. As I knew the assignment would be for four years, I wondered aloud whether there was a ticket for my wife as well. Landale excused himself and said he had forgotten I was married, and another ticket would be issued forthwith! The Jardine Matheson marriage policy stated that one had to get permission before marrying. For a recruit in the cadre to be married on arrival was unheard of. Perhaps the human resources director could be forgiven his oversight.

We arrived at Bangkok with my pistol again nestled against my genitals. The airport's name seemed particularly appropriate! An incident occurred on day two after our arrival. The local English newspaper, the *Bangkok Post*, announced on its front page an amnesty for all firearms if they were surrendered before the end of the week at the nearest police station. If they were not handed over and were found later, the consequences would be jail. It was time to say goodbye to my lovely P.K. I took it to the nearest police station, in slight trepidation in case I was asked how I got it into Bangkok in the first place. There were no questions, but they took the gun and I was ordered to reappear in seven days.

Seven days later I was back at the cop-shop. The gun was returned to me with a licence and the licence number stamped on the barrel. Thailand is a good place to have a pistol, but little did I know then just how useful it might turn out to be.

At Jardine Waugh, I was formally appointed as ICO (In Charge Of) the building and industrial supplies department, a very lofty position. It comprised a salesman called Khun Prakorb, a secretary named Pimpa and me. My office was the size of a lavatory (in fact a conversion from), but it did not reduce my enthusiasm for the task ahead, even when I entered the office on the first day to find a dead bat hanging from the empty metal 'handy-angle' bookcase.

I was taking over the post from my predecessor James Young, who had been doing the job for five years and who was going to show me the ropes. Unfortunately, he committed suicide the day after I arrived: nothing to do with me, but not a very good omen.

There was a lot to do and a lot to learn.

You name it, the industrial supplies department handled it. Khun Prakorb ran a dealer network, through which we distributed sanitary ware from Armitage Ware, nuts and bolts from Guest Keen and Nettlefold and Avery weighing machines. We flogged Hardoll petrol pumps to the Shell Oil Company. I was importing tin plate and iron ingots from BHP in Australia and even asbestos from the American Smelting and Refining Company (ASARCO), which we sold to the Siam Cement Company in which the Thai royal family was the main shareholder. I was doing business with the king on day one!

Early on, Jeffa and I met Charlie and Ginny Kirkwood. Charlie was the foremost American lawyer in Bangkok. The Americans had arrived to build airbases in support of their Vietnam war effort, which was just warming up in 1966 and through him I very quickly established a network with many American firms, principally architectural engineers (A/Es) who were responsible for the design of the airbases. These firms were huge and run by individuals who had the responsibility of designing and indeed spending millions of dollars building the bases. Companies like De Lieu Cather and Utah Martin Day had been formed as joint ventures between American contractors to come and reap the benefits of this war in Asia. Somebody always makes money in wartime.

Through the wonderful friendship of Charlie and Ginny we were introduced to a whole new circle of American friends, two of whom were Brian Smith and Fred Gulden. They were architectural engineers and contractors but had no idea where to source anything in Thailand. I became their source as I took on new agencies every week, often steered in the right direction by the A/Es to American supply companies like Soule for steel-frame buildings and Detroit Diesel for standby diesel generators. It was Fred Gulden who introduced me to an American company called H.H. Robertson and over time, through them, I really learned to understand the contracting business. Their representative was Ron Gebhardt.

H.H. Robertson produced Galbestos (a corrugated cladding for industrial buildings made of galvanised steel sheeting coated with asbestos and an outer cover of coloured silicon), glass curtain-walling, industrial ventilators and raised flooring. They had recently supplied the raised flooring through which all the electric wiring in a building passes, for the iconic twin tower skyscrapers in New York: those same towers that would come crashing down thirty-five years later under the impact of two aircraft sent to destroy them by the evil monster Osama bin Laden, leader of the Al-Qaeda terrorist group.

Ron Gebhardt, Brian Smith and Fred Gulden taught me the fundamentals of the contract supply business, which would stand me in good stead for a lifetime. They had patience and were unforgettably kind to me.

Dealing in the contracting business involves far more than the contractor. At the top of the ladder is the owner of the project, the financier. He appoints the architect and engineer, and a project manager. Then there is a contractor, who may often be one of six or more tendering for the project. Having won the contract, he may appoint subcontractors and there may be others who have to approve the product, such as the fire department. There are a lot of people needing to be convinced that your product is better than your competitor's and there are many who are looking for an alternative to yours, even though yours may have been specified by the architect, because they can demonstrate financial advantages to the owner.

A good place to start is the architect. I got to know all the major architects in Thailand. The architect must be persuaded, when drafting his specifications, to match those of your product in a manner that will pre-empt the specifications of the competition. The same goes for the engineer, who will want to have his say. Everybody has an opinion in this game. That is what they are paid for. The engineer adds structural knowledge, fire protection, durability against weather conditions and bombs, if it's in a war zone. The project manager is all this and more, including budget control (his master's money), and is the direct line to the owner who, very often in my case, was the Officer in Charge of Construction (the OICC) from the US Navy. I was soon doing very serious business with these contractors, building airbases at Udorn, Sattahip and Kham Paeng Seng, all on my salary of £800 per year but making millions for Jardine Waugh.

Ron Gebhardt was my guide in this labyrinthine and complex maze of interested parties. I loved it. The fundamental ingredient of success was trust (learned in days gone by in Denmark). The players had to trust you and the products you represented. You would be there when things went wrong. Your neck was the one they could grab when there were delays or disappointment in expectancy. Your neck was available at all times. Everybody's backside had to be covered and if the axe fell, it fell on me. But trust broadens shoulders. To know that you are trusted is also a great source of energy. Ron Gebhardt will never be forgotten. Nor will Brian Smith and Fred Gulden.

Meanwhile Jeffa, who did not want to spend her days lounging by the pool with the other ex-pat wives, and was a professional textile designer, had begun designing fabrics for Jim Thompson. We had met him through an introduction from her father, whose own grandfather had sold textile machinery to Jim Thompson's father. Jim Thompson was a great man and very kind to us. The first time we had dinner with him he kept calling me Patrick and we discovered he had met my father many years earlier and was mistaking me for him. A strange world, as we are constantly reminded.

Jim Thompson had built the Thai silk business from virtually nothing after the war. Years earlier he had narrowly escaped trouble when King Ananda was found shot through the head in his bed one morning. The military decided it was a coup d'état perpetrated by Pridi Banomyong, the Prime Minister at the time, who they accused of being a republican and against the Thai monarchy. In fact this was not true. What he wanted was a constitutional monarchy, as we have in the UK.

Pridi, supported by the British Ambassador, escaped with the help of Jim Thompson. At that time no country would give sanctuary to someone accused of regicide, except China. They got him to China. That of course enabled the military to enhance their accusations by saying he, Pridi, was a communist. France eventually gave him sanctuary and he died in Paris years later.

There were many theories about the death of King Ananda. One such was that his younger brother, Bhumipol, who succeeded Ananda as king and died in 2016, had shot him by accident. They were often playing with pistols with live rounds and perhaps the gun had gone off by mistake. Yet another theory was that because the brothers had been born of different mothers, then perhaps Bhumipol's mother, who was ambitious for her son, may have been behind the accident, which perhaps wasn't an accident after all.

All this was unacceptable to the Thais and the military accused two bedchamber servants of carrying out the assassination on Pridi's orders with the involvement of the palace secretary, an ex-navy captain. The servants were acquitted after a trial lasting three years, but the prosecution ordered a re-trial. The total trial time, after several acquittals followed by constant appeals from the prosecution for re-trial, was eleven years, at the end of which the servants were finally found guilty and executed. The navy captain was also found guilty but fled Thailand, aided by the British Embassy, with Jim Thompson again suspected of playing a role.

Many years later Thompson, who had worked with the OSS, the forerunner of the CIA, 'disappeared' while on holiday in the Cameron Highlands in Malaysia. By a strange twist of fate, Jeffa and I were on holiday in Malaysia at the time, staying in the villa next to his. There were many theories as to what might have happened. The soldiers searching for his body found an airplane which had crashed in the war, just fifty yards from the path, and had remained undiscovered for all those intervening years, such was the density of the bush there. But Jim Thompson's body was never found. The story went around the world. It was stranger than fiction.

⌁

Thailand for us was exciting and great fun, and they were happy carefree days. We had found a small house with a garden surrounded by paddy fields on the outskirts of the city. We had no telephone at home and no television, both of which were unheard of in Thailand in those days unless you paid US$20,000. But it was our first home and we loved it. We could make overseas telephone calls from the office, but we had to book the calls two days in advance. Not because the office insisted, but because it took the Thai telephone company that amount of time to arrange the call.

I played rugby, squash and golf, and used to shoot snipe at weekends with my friend Kim Fraser. No licence was required and we just walked through the paddy fields, without permission, and shot the birds when they 'upped' and flew off. We used to pick up a couple of Gurkhas, off-duty security soldiers at the British Embassy who acted as beaters for us. They loved the chance to get out of the Embassy for a few hours. All above board. In the evenings we would invite thirty people over for barbequed snipe, all washed down with gallons of Singha beer. What a happy life.

Jeffa continued to develop her fabrics and soon had her own business, 'High Thai Fabrics'. She was designing fabrics on our dining room table and then having bolts of the fabric produced by the Shinawatra company which she then sold to retailers. The Kirkwoods were our partners in the business.

One day I came home to find her looking forlorn. There was a credit rating problem. Not Jeffa's forte. She was happy to sell to anyone and be paid later. A retailer was refusing to pay her some months after he had filled his shop with High Thai fabrics. I told her to go and get her fabrics back, but no, the shop owner had refused to surrender them and said he would pay her when he was ready to do so.

It was time for the licensed P.K. Walther. We set off in a small truck to the retail shop. I walked into the shop with my gun in hand. The owner was standing there with his wife. He saw the gun and in the same instant dived headlong straight through the open window. Gone into the darkness. Never to be seen again. Luckily, we were on the ground floor! His wife was a gibbering wreck. I told Jeffa to help herself to her fabrics, which she did and home we drove to a nice gin and tonic. The Murray Debt Collection Agency was founded – triple AAA on the first job.

⁓〜⁓

Jardine Waugh had a cash sales business in the rural zones of Thailand. A truck would go up country laden with goodies. The most popular item was Jacob's biscuits. The Thais had no taste for the biscuits, but they loved the tins in which they were packed, which could be used for water storage. I once received a long-distance call from one of our salesmen, lamenting he had lost all the cash in a casino and would not be returning. He had sold the truck and all the merchandise and now he had no money to return. He was apologetic and said he was on his way to a monastery to become a monk and get forgiveness. I told him when he got it to come back to Bangkok and we would have a reception for him to celebrate his 'forgiveness'.

Never saw him again.

I became the agent for Mather and Platt pumps and fire sprinklers and got orders from the US armed forces. Bill Mather was over the moon and telling anybody who would listen that his son-in-law had secured their first order in Thailand since the firm was founded. This was probably the moment when he finally forgave me for rushing off to the Manneken Pis for that rendezvous with Soto.

Charles Letts visited often and was always encouraging and full of enthusiasm about what I was doing. A director from Jardine's in Hong Kong called David Edwards was also a regular visitor and we became good friends, although Charles was only lukewarm in his opinion of Edwards. Having said that, Edwards constantly reported back to Hong Kong that I was doing a great job and making millions for the company and that I was the only member of the foreign staff who was fluent in Thai.

I was, and could read and write it. Over the years, my good ear had served me well. During my time in the Legion I had learnt French, obviously, but also German because of the number of legionnaires who were German. I could also play the piano – by ear – and have always maintained music and languages go well together. Thai was another ball game. I employed a local to come to my office for two hours every day to teach me the language. It worked. When our principals visited, (the representatives of the companies for which we acted as agents and distributors), they were quite impressed that I could speak the lingo. It helped the relationship. We could lose an agency if we did not perform and there were plenty of competitors who were more than willing to take the business from us, such as the Borneo Company, Leonowens, the East Asiatic Company and others.

We were expected to meet our principals at the airport, no matter their arrival time, and never lose sight of them during their visits. Constant entertainment at home and in restaurants was required, all the while demonstrating what a wonderful job we were doing with their products, as if there was nothing else in our thoughts or lives except them. Great, when you're dealing in lavatories (Shanks for the memories)!

I was the agent for Cement Aids, a product for keeping cement moist without the necessity of adding water when it is being transported. When cement is mixed with water, it makes it workable and prevents it hardening. When it is being transported to a distant site it is constantly turned to keep it workable, but sometimes the distance is too far and the cement begins to harden. If more water is added, it keeps it from solidifying but at the same time it weakens it. Special additives can be used that keep the cement moist without loss of strength. These additives are called retarding agents because they delay the concrete from hardening. Cement Aids was the Australian company that made such additives with a secret formula. The World Bank had sponsored the construction of a dam in Laos across the Mekong river and a Japanese company, Hazamagumi, had been awarded the contract to build it, at a very low price.

Too low.

I was responsible for all our business in Laos, primarily because I was the only one in the company who spoke French. The dam was going to require tons of retarding agent and I was on the case. We were also the agents for Leyland Trucks in Laos under a British aid scheme which enabled Laotian companies to apply to purchase British goods at UK government subsidised prices. My job was to get the Laotians to 'apply' for Leyland Trucks and then work on the people at the British Embassy to persuade them to place Leyland trucks on the priority list for government aid. We sold hundreds of Leyland trucks with the kind assistance of British aid.

Our man in Laos was Zima Wong. He was the original Mr Fix-it: a small man with a brown trilby hat permanently on his head and a large cigar protruding from his mouth. Anything I needed was available in a minute, through Zima Wong. I soon needed transport to the Nam Ngum dam, 200 miles north of Vientiane, the commercial capital of Laos. There was no tarmac road to the dam, only a long winding laterite track through miles of forest. The trees clung tightly to the borders of the track, creating the impression that one was driving through a tunnel. Zima provided a Leyland truck and driver and soon I was on my way to the Nam Ngum dam

There was a problem. There's always a problem! The Pathet Lao was a communist organization in Laos, supported by Mao Zedong in China, fighting on the side of North Vietnam against the Americans defending the South. The Pathet Lao used terrorist tactics, blowing up buildings and ambushing convoys on the road to the dam among other things, to make their point. The Americans had a CIA base in Laos, masquerading as an 'economic aid foundation'. It was a good source of information for me. I was supplying them with air-conditioning units, *en passant*. The British Embassy were also well informed on Pathet Lao intelligence.

Driving to the dam site, often at night, reminded me of an old French film called *The Wages of Fear* featuring Yves Montand. It is about some guys in South America driving nitro-glycerine to an oil depot 150 miles away which is on fire. The only way to extinguish the fire is to 'blow' it out with the nitro-glycerine. But if the trucks had an accident or a substantial bump on their way to the oil depot, the nitro-glycerine would explode. In the movie, it did, and they all got killed.

Every minute in the truck on my way to the dam, I felt like those truck drivers. At each corner in the tunnel of trees, I expected to be greeted by a barrage across the path with lots of men in green denims brandishing Kalashnikovs. I had my passport open, pressed against the front windscreen, held in place by my foot, showing that I was a Brit, not an American, hoping they would note that before they started shooting.

On my first arrival at the dam site in the middle of nowhere in dense jungle, I met the senior project engineer, a Japanese man called Mr Tanaka. I had brought some samples of my Cement Aids and he asked me to assist and indeed organise various tests. I hadn't a clue what he wanted, but by the time we had finished lunch we were already friends and thus began a long, wonderful business relationship that continued for all my working life in Asia. A handshake on a deal with the Japanese was better than any lawyer could craft with a contract. Their word was enough. They were the best.

One day, on a visit to the site, Tanaka told me that decision time was coming up and the contract for the retarding agent was to be awarded shortly. A Canadian engineer from the World Bank, the sponsors of the dam, was coming to the site and various contracts would be agreed and signed.

Tanaka had stressed that it would be hugely to my advantage if I was at the dam site when he arrived, so I prepared to fly up to Laos yet again.

Three weeks later, waiting for my plane at Bangkok airport, I found myself standing next to someone who looked familiar. I suddenly recognised him and went up and said, 'Lieutenant L'Hospitallier, Légion Étrangère?' He was staggered. I said, 'Legionnaire Murray, I was in your section in the 2nd Para Regiment in Algeria.' He nearly dropped dead. 'C'est toi l'anglais?' he said. I was indeed the English one. The only one in the entire regiment. I hadn't seen him for seven years, since he was snatched away after the coup d'état against de Gaulle. He had been living in Cambodia, advising the Cambodian army on parachute training. I thought this was a good omen. It was, and we have remained friends for fifty-five years.

When I got to Laos, I immediately checked in to the British Embassy and was warned in no uncertain terms that it was out of the question to go to the dam. The convoys were constantly under attack by the Pathet Lao. Bad news. I adjourned to the Lane Xiang hotel.

In the evening, as usual, the bar was full of furtive-looking groups, the Russians in one corner, the Chinese in another and the French over there, all whispering and speaking out of the corner of their mouths. I was at the bar wondering how I could get to the dam. Next to me at the bar was a Frenchman on his own, quietly sipping a glass of the local brew. I asked him to pass the nuts and within a few moments we were chatting. He asked me what I was doing in Laos and complimented me on my French and one thing led to another. When he learned that I had been in Algeria, he became excited. It turned out he had flown my regiment on many sorties. He was now a pilot with a private three-seater Cessna plane, and after a few more rounds of hooch, he offered to fly me to the dam site the following morning. This coming so soon after bumping into L'Hospitallier started to restore my faith in God and make me understand that he did indeed have a plan. The next morning, we flew to the dam, to a welcome from Tanaka that was ecstatic. I was awarded the contract to supply the retarding agent for the project! Signed and sealed.

Meanwhile back in Bangkok, Jeffa had come downstairs in her dressing gown to pick up the Bangkok Post which was delivered each morning to our front door. The headlines threw in her face the news that there had been a Pathet Lao attack on the road to the dam in Laos and a convoy had been ambushed with twenty-three people killed.

Total panic.

She immediately telephoned my boss, Alasdair Lapping, who telephoned the British Embassy in Laos. Yes! They had seen Simon and warned him on no account was he to go to the dam. The embassy telephoned the Lane Xiang hotel immediately, only to be informed that Mr Murray had left the hotel and was no longer in residence, but he had not paid the bill. Assumption? He was coming back – hopefully. But he may have been in the convoy to the dam and therefore not coming back. My demise was apparently the story of the day, the sole subject of discussion at the British Club and circulating rapidly among the British expatriate class in Bangkok. Poor Jeffa was distraught. Murray, who spent five years in the French Foreign Legion, now dies for Cement Aids!

Meanwhile, I was at the dam celebrating the award of the contract with Tanaka-san, completely unaware of any of this. There were no telephones on the dam site and the news of an ambush, relayed by radio, was not totally out of the norm; the Japanese assumed it had nothing to do with Simon Murray anyway – 'he's here with us' – so nobody told me anything about the ambush.

It so happened that Hazamagumi, the Japanese contracting company, had greatly underestimated the cost of building this dam. Nor had they expected that every other night, the Pathet Lao would be firing bullets across their campsite. On top of that, half the workforce was down with malaria and the conditions, including the food, not to mention the water, were appalling. I knew because I had frequently stayed at the site in one of their dormitories. The camp dormitory made the Foreign Legion barracks look like Claridge's.

The result was that the Japanese were trying to get out of the contract as it existed and had laid claims with the World Bank. The World Bank, in response to these claims, had sent in a group from the World Health Organisation to see for themselves how far the claims were justified. The day after the ambush, a large aircraft arrived with a team from the World Health Organisation, and they were welcomed at the dam site with an outdoor cocktail party hosted by the Japanese, to which I was also invited. Among the guests who attended the event, I noticed the British Ambassador from Bangkok. I did not know him personally, but I recognised him from newspaper photographs. I introduced myself. He practically fainted and let forth a roar of surprise which contained much happiness.

'Simon Murray!' he shouted. 'You're dead! Everybody thinks you're dead! How wonderful you're here alive. My God, you must return at once with us in the plane when we go back to Bangkok tonight.' My arrival in Bangkok made the 'return of the prodigal' look like a non-event – talk of the town for weeks to come. Jeffa of course has never got over it.

Thailand was full of interesting days. I got into a couple of fights while we there and we had some downs, but overall they were days to remember with a smile. I made truckloads of money for Jardine's with major contributions from construction projects: the American air bases at Sattahip, Kam Paeng Seng, Udorn and others; the new Dusit Thani Hotel; the Peninsular Hotel; the Boon Rawd brewery (the production centre of Singha beer), and by selling thousands of weighing machines for Avery and even more lavatories for Armitage Ware, who now owned Shanks. They were prosperous days for everyone, thanks to the Americans.

The Thais are wonderful people, and we loved them. But they could be turned off by insults or loss of face, like most people. The head of our engineering group was Alasdair Lapping, a brash Geordie from Newcastle. He had little patience with the Thais and particularly our senior Thai director, Khun Suchart. Suchart was a favourite of Charles Letts.

During the Second World War, Charles had been a prisoner of the Japanese in Thailand. At night he had on many occasions managed to get out of the prison and had gone to get food from the local Thais and brought it back to the camp. He was a real hero. He would have been shot if he had been caught. One of the Thai families who had provided the food was Suchart's. Charles and Suchart were friends for ever.

But Lapping was contemptuous of Suchart, often in front of others. He did business by the book, whereas Suchart used some old-fashioned methods, regarded as the norm in Thailand at the time! Suchart, in response to Lapping's attitude, let it be known amongst the locals that he disliked him intensely. Lapping started to encounter problems. Irritating problems, like

Heavyweight ancestors: Sir William Mather

Foreign Legion days

With K.S. Li: good
friends and great
business partners

Chinese entrepreneur Li Ka-Shing's UK ambitions are hot gossip,
but his right-hand man says the commitment is still to Hong Kong

THE DRAGON'S NEXT MOVE

Like all the best offices in Hong Kong, Simon Murray's suite atop the Hutchison building looks out over the Crown Colony's spectacular harbour and to the Kowloon waterfront, the mountainous New Territories with hints of China beyond. It is a dramatic view for a man who likes business on a dramatic scale.

Seven years after he stormed out of a 14-year stint with neighbouring Jardine Matheson when a promised promotion failed to materialise, Murray has assumed one of the most powerful business roles in Hong Kong as right-hand man to the fabled Chinese entrepreneur Li Ka-Shing.

From his lofty perch in Hong Kong's booming Central district, Murray directs the expansion of the Hutchison Whampoa part of Ka-Shing's interests with an emphasis on urgency and big deals.

Murray still betrays a little of the upright starchiness of his days in the early '60s as a paratrooper in the French Foreign Legion. He is smart and officious. With US$1bn to spend on corporate aggrandisement, should he need it, he can afford to strut a little these days.

His and Ka-Shing's predatory ambitions have caused flutters in boardrooms in more places than just Hong Kong. In Britain it is the attention that Hutchison has paid to the Pearson publishing-to-oil group that has aroused interest. But with broad designs on the energy sector and

Hutchison Whampoa's Simon Murray ... causes flutters in some boardrooms

Hutchison's first strike in Britain could be anywhere

companies with branded products, Hutchison's first strike in Britain could be almost anywhere.

Like most business leaders in Hong Kong, Murray denies that his growing interest in investing overseas has anything to do with the territory returning to Chinese control in 1997. Indeed, both Hutchison and Ka-Shing's main property flagship company Cheung Kong are still actively enhancing their core businesses in Hong Kong. Hutchison and its 23.5%-owned Hong Kong Electric group have thrown HK$15bn at their businesses in the colony over the last two years.

With a combined market capitalisation

of HK$75bn Cheung Kong and Hutchison represent 17% of the Hong Kong stock market's value. The companies can hardly walk away from this unique enclave of capitalism.

"Our strategy is to support our existing businesses," insists Murray. One of the remaining vestiges of the old "Hong" dynasties in the territory before Ka-Shing gave it the Chinese stamp, Hutchison's business falls into three main groups: property, shipping-related services and finance & investment. Trading, retail and quarrying make a smaller contribution.

The best-performing sector in the '80s has been shipping, where Hutchison has done well out of its container terminal, the largest privately owned one in the world. Like New York, Hong Kong handles two million containers a year and half of those come through Hutchison's terminal. The group is now reclaiming land to build a second terminal at a cost

of HK$2bn. In property, Hutchison and Cheung Kong together build 30% of all the flats in Hong Kong; by hanging on to the commercial development they have a reputation for not just making residential sales and running but of subsequently attracting business and retailing interest.

Other recent developments include

Cavendish likely to surface in takeover move

entry into the cellular telephone market through a joint venture with Motorola, an interest in radio-paging and a partnership with British Telecom in the bid for Hong Kong's cable television rights.

The recent purchase of a controlling

Venture to launch Asiasat I

BRITISH telecommunications giant **Cable and Wireless** and Hong Kong's **Hutchison** group, controlled by business tycoon Li Ka-shing, have joined with the influential **China International Trust and Investment Corporation** (CITIC), to launch China's first domestic satellite for Asia.

The three equal partners signed an agreement in late February for a new joint venture consortium to launch a refurbished *Westar VI* communications satellite into orbit in April next year, using China's *Long March III* rocket.

At the contract-signing ceremony for the HK$1.17 billion project, Mr Min Yu, head of CITIC Technology, a CITIC subsidiary representing Chinese interests, said that the satellite, to be named *Asiasat I*, would fill a telecommunications void in the region.

He said that *Asiasat I* would be available to Asia-Pacific countries from Thailand, Pakistan and the Philippines to south Japan and even Taiwan, besides Hong Kong and China itself.

Mr Yu added that China will enter into more joint ventures with foreign conglomerates to put more satellites into space.

Cable and Wireless director (Hong Kong) Mike Gale said that the first control and monitoring facility would be in Hong Kong, but participating countries will also own and operate their own networks with the use of facilities provided by the consortium.

The former *Westar VI* satellite is being modified by its US maker, Hughes Aircraft. It had been launched by the US space shuttle but later salvaged from space in 1985 after failing to get into proper orbit.

Managing director Fung Hak Ming of Cable and Wireless, Hong Kong, said that after modifications to meet the new owners' specifications, *Asiasat I* would be practically new because it had never been used before.

The exact location of *Asiasat I* is yet to be worked out but it will be 36,000 kilometres above the equator in fixed orbit over Southeast Asia, with a *footprint* over many countries in the region including China.

With *Asiasat I*'s life expectancy of eight years, the consortium expects to recoup its capital outlay in about four years.

Engineers present at the contract-signing ceremony pointed out that the indicated lifespan of *Asiasat I* only referred to the maker's guaranteed term, which might well be extended in reality.

Mr Rick Siemens, group managing director of Hutchison Telecommunications, added that partners of the consortium are viewing the joint venture as a continuing one, so that before one satellite goes out of service another or others may well have been launched into service.

The C-band *Asiasat I* with its 24 transponders will be able to carry all types of domestic telecommunications signals. These will include public and private telephone services, data communication, television distribution, VSAT (very small aperture terminal) data operations and telemetry.

A spokesman for the new consortium said that the satellite will allow provision of telecommunications in areas where the use of land-based systems has been physically difficult to establish.

"For the first time an array of domestic telecommunications-based services will become routinely available. The impact on social and economic development in the participating countries will be dramatic," he added.

"We expect increased use of telephone, television and data communications, but there are myriad other uses for the satellite – for example, distribution of newspaper copy transmitted for production in remote locations," he said.

The spokesman also remarked that the joint venture "...is a business venture in the strictest sense" because each participant brings unique resources to the project, and each will make a significant contribution to it.

Chief engineer Chen Shouchun of China Great Wall Industrial Corp, which will supervise the *Long March III* launch programme, said China was poised to launch *Asiasat I* from Xichang in Sichuan province where communications satellites are launched.

(China's other space centre is in Jiuquan in western Gansu province.)

Detailed financing plans were not disclosed, but spokesmen said that a combination of equity investment and long-term debt would be used. Individual user tariffs would be charged for the use of *Asiasat I*, as is common in industry.

The track record of China's *Long March* launch programme is good but insurance cost is still expected to make up more than 20 per cent of the cost of the venture.

At press time, the consortium had joined two Bangkok-based partners, Loxley and Piyanant, and submitted a tender for a turnkey project in Thailand, to be awarded in August.

Winner of the tender would have the right to operate satellite communications services in Thailand for at least 30 years.

The winning group would also be required to buy and launch the orbitor, according to group planning director of Hutchison Telecommunications, Robin Maule.

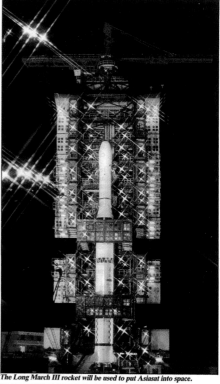

The Long March III rocket will be used to put Asiasat into space.

ASIASAT I Coverage

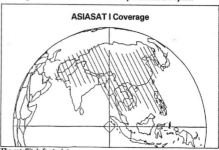

The satellite's footprint.

Launching Asiasat in China – a great leap forward for telephones and television

On the Great Wall of China with David Tang

Marathon des Sables – 250 km across the Moroccan desert

The MacLehose Trail in Hong Kong

In the Legion with Soto and
Vignaga and again at a reunion
25 years later (above)

Rolling down the Champs-Élysées in a tank on Bastille Day

flat tyres on his car in the car park and a constant unavailability of things he needed.

Unfortunately, the cold war between Lapping and Suchart spread to all the locals and expats, known as farangs. This was not Suchart's intention, and he and I, for instance, had an excellent relationship. But some of his sycophants had misread the boss's intentions and pushed the anti-farang message too far. Things came to a head one day when I had to deliver a government tender to the railway department in a hurry. I needed a car fast and asked Suchart if I could borrow his driver and car. His office was on the top floor of the building overlooking the compound where we parked the cars. The drivers spent their days in a hut in the corner of the compound smoking their weeds and waiting instructions. Suchart's driver was a Thai boxer, tall for a Thai and in reality his bodyguard. His name was Poon. Suchart immediately told me to get Poon to drive me to the government offices to deliver the tender. We were going to be late.

I approached the drivers' hut where Poon was holding court as usual and asked him to get the car ready. He waved his hand and said, 'No petrol.' I responded politely but with a degree of acidity, 'Well go and get some.' 'No money' came the reply with a sort of 'so stuff you' tone attached. 'Well go to the accounts department and get some for Christ's sake!'

And then from Poon, 'Go and get it yourself.' This time in a 'Fuck you' tone.

It is not only Asians who lose face. This was a huge loss of face for me in front of the gang of smirking drivers. I stood there for a moment, wondering how to respond. I finally turned and went back up to Suchart's office and told him his driver had gone mad. He exploded in fury when he heard what had happened, opened his window and screamed across the compound to Poon to bring the car to the front of the office and drive Mr Murray to the railway department 'NOW!'

I went slowly downstairs and there was Poon waiting in the car looking like a man about to commit murder. I tapped on his window, which he lowered, and I leaned down close to his face and said in a low voice, so that Suchart, who was watching the whole scene from his window above could not hear, 'Take your car and shove it up your arse, I prefer to take a taxi than drive with a dick like you, and I'll see you at six o'clock tonight behind the warehouse.'

I was young at the time and relatively fresh out of the Foreign Legion. Poon let out a great roar and leapt out of the car screaming, 'Not tonight… NOW!' and thumped me in the chest and started kicking the hell out of me, Thai-boxing style. Suchart was hanging from his window by his shoelaces, yelling hysterically at Poon to stop, but he carried on. I was standing there taking the kicks while holding my briefcase.

Finally, enough! I dropped my briefcase and caught Poon's foot in my arm so that his legs were at a perfect right angle. I kicked him in the crotch with the point of my foot (not the upper part), so that my foot went halfway up his orifice with more force behind it than needed to kick a rugger ball between the posts from the halfway line. He went down like the proverbial pole-axed ox, letting out a great hiss that sounded like a burst water main. I then slammed him in the mouth with my elbow and grabbed him in a neck hold and squeezed with everything I had. After a minute or two I realised I was killing him. His face was a deep purple colour and blood was pouring out of his mouth all over my shirt. I quickly released him and jumped up. He staggered to his feet, glared at me like a mad bull and rushed out of the compound into the Bangkok traffic, never to be seen again.

Kim Fraser, my colleague, had watched the whole thing through his nearby window and later declared to all and sundry that it was the best spectator sport that he had seen in a lifetime.

We failed to deliver the tender on time.

Expensive spectator sport!

I received a telegram one day to say my father had died. I had met him once in my life and we had lunched together. Not much to hang a memory on.

The finale in Thailand was the birth of our first-born son and heir. We named him George, after Jeffa's American family and my grandfather George, and Justin as a name we liked. He weighed in at nine and a half pounds. Welcome to our world, Just.

The day came for our departure and after four years at the coalface, we left with sadness mingled with excitement for a six-month pre-paid holiday, now blessed with a seven-month-old son. One of the saddest things was saying goodbye to our dog, Rug. We could not take him with us, and we gave him to an Irish friend. Liam came to the house in a small open truck full of kit and he put Rug on the back and drove off. Seeing Rug standing on the back of the truck looking at us with so much misery on his face was eye-watering stuff. They will always be a man's best friend. Rug will never be forgotten, nor will those sunny days in Thailand.

CHAPTER XV
THE CRESTA RUN

Six months' leave, paid in advance – what could be more exhilarating than that? One sobering fact was that my annual salary was £1,350 at the time, thanks to an annual increment of £50 per annum over the previous three years and an upward adjustment of 25 per cent for the devaluation of sterling announced by the British government in 1967. The Jardine's salary was, to be fair, supplemented by free accommodation. However, the accommodation allowance did not carry through when we were on leave. Nor indeed did it carry through to the provident fund calculation on retirement. So, caution was always indicated when dispensing cash.

We raced to St Moritz in Switzerland for a skiing holiday with Jeffa's parents. Good intentions on day one. I had never skied before in my life so was on the nursery slopes on arrival. Jeffa's father introduced me to the Cresta Run. It was love at first sight, which dimmed just a little after the first ride. Terrifying.

The Cresta Run is unique in the world. It is an iced track, two metres wide, with vertical sides, which careers down the mountain at 45 degrees for about a kilometre, and is the most pants-wetting experience of a lifetime. It makes parachute jumping at night feel like jumping out of bed in the morning. The rider lies on a toboggan (known as a skeleton), weighing 60kg, with a sliding seat. To increase speed, the rider pulls himself forward and to reduce speed he pushes back on the sliding seat and drags his feet behind him. His boots have spikes on the toes, and they act as a braking system, to some degree.

The weight of the skeleton and the speed at which it is travelling after the first fifty yards makes braking a very tiring exercise, and after a short while one's feet simply bounce off the ice, unless you have the leg muscles of a rhino. You are then increasing speed and you are essentially no longer in control of your vehicle. The track winds around prolonged curves, the most notorious of which is called 'shuttlecock'; one has to use all one's strength to steer the skeleton around these corners, leaning over with your body and raking like hell with your feet, if still possible, in order to stay on the track. At peak speed you are hitting eighty miles per hour and your nose is three inches from the ice. The track ends with a gradual ascent, which slows you down eventually to a merciful stop. Many riders exit at 'shuttlecock' corner and the ride is over as you are jettisoned out of the track into nowhere and end up buried in a pile of snow, if the gods are smiling.

You are instructed on 'take-off' that in the event that you are thrown out of the track, it is critical that you throw the skeleton from your body to avoid it falling on top of you. 60kg of metal hitting you at 70 miles an hour can cause damage. Serious damage. Having said that, although there have been over the years many broken ribs, wrists and legs, only seven riders have actually been killed on the run.

As a beginner, a novice rider starts at the halfway point, known as 'Junction'. Over a number of years, as you increase your speed and demonstrate control, you are eventually invited to go from 'Top'. From Top is a whole new experience and is not for those that fear death. I rode the Cresta for seventeen years.

After the séjour in St Moritz, we travelled to the States where Jeffa had lots of relatives through her American mother. I met her grandmother, whose sagacious advice on our wedding day has proven to be accurate.

Out of the blue one day I got a letter from Roland Gagnon, the export director of ASARCO, for whom I had acted as agent in Thailand for the distribution of asbestos over the previous four years. I had apparently made their first ever sale to the Siam Cement Company. It was an offer of a job as sales director for Europe, based in London on a salary of US$10,000 plus a car. They flew Jeffa and me to Canada and we motored to the Tetford mines, nerve centre of ASARCO, where we were treated to a warm reception; needed as the temperature was thirty below. The job offer was confirmed. We would live in London and be responsible for European markets.

I rang David Edwards at Jardine's in Hong Kong. He was now a full director of the company and I told him I was considering ASARCO's offer. He reacted energetically, telling me I should do nothing until he got back to me after he had discussed it with his fellow directors. He said I was highly regarded in Hong Kong, my tour in Thailand had gone exceptionally well, they had something very exciting for me... and I must wait.

I waited.

CHAPTER XVI
HONG KONG

David Edwards eventually came back full of enthusiasm and a job offer as managing director of a Jardine subsidiary called Harry Wicking. Harry Wicking was a trading company importing a mass of different products, many of which were competing with those marketed by Jardine Matheson themselves. In this way, I suppose, they covered the ground and made sure nothing slipped through the net. My salary would be £2,500 per annum plus a bonus and the usual perks of accommodation, medical cover and school fees for two children until the age of eighteen.

Shortly after the call from Edwards, I met Ralph Bateman at a cocktail party hosted by Jeffa's father. Bateman was the chairman of an asbestos mining company called John Mansfield, one of the largest in the world. Bill Mather told him, as he introduced me, that I had been offered a job by ASARCO and to my surprise, Bateman started to warn me off. He wasn't running down ASARCO, but was talking in a rather subdued tone against asbestos. It was unclear what he was warning me about exactly. It was something against the asbestos industry as a whole. It was the final prompt that made me opt for Jardine's. It turned out to be a lifesaver.

A few years later, asbestos was confirmed as a cause of cancer. Over the years it had been used in multiple manufacturing processes such as asbestos cement roofs and fire-proof products. Suddenly the class action lawsuits were flying. Lloyd's of London, the largest insurance company in the world at that time, was on its knees with claims from companies involved in asbestos. Another fork in the road where I was lucky.

I forgot about asbestos and decided to head for Hong Kong, to be appointed by Jardine's as managing director of their Harry Wicking subsidiary, on a fraction of the salary offered by ASARCO. But money isn't everything, as they say.

Harry Wicking traded everything from Terry's chocolates, Robertson's jam, Clarks shoes, railway sleepers from Australia, wooden floor tiles from

Burma, suiting material from Burlington Mills in the States, artificial aroma products for perfumes and food stuff from Bush Boake Allen, weighing machines from Avery, perfumery products from Christian Dior, ties and foulards from Hermès, explosives from Dupont and a host of other things. David Middleditch's predictions at Matheson's in London had proved accurate. My Legion training in explosives would come in useful after all.

In addition, I was instructed by Edwards to create a hotel supplies company in response to the hotels which were due to be constructed over the next few years in Hong Kong. I had a staff of twenty-five to help me with this challenge. Edwards declared my budget for starting this hotel supplies enterprise to be the sizzling sum of US$20,000. I started off with a trip around the world, staying at many different hotels and blowing $40,000 in the process. But I learned a lot about hotels.

No two hotel managers agreed on anything. One would stress the importance of bathrooms. That is what guests remembered. Another would make the point that bedrooms should not be too cushy, otherwise guests would remain in them all day and tap room service. How do you make money carting a cup of coffee to the twentieth floor every three hours? Ashtrays should be cheap because they are stolen. Ashtrays should be expensive because they end up on armchairs in the drawing rooms of grand houses, are a good reminder of people's holidays and, as such, are an advertisement. Beds should be soft and comfortable. Beds should be hard, good for bad backs. By the time I had finished my 'tour du monde,' I probably knew more about hotels than most students graduating from the Lausanne Hotel Management School.

Apart from hotel supplies, most of what Harry Wicking marketed was done through dealers, who opened letters of credit on our principals' accounts. We lived on commissions. My staff were well capable of handling the dealer business, but one or two things required the boss's direct involvement. This was when we were financing the trade ourselves and the risk increased.

Jardine Matheson was very risk averse. That is why they controlled the largest property company in Hong Kong (Hong Kong Land) with a tiny 3 per cent shareholding and reaped a fraction of what they might have done had they held a reasonable stake and accepted the risks.

One of the activities we financed ourselves at Harry Wicking, thereby braving the risk, was suiting fabric from Burlington Mills, in the States. At the beginning of each year we had to commit to the purchase of a million dollars of prime suiting fabric at a price of US$5.50 per yard. Serious 'bread' in those days. In return for this commitment and only if we made this commitment, we would be offered 'seconds' from time to time during the year, at greatly reduced prices. 'Seconds' were bolts of fabric with defects that could not be sold to the big textile manufacturers in the States but could be sold to the tailors in Hong Kong, who had no problem cutting round the defects by hand. The price of the seconds averaged $2.80 per yard, a massive discount to the prime product. This was where we could make a return. I sold prime Dacron to my dealers at cost. They hated buying it because they knew the seconds were coming later at less than half the price. They would argue for hours trying to squeeze me down on the quantity I was trying to force on them. But they also knew that unless they bought the prime, I would not offer seconds later. They were in the same 'vice' that I was in with Burlington.

During the year I would receive periodic telephone calls from a Walter Rosenbaum in New York, usually around midnight – a convenient time for him but a bloody awful hour for me – offering me 400 bolts of seconds for immediate delivery. Price $2.50 per yard. All colours and some 'fancies' (pinstripes). Three and a half yards of material are required for one suit.

400 bolts of fabric could be 4,000 yards of cloth. 'Seconds' could have 10 per cent defects. It was all guess work. No guarantees on anything. I could be buying gold or garbage. Fabric with very few defects and lots of pinstriped cloth or black colour full of holes… My tailors loved all colours except black and raved about 'fancies'. I supplied about sixty tailors in Hong Kong. Having sometimes made a commitment of well over $200,000 in the middle of the night and not all that sure of what I had bought in terms of colours of the cloth etc., I had to take the following day at a run and get around the market and offload this stuff. Not easy when nobody has a clue what they are buying.

Of course, I always bargained with Rosenbaum. It usually went like this against his opening offer of $2.50:

'Walter, how about I take the lot for $1.80?'

From Rosenbaum: 'Not a chance, Simon. If you don't want it, I can sell it in Puerto Rico and they will sell it in your market.'

'Okay! $1.90 and that's it.'

'Simon, we've been doing business a long time. Because it's you, I can let you have it for $2.'

'All right Walter. It's colours and fancies right? Very little black?'

'Yes... err... only about 10 per cent black.'

'Okay $1.95, and Walt, that really is it... and it's one o'clock in the fucking morning here, Walt.'

'Done.'

I would then give my tailors the same treatment that Rosenbaum had given me, but I'd ask for $3.50 and if they didn't like it, I would threaten to sell it maybe for less to Tailor Wong next door. I felt awful, but it had to be done. And then when the cloth arrived six weeks later, 20 per cent would be black cloth. The dealers would scream at me and I would shout at Rosenbaum... and on we went throughout the year.

The hotel supplies business was much more fun.

In 1970, the visitors arriving into Hong Kong numbered 400,000 per annum, compared to 56 million visitors today. In the early 1970s, the mainland Chinese were not allowed in and a barbed wire barrage along the frontier guarded by Gurkha troops ensured they didn't get in. But hotels were being built en masse. Not just in Hong Kong but in the whole region: Singapore, Thailand, Malaysia and Indonesia.

In Hong Kong, the Excelsior Hotel, built by Hong Kong Land and Trusthouse Forte in a joint venture, was going to be a thousand-bedroom hotel. Probably the largest hotel in the world outside America. I was rushing round the globe getting exclusive representation for beds, wallpaper, soap, ashtrays, carpet, towels, bed linen, cutlery, glass, coat-hangers and anything else that goes into a hotel. My first order came from the new Lee Gardens Hotel built by Swire's. I got the cutlery contract for US$50,000. Huge excitement. We were in business.

We won many contracts for hotels such as the Shangri-La, the Park, the Excelsior, the Hyatt, the Sheraton, the Hilton and others. These hotels in many cases were regional and having secured business in one place, the relationship flourished around the region.

Of all the contracts we won, three stories stand out.

The Excelsior was the challenge of a lifetime. The manager was Sami Zohgby. He was a Trusthouse Forte man of great experience and he knew what he wanted. We clicked on day one. He was full of good advice and guidance.

The first contract I was chasing was the bed contract. 1,000 rooms with two beds in each room was a very fat order: 2,000 beds. The biggest single order for beds ever in Hong Kong. All the bed manufacturers were already represented. I had to go and find a new source. I set off to Japan and the trail led me to the Nihon Bed Company. First, a sample and an okay from Zohgby on quality. I got it.

Then the price. We won the contract. Over US$3 million.

Then the problems.

Shipping, and where to store the beds and the labour to get the beds into the rooms before the hotel opened. The Japanese in those days always quoted in US dollars. I was selling in Hong Kong dollars. The exchange rate was ¥360 to US$1 and having secured and signed the contract, the US dollar/yen rate changed, with the yen rising in strength against the dollar. In other words, fewer yen for their dollar. Nihon were going to be seriously out of pocket in yen terms. At the same time the Hong Kong dollar had dropped against the US dollar, so I was making an extra bomb in Hong Kong dollars. My currency. Nihon bed officers came over to Hong Kong and were on their knees for a price increase. I could afford it and gave it to them, though contractually I didn't have to.

They threatened to build a statue of me in their compound!

Sami arranged for me to store the beds in the Excelsior grounds in the containers in which they had arrived, but the container company demanded rent on the containers after three days. We had a typhoon on the third day. I started paying rent and my profit was being eroded by the hour. The lifts in the hotel, being supplied by Jardine's, were not ready. I had to hire 200 coolies to carry the beds up 30 floors into the 1,000 bedrooms. I discovered there was more to supplying 2,000 beds to a hotel than signing a contract. Nevertheless, we made money. Good money and I got seven more contracts for the Nihon Bed Company. The statue is probably up by now.

And then there was the wallpaper contract.

The interior designer of the Excelsior Hotel was Bonnie Roberts and she was not to be messed with. Vernon Roberts, her husband, was the general manager of Hong Kong Land, 50 per cent owners of the hotel. She was also the agent for some of the products that she had designed for the hotel, including Sanderson's wallpaper, and receiving a commission as such. Massive conflict of interest. The wallpaper contract was huge, and she had specified Sanderson's most expensive wallpaper in a complicated design that was almost impossible to replicate. I had made friends with the son of the biggest company in Taiwan, the Formosa Plastics Company, and he said he thought he could take a shot at the wallpaper contract against the wishes of Bonnie, who simply wanted to give the contract to Sanderson's and collect her commission.

Hotel manager Sami was persuaded by me that we could do the job for 50 per cent less than Bonnie. He decided to go through a tender process, otherwise it would look terrible, even though Bonnie didn't care what it looked like. I submitted a price well below Bonnie's. She was bidding in the clouds assuming nobody could match her Sanderson specification. I won the tender, subject to samples matching the specs.

Then came the hard bit.

The day dawned when we had to submit samples. The Sanderson designs were complicated, and the colours were, in the main, blue and white. Paradoxically, two whites are almost impossible to match. I arrived at the meeting; Sami was at the head of the table. Architects and engineers filled the room, with Bonnie Roberts and her team occupying the middle and looking very prominent. This was the committee that awarded contracts. The Sanderson sample was on the table and I was asked to put mine beside it. It was close but not close enough and Bonnie let out a great cry of condemnation.

'Oh No! No! No! That will never do,' she bleated.

Everybody nodded in sort of agreement. Nobody was going against the boss's wife. Sami said rather sadly, 'I'm afraid you'll have to do a little better than that, Simon.'

'No problem. Give me another week', I said.

The boys from Formosa were fantastic and said it could be done. I went over to Taiwan to have a look at their operations. They were very impressive, and I felt they could do it.

A week later, the same meeting with the same result. We were nearer but not 100 per cent. It was never going to be a 100 per cent match. I asked for one more shot. Bonnie objected. Sami agreed and overruled her. I was after all representing a Jardine's subsidiary, and Jardine's were shareholders in the project through Hong Kong Land.

Ten days later I was ready. Before going to the meeting I went into the mock-up bedroom in the Hong Kong Land offices and stuck a square foot piece of my wallpaper on top of the Sanderson's wallpaper that was already there. In the meeting room everybody was on red alert for a row. Bonnie demanded to see the sample. Sami said, 'Last chance Simon.' Great tension in the room. I said the sample is in the mock-up room. Confusion followed. Bad looks from Bonnie. Sami said with a smile on his face, 'Okay let's go and take a look,' and all fourteen of us trooped down to the mock-up bedroom. When we were all in, Sami said, 'Okay Simon, so where's the sample?'

And I said, 'You tell me.'

They searched and searched every square inch of the walls, but they couldn't see it. And when they finally gave up the search, I walked over to the wall and peeled it off and said, 'I think it matches.'

Sami let out a great roar and laughed his head off, shouting 'Well done Simon. Fantastic. I guess you win.' Everybody joined in except Bonnie, whose face was as black as thunder. I haven't seen her since and that was fifty years ago. We had secured the largest wallpaper contract ever awarded in Hong Kong – maybe in the world.

And on it went. The Harry Wicking hotel supplies company was soon renowned. Hotels kept going up and so did our profits. By the time I was ready to move on, Harry Wicking hotel supplies was the largest business of its kind in Hong Kong, supplying everything from kitchen equipment to carpets, beds, linen, cutlery, furniture, soap, ashtrays, prints, and even flowers. And Hong Kong's tourist numbers went from 300,000 to 10 million per annum in 5 years. Hong Kong hotels grew and indeed spread throughout the world: the Peninsular, the Mandarin, the Shangri-La, the Marriott, Rosewood, Hyatt and on and on; they kept building. But not everything had a bouncy ending.

I discovered an Italian manufacturer of unbreakable wine glasses. When I went to visit the company in Rome, they dropped the glasses on a concrete floor, to demonstrate how unbreakable they were. Very impressive and a hotelier's dream.

I was doing business with a Mr Chan Chak Fu, who was building the Indra Hotel in Thailand and the Park Hotel in Hong Kong. I had already secured contracts for these hotels, including for soap. Soap is an infinity contract: disposable. I told Mr Chan about my wine glasses and delivered samples. I dropped one on the floor. It didn't break and he was extremely excited and called his entire senior management into the colossal ballroom of the hotel and proceeded to lecture them. 'This is Simon Murray', he said. 'He travels the world over and finds amazing products at good prices. We need more people like him in the hotel business. And now he has found a source of unbreakable glasses. We lose thousands of glasses through breakage every year and now finally the solution. Simon, please demonstrate the quality of the glasses.'

With an introduction like that, it set my energy levels at full throttle and I threw a glass high into the air to the gaping astonishment of the twenty-three people in the room. It crashed to the floor and shattered into a million pieces. Mr Chan walked out, leaving everybody in hysterics, except me. End of glassware business. End of contracts with Mr Chan. Nearly the end of me.

I even introduced the 'bell captain' into several hotels. These days it is simply known as the 'bar' in the bedroom and is a fixture in all hotels. In those days it was a novelty. It was essentially a vending machine that automatically debited your room service account when you selected something from it. It was perceived as a huge saving to room service costs and of course a great convenience to the people in the room, who did not have to wait for service.

And then, one day, a promotion. I was assigned to Jeremy Brown, the number three director, as an assistant director, leading to a substantial increase in my salary. All the directors were assigned executive assistants known as EAs. David Edwards called me in to his office and asked if I would like to be his EA. I told him I was already acting as such for Jeremy Brown. He said he was aware of that, but he could arrange for it to be changed, if I agreed. This put me in an awkward position. Apart from anything else, Jeremy Brown was senior to Edwards as deputy managing director of the group, while Edwards was the trading director. I did not want to upset Brown; he would lose face and I would certainly lose marks.

I told Edwards that having accepted the position with Brown, to now turn around and say I would prefer to work with him, would be embarrassing. Edwards tried hard to persuade me that it didn't matter, but I felt differently and refused to budge, and when I wouldn't change my mind, I detected a complete change in his attitude towards me. He didn't like it at all and read it as a snub. This was the beginning of a slow-burning long slide in our relationship.

These were bouncy days in Hong Kong. The stock market was booming with new penny stocks coming to the public markets every day. I had become friends with Michael Stapleton – 'Stapes' – a long-term Hong Kong player. He knew everybody and was the man about town and already a legend in his own mind, driving around in an E-Type Jaguar with a Ferrari on order. An 'It' man, never without a good-looking girl on his arm.

He was a shipbroker and I met him when he was a bit down, having fallen out with his boss and started his own company with a partner who had been with him at the previous company. This partner, called Regan, ratted on Stapes when they were only a few days into their new company and crawled back to their old boss to provide him with enough information to sue Stapes. Stapes was sued for having left the company with confidential information, a list of clients and all the usual rubbish, which was in his head anyway. The lawsuit went nowhere but obviously worried him at the time. He lost some of his 'gung-ho' and it was at this moment that we met one day at the bottom of Pedder Street and wandered over to the Captain's Bar, in the Mandarin Hotel, for a few drinks. Out poured all his problems and I was sympathetic, and it went from there into one of the great friendships of my life.

The Captain's Bar was the waterhole for the ex-pats at the end of the day. The discussion points at the bar circled mainly around the stock market. What stocks to buy in the morning. The newly listed companies had strange sounding Chinese names, companies about which we knew nothing, but anything newly listed increased its quoted value within a week. Lunch would begin with someone announcing, 'New listing today, guys. It's called Luk Fuk Yu. Coming to the market at eleven cents.'

'What do they do?' from the mob.

'God knows,' the answer would come back.

Immediately everyone made a mental note to call HSBC in the afternoon and get some Luk Fuk Yu shares.

We had lunch at either one of two restaurants every day: Young's Restaurant if it was to be Chinese food and Jimmy's Kitchen if European. Jimmy's had originally been created by his father to cater to English merchant sailors coming through Hong Kong, who wanted English grub. That had occurred years before and it had now moved upmarket to some degree. Jimmy's had nine tables and we used to book a table for a year at a time with the unwritten understanding that we would call before eleven o'clock if we wished to cancel on a particular day.

Stapes's brother David was a partner at W.I. Carr in London. They were also one of the main stockbrokers in Hong Kong. David fed us the information on stocks coming to the market. We all had accounts with the Hong Kong & Shanghai Bank through which we bought our shares and against which the bank would automatically advance us a loan of 50 per cent.

This was capitalism at its best. The first stock I bought was Jardine Matheson, but soon I was riding a value mountain twenty times my salary, with a debt valley ten times my salary. The bank didn't seem to worry and anyway the stock values went up every day.

In 1972, I was on leave with Jeffa in Switzerland. Jardine's had changed the leave arrangements so that we now took two months every two years instead of six months every three years. Just before we left, I had bought shares in Swire's. The company in those days was known as Butterfield and Swire or simply B and S. I paid HK$16 per share.

We were staying in a chalet in Switzerland having a wonderful time. I had left the nursery slopes far behind. At the bar in the evening people were coming up to me and congratulating me for living in Hong Kong, where apparently there was this amazing stock market that only went up, never down. I would offer them a glass of champagne and was beginning to feel more and more like Croesus in his prime. And then out of the blue one morning came a telegram from Stapes. This was a long time before mobile phones, faxes and telexes. The telegram was brief. It said, 'BANDS 156 have a good holiday.' I had no idea what this was except that it sounded musical.

An hour later, I was 'shussing' down a vertical slope and it hit me: 'BANDS' was Butterfield and Swire, and the shares I had bought before we left Hong Kong at HK$16 were now at $156. I crossed my skis in that moment of exhilaration and rolled down the mountain into a crumpled heap at the bottom.

Jeffa came tearing down in a total panic, screaming, 'Are you okay darling... are you okay?'

I was okay and managed to gasp, 'We are rich.'

I called W.I. Carr and told them to 'sell', thank God.

Feeling so prosperous, we extended our Swiss holiday for an extra month before returning to London.

CHAPTER XVII

WATER INTO WINE

On my return from our wonderful holiday in the Swiss mountains, I had been invited to lunch with W.I. Carr in London before returning to Hong Kong. It was not my first visit, but instead of the usual jocular mood, everybody was quiet and drinking water instead of Château Latour, which was the norm.

'Anything the matter?' I asked.

'Haven't you heard?' came the reply.

'No. What's happened?'

'The Hong Kong stock market has fallen 50 per cent in the last week.

I hadn't read a newspaper in over a month. This was a knife straight into the chest.

'Jesus Christ. I better get selling now.'

The W.I. Carr boys, though clearly 'zapped,' were nevertheless cautiously of the view that the worst was over. The Hang Seng Index had hit the ceiling at 1770 and fallen to 840 in five days. Their opinion was that this was the bottom and it would steady up at this point and climb. The following day it rose to 883. They were right?

Wrong! It was a 'dead cat bounce'. Jeffa and I flew to Hong Kong the following day, a fourteen-hour flight. By the time we hit town, the market index had collapsed to 440. I thanked God again that I had sold the B and S shares.

On arrival in Hong Kong I told my broker to sell my Jardine shares 'at any price'. In the evening I called to find out the price at which he had sold. Imagine how I felt when he replied, 'I haven't sold.'

WHAT?????

'No buyers… *at any price.*'

I was out of the market two days later with my bank balance, after paying the overdraft. Empty. Broke. But at least I was still alive. Many were not.

The market index sailed on down to 152 — a drop of 91 per cent. The horizon was black with people running for the airport. The suicide rate went up 300 per cent. The pavements were covered with the blood of people jumping out of windows. They were bad days.

The cause of this stock market 'Hiroshima' was my very own company, Jardine Matheson. JM had sold 7 per cent of the company's shares, through a private placement, to the Prudential Insurance company, with the proceeds of which they had bought a property company in London called Reunion Properties. This was interpreted by many in Hong Kong, particularly the Chinese, as the beginning of their exit from Hong Kong. Jardine's doing a runner was very bad 'joss'.

In 1842 the Opium War was terminated by the Treaty of Nanjing with China surrendering Hong Kong Island to the British in perpetuity. The island was regarded by the Chinese as a 'barren rock'. The British wanted more territory over time and felt too closed in, surrounded on all sides by the Chinese. In 1898, China agreed to lease an additional 400 square miles of what became known as the New Territories to the British, for ninety-nine years. This enabled the British to own more of the area, with the Kowloon (nine dragons) peninsula and a number of islands, including Lamma and Lantau, thrown in for good measure. The first question asked by anyone arriving in Hong Kong was and always had been, 'What happens in 1997, when the lease runs out?' The answer was always: 'Oh! Nothing to worry about; they'll extend it. Hong Kong is very useful to them, their eye on the world. A pot of silver for them, the golden egg,' and so on.

But the boss in China was Mao Zedong. He undoubtedly had a different view on all this and above everything, he was not a man to lose face and he believed in his legacy, which was certainly not to give away land. Under Communist Party rule, every square inch of land in China belongs to the state. Item one in the rulebook of communism.

And so it remains.

But even as early as 1972, many people in Hong Kong had an eye on 1997 and could feel the clock ticking. Of all the people in Hong Kong who were perceived to know what was going on, it was the Princely Hong, and here they were, apparently, preparing to move out. A first step towards the exit. Panic was triggered.

For the next twenty-five years there was a gradual seepage of Hong

Kongers. Today 49 per cent of Vancouver's population is Chinese because of this. The foreign companies in Hong Kong ruled the waves. Jardine Matheson, B and S, Hutchison Whampoa, Dodwell's, Inchcape, Wheelock Marden, The Wharf Company and of course Hong Kong Land. Two local companies were also in this league: Y.K. Pao and C.Y. Tung. They were shipping companies. In the seventies, they were the biggest shipping companies in the world. Hong Kong was also becoming one of the largest transit container ports in the world and still is. One level down were some growing Chinese companies, but they were not yet in the 'club des riches'.

K.S. Li was a plastic flower manufacturer. His company was Cheung Kong; he had sold the factory building to Swire's for a huge amount of money and became a property enthusiast. When the market collapsed, he was buying, with little downside.

Other Chinese companies followed, such as Sun Hung Kai, Hynan, Henderson Land, Nan Fung, New World, Sino Land, Great Eagle, and Kerry – run by the amazing Robert Kuok who had arrived from Singapore and built the Shangri-La hotels. These companies had much greater faith in the future of Hong Kong than the 'Gweilo' companies, as the foreigners were known. Perhaps they had less to lose. Over time, the property companies dominated the Hong Kong economy and the local Chinese companies who had a greater appetite for risk completely outflanked the foreign companies.

There were takeovers as the Chinese companies bought out the foreigners. Cheung Kong bought Hutchison; Y.K. Pao bought the Wharf Company and its ferries, controlled by Jardine's; Inchcape, Dodwell's and Wheelock Marden were all devoured. Hong Kong Land remained the giant of the central district of Hong Kong, but the rest of the city and the Kowloon side, outside the centre, grew at a rapid pace.

Nevertheless, Jardine's maintained their title as the Princely Hong – for the time being.

I was now working for the deputy managing director of Jardine's, Jeremy Brown. All our principals, when visiting Hong Kong, filed through Jeremy Brown's office prior to a grand lunch in the Jardine's directors' dining room. My job was to brief Jeremy on the people coming through. How we were doing with their merchandise, profits, problems, identify any likely 'flak' coming in and to make sure our relationship with these principals continued to go well. They were, after all, our food line. It was good for me, in that I got to know everyone, all the key people in the many companies we represented; even better, they got to know me. We had businesses all over Asia and I travelled everywhere and made friends and business acquaintances. In Malaysia one of the Sultan's sons, called Tab, became a great chum. He was a player, loved the bars and night clubs as well as horse racing. The finance minister, Tengku Razaleigh, was also in the gang. Jardine's had a car distribution company, 'Cycle and Carriage', who were great partners for us. This company would later become a Jardine jewellery box.

In Indonesia, we had local partners who became real friends over time – the Ciputras. And the same again in the Philippines, where we had forestry and sugar interests. Jardine's also had a joint venture with MacMillan Bloedel in Canada, the largest forestry company in the world. I wouldn't say we planted every tree in Asia but we had a good share. Wandering around Asia, often alone, compiling facts and figures for Jeremy Brown, was fun and would stand me in good stead over the years. We all know it's not *what* you know, but *who* you know that matters in the long run.

We also had a joint venture with the Olayan group in Saudi Arabia, so that was also on my patrol path, and on into Iran, where the Shah was still in control and where we had a joint venture with a company selling whisky. Sounds rather strange today. The reality is they drink alcohol like we drink lemonade, when nobody's looking.

I made my first visit to China at this time, carrying Jeremy's bag to the Canton Fair. This was an annual fair that enabled China to show her wares to the world at large. All foreign visitors were locked in the same hotel and we were escorted everywhere we went. The Cultural Revolution was at its height. Thousands of young Red Guards were wandering around in gangs. There were huge posters everywhere of revolutionaries armed with pitchforks seemingly fighting a revolution. The streets were jammed with bicycles. No cars. There were only eight private cars in Beijing at this time and clearly none in Canton. We could wander, only if we were accompanied by a 'guide'.

The Chinese were selling locally made cosmetics and watches wrapped in brown paper and I explained through my 'escort' that presentation and packaging was an important part of the marketing of luxury goods. The seller lectured me in return that it was a complete waste of money, that the customer paid for all the fancy packaging. And I suppose he had a point. He also suggested that it was perhaps also an attempt to disguise the quality of the goods by wrapping them in gold paper and fancy boxes instead of ordinary brown paper. Tell that to Cartier!

One incident was unforgettable.

You could send letters and postcards. The stamps were sold separately and having got the appropriate stamp depending on the country to which the letter was going, you then walked over to a stall with a security grill in front and passed the envelope through the grill, where it was 'stamped' and thrown into the dispatch basket. Job done.

I addressed an envelope to London, got the stamp and went to the security grill. I asked the man behind the grill if he could 'stamp' it and give it back to me, instead of throwing it into the dispatch basket. Problems!

Lots of discussion with my guide. I claimed that if I took the letter myself, having paid for the stamp, I would be saving them the air freight. The man behind the grill was okay with this idea but pressed me on why I needed the letter to be stamped – difficult to explain. He decided to call his superior. The superior was also confused. I said I wanted to avoid the risk of it getting lost if it was sent by air, but it was very important that it was properly stamped as having been sent from China. A third person was called and eventually after half an hour they agreed to stamp it and give it back to me. I now had a letter sent from China in 1970 during the Cultural Revolution.

Forty years later I showed the letter to my granddaughter, Nicola.

'Oh my God' she said. 'Grandpa, you were in China in 1970 in the Cultural Revolution.' I said, 'Yes, but look at the address.' The address on the envelope was simply: 'Mr Simon Murray, London. England.' Nicola was overwhelmed and said, 'But how did they find you with only your name and "London" on the envelope?' And then, after waiting forty years, it was my great pleasure to say, 'In those days in London, I was very famous.' And so have I remained in my granddaughter's eyes ever since.

That's called thinking ahead!

A year after working as Brown's executive assistant, I was posted to Matheson's in London, where the senior Keswicks were ensconced, and where the ex-chairman of Jardine's, Michael Herries, and three other directors resided. It was also a burial ground for retired directors from Asia. Paradoxically they were assumed to have lost touch with the realities of Hong Kong after a while, although there was a weekly telephone call. But London was also the first port of call for many of our principals, who could be deterred by a visit to sleepy Matheson's and might as a consequence be moved to make some changes in their distribution arrangements in Asia, to a company like Hutchison – Jardine's main competitor. It was decided to send a fresh young buck from the front, who could go into bat for the firm in London where we needed more up-to-date knowledge of what was actually happening in Hong Kong and other parts of Asia.

Under Brown, I had travelled all over Asia, dipping into all our businesses there, and I probably had a deeper understanding of what we were up to and how the businesses were going, than anyone in the company, including Brown himself. He got his reports from me. And so it was that Murray was deemed the man to go on the board of Matheson's. Not everybody thought it was a good idea. Herries, now the chairman of Matheson's, thought it was unnecessary and regarded me as some sort of Hong Kong spy. Not far wrong in fact. He was even more annoyed that he had not been consulted over my appointment. I had been thrust upon him.

When Herries had retired from Hong Kong two years earlier, the board had been divided as to who should succeed him. The candidates were Henry Keswick, founders' kin, and David Newbigging. Newbigging was a few years older than Keswick and had been in the firm longer. Eventually the Keswicks had their way, although there was a degree of compromise. Henry was made 'senior' managing director and Newbigging, just plain managing director; John Keswick in London became the chairman. Some people were unhappy about this. Charles Letts had resigned over it. I had lost my mentor and real friend in the company at senior level and was in an environment of crispy discontent.

Another fork in the road.

Off to London. Lots of excitement. Jeffa and I rented a house in Chelsea owned by David Newbigging. When I say we rented a house from David Newbigging, we did not pay the rent. Jardine's paid the rent. As far as Jeffa and I were concerned, no problem at all. The house was perfect, indeed rather grand.

Living in London, apart from anything else, gave us great times with our children. We had now three adorable children, Justin and Suzanna, who went to school 200 yards away at the Vale School, and Christy. This was a close family of five, that I had never experienced myself when I was young.

The office was something different. At Matheson's, in its sombre setting on Lombard Street, the days began with 'prayers'. Not biblical, but a meeting attended by all the directors. The senior Keswick brothers, Tony and John, would be there and good old Middleditch, who could hardly believe I had arrived on the London board. It seemed like only yesterday he had been interviewing me for a job.

Herries chaired the meetings and began reading out the telexes from Hong Kong, requesting London to do this and that and to contact this principal and that one and run around in Europe, where all the firms we represented were located. He passed all this to me in a tone as though he was giving orders to a serf. He would often throw in extra duties like 'Oh Simon, the lavatory seat is falling off in the loo, could you get it fixed. Thanks,' which would ensure that I did not get above my station.

In spite of Herries, the two years in London were fabulous. I got to know everybody in the city. The senior directors of all the big companies we represented in Asia were invited to Matheson's directors' lunch on a daily basis. The heads of Rolls Royce, BAC, the banks, the law firms, the booze companies, Guinness, White Horse Whisky, Unilever, investment banks, Westland Helicopters and the rest.

The daily directors' lunch began with a healthy, refreshing round of gin and tonic. By the time all the guests had arrived, this had been doubled. We sat down at the table where the sherry was already waiting for us in our glasses. Then the white wine was downed and the red circulated. Lunch ended with cheese accompanied by Madeira. The Madeira was pushed around until the decanter was empty, and woe betide anybody who did not keep it moving. After lunch we would return to our offices: the oldies for a nap; me, feeling very fresh and ready to go.

In contrast to my rather brittle relationship with Herries, I enjoyed a close relationship with Middleditch and John Keswick the group chairman.

J.K., as he was known, became another surrogate father following in the paths of Peter Clapham, Charles Letts and also the wonderful Alfred Hecht.

I had first met Alfred when he came out to Thailand with his friend Frank Lloyd, the father of a great friend of mine at Bedford School, Gilbert Lloyd. He was a picture framer by trade and a talented one too. He worked closely with all the great artists of the day, perhaps most notably, Francis Bacon. He and Bacon became friends and Bacon gifted Alfred many of his paintings. In turn, following a long and happy friendship, Alfred offered to leave some of these paintings to me in his will. But I had to politely decline. Bacon's work often included rather grotesque, distorted nude figures. Jeffa summed it up best: 'It's very kind of him darling, but I don't think I could live with those pictures on our walls.' Bacon's works sell for eye-watering figures these days: what a deal to miss!

J.K. became a real friend. He invited Jeffa and I to shoots and dinners. I travelled with him as bag carrier and information source on trips all over Europe to visit our principals. He was hysterically amusing. He knew everybody. He was regarded as one of the world's foremost experts on China, where Jardine's had thrived long before the arrival of Mao Zedong in 1949.

A Chinese friend who knew Jardine's of old when they were headquartered in Shanghai, said to me once, 'What Jardine's has here now in Hong Kong is like the porter's lodge in comparison to what they had in the old days in Shanghai.' It all ended in 1949.

John Keswick had written a book on China. It was modestly titled *What I know about China*. It was a best seller. It had 200 blank pages! Brilliant, and a testament to his modesty.

He disliked Herries intensely; a feeling which was mutual and which drew J.K. and I together even more. Nothing like a common foe to bind people together.

Sometimes, after the morning prayers meeting, we would all walk out of the boardroom but Herries would quietly signal us to hang around. He would wait until J.K. had walked down the passage to his office and then usher us back into the boardroom to say what he really wanted to say and make sure J.K. did not get involved. I found this very embarrassing and of course J.K. knew about it. Herries resigned a short while later and became chairman of the Royal Bank of Scotland.

One of the functions of Matheson's was the recruitment of the cadre for Jardine's every year. We hired five young students from Oxford and Cambridge. We paid a number of visits to the two universities and probably interviewed in all about fifty who had applied. We also searched for other staff as requested by Jardine's, which could range from engineers to hotel managers. One day came a request for a marketing manager. The search would begin through our friend Dickie Dutton, a headhunter, who would narrow it down to two or three who would be handed over to Middleditch and myself to make the final decision.

Middleditch, on his way out to lunch one day came to my office and said, 'Look, I've got this guy coming in at 2:30. He's a marketing man that I think will suit them in Hong Kong. I've got another meeting outside. Can you take a look? Here are his papers.'

I looked at the papers. Brian Skinner. Ex-ADC to General Pugh, 2nd Gurkhas. The old world just keeps on turning. He came into my office and I apologised that Middleditch could not see him but had asked me to do the interview. He didn't recognise me, and I did not tell him that I recognised him, helped of course by the fact that I knew he was coming. It had been nearly fourteen years since we had last met. I got him seated and after the usual platitudes, I said, 'Brian, as long as you can confirm to me that you do not spend your free time reading Hank Jansen novels and that you do not smoke black cheroots, the job is yours.' His mouth dropped open. He was staggered. 'Simon Murray,' he gasped.

'Yes sir.'

'My God, we thought you were dead. This is wonderful!' he shouted.

It was a good moment. Big hug. He got the job.

Whilst these were good days for Jeffa and I, they were not good for London. In 1973, the Organisation of Petroleum Exporting Countries (OPEC) suddenly raised its ugly head and declared the price of oil up from US$3 a barrel to $12 in one day. It may seem cheap by today's rates but it was an overnight rise of 400 per cent and shook the world to pieces.

In England inflation rose to 27 per cent and interest rates hit 19 per cent. We started to look like the 1923 Weimar Republic. Hundreds of businesses were going bust on a daily basis. It was catastrophic. The coal miners decided it was a good time to strike for more pay. The electricity supply was cut. In the winter months after 4pm, we had to work by candlelight. England was in the pits, literally. Property prices collapsed. The Church of England announced that it had lost four billion pounds.

Jeffa and I took advantage and accepted the risk and bought a little cottage in the deep countryside of Kent. It cost £27,000 and with a 50 per cent mortgage from good old Midland Bank, it required only £13,000. I didn't have it, but Jeffa's father had given her shares in Mather and Platt on her twenty-first birthday. We sold half of them. The deal was done. We owned a house.

We sold it fourteen years later for £360,000 and bought Hemington House in Somerset, a beautiful old rectory standing in ten acres. Those vicars lived well in days gone by and there is money in bricks and mortar. Britain would remain paupers yet for three years, but the world resurfaced from the oil crisis in 1975.

At Matheson's, even in those dark days of the 1970s recession, I was also in charge of the entertainment of our Asian customers, who periodically came through London, wining and dining them and keeping the relationship warm. They included heads of our client and distribution companies, politicians from all the Asian countries and anybody who could be useful.

One day I had a call from Harrods.

'Mr Murray, we have a gentleman with us, a Mr Tengku Razaleigh, who has purchased some shirts and said we could send the bill to you at Matheson's. Will that be okay?'

'Yes that will be fine,' I replied, and then, just as I was about to put the phone down, I said, 'Oh, by the way, how many shirts has he bought?'

'128', came the reply.

Christ, I thought, Herries will love this.

These visitors from overseas were supposed to pay Jardine's back in Hong Kong. Whether or not they ever did, I don't know. I never asked just in case they hadn't and Herries would certainly have slapped the bill on me.

Many years later, long after I had left Jardine's, I was in Paris and had just bought a rather smart jacket in a very upmarket shop in the Champs-Élysées. The shop owner was having trouble with my credit card, which was not functioning, and as I apologised, a voice from behind me said, 'Don't worry, we will pay for Mr Murray's jacket.' I turned round and there, with one of his men, was Tengku Razaleigh.

Grand reunion, never forgotten.

~~~

One of my most memorable tasks at Matheson's in London, was solving our problems due to the Bordeaux wine scandal, which rocked the drinking world. It was noticed that Bordeaux was selling far more wine than it produced. Distributors like Jardine's and many others bought wine on an annual basis, but left it to mature in the vats of the merchants in Bordeaux until it was ready for drinking. But we paid up front. At any one time, we could have had ten years of potential wine revenues sitting in the vats of the Bordeaux wine merchants.

Jardine's had about £7 million of wine 'laid down' in the cellars of their principals, Cruse Frères et Fils, one of the largest merchants in Bordeaux. In 1973 that was quite a lot of money and a copious supply of wine. The sale of French wine was increasing dramatically to Japanese and Chinese consumers and the merchants in Bordeaux were maximising their returns by increasing their sales of wine, not by planting more grapes, but by adding Algerian red.

The balloon burst. The whistle-blower was a Madame Bert when she discovered her husband had a mistress. Monsieur Bert was the agent for Mascara wine from Algeria, much of which I had swallowed in my Legion days. Bert was making a fortune selling it to the merchants in Bordeaux, who were mixing it with the local Bordeaux brew and flogging it to their unsuspecting distributors like Jardine Matheson, who were in turn selling it to the unsuspecting Chinese and Japanese.

The mayor of Bordeaux, Chaban Delmas, was, as it happened, running for President of France when this massive calamity for Bordeaux hit the headlines. His opponents in Paris wasted no time in making sure this story blossomed, and soon the scandal went global. The 'claims' were about to begin. Insurance companies were alarmed. Jardine's was in a blind panic. The claims were that Bordeaux wine merchants had been mixing Algerian wine with Bordeaux wine and selling it in the Château-named bottles as pure Bordeaux. The 'claims' would go down the distribution chain. Everybody could be hit with class-action lawsuits.

The order came from Hong Kong and I was handed the task at our morning meeting to go to Bordeaux and solve the problem, but above all get our wine back and make sure it contained nothing except Bordeaux grapes. I was probably the right man for the job in that I spoke French fluently and knew the Brothers Cruse, our principals, well; of course, I was very familiar with Algerian wine: a good conversation piece. I was soon on my way to Paris with an introduction to a French lawyer.

It seemed that if our wine was still in the vats when Cruse Frères et Fils went bankrupt, which was now a certainty, then we would just be another creditor in the long queue. To avoid this, the key was to persuade the Cruse Brothers to take our wine out of the 'Bordeaux' wine vats and bottle it with Jardine's labels on the bottles. Thus, the wine would belong to us and not Cruse, and we would avoid the queue of creditors when they came charging in after the bankruptcy.

I went down to Bordeaux. Henri Cruse was welcoming as we sat in his offices in Bordeaux and he immediately understood what needed to be done. In the middle of our talks, his older brother, Lionel, came in from a hard day in court. The court process was already in full motion. He looked exhausted. I greeted him and offered him a glass of wine. He declined and said, 'I never touch the stuff. I prefer whisky!'

Henri suggested a tour of the cellars to give me some idea of the problems involved in bottling all our wine, which they had agreed to do after five hours of discussion. In the cellars were these enormous vats. Some of the vats had labels, one of which I read as '*assez bien pour Japon*'. This could have been loosely translated as 'good enough for Japan'. Jardine's main market.

It took three days to bottle our wine. My friends at Hennessy, the cognac company, for whom we also acted as distributors, helped me find storage and hire about a hundred trucks to transport the wine to an independent merchant. The merchant turned out to be the supplier of wine to our main competitor in Hong Kong, Caldbeck Macgregor, but I don't want to go into that now.

I was a hero.

But a better wine story was when I was invited by my friends the Bartons to their wonderful Château for lunch one day in 2006. They produced Léoville Barton wine, renowned around the world. There were eight people around the table including the owner of the Château Pétrus wine estate, Nina Rothschild, Anthony Barton and myself and others. I was facing Anthony across one end of the table and halfway through the meal, he asked if everybody was enjoying the wine. An enthusiastic positive response came from all.

'Any ideas what it is?' from Anthony and round the table one by one he went with his question. I was going to be the last.

Pétrus said, 'I must say it is absolutely wonderful. Strong and great bouquet. I think maybe quite young, say around 1994?'

Sitting so close to Anthony, I thought I saw a faint shadow of disappointment flicker across his face and then we moved on to Nina. 'Oh No! No! No! Much older; 1982 would be my guess, the best year in a very long time.' A smile from Anthony. And on it went, gradually coming towards me. I didn't have the faintest idea. Not even a trace of an idea. I could easily follow Nina and thought about it. But it would be seen as wet if I simply followed her.

I did know that the best year for Bordeaux wine since the war and the one recognised as such by all the experts was 1961. I had read that somewhere years ago. How could I go wrong with my host if I suggested that, even if all the guests burst out laughing? They would think I was joking anyway. So there I was, putting on my most thoughtful expression. I said, 'Do you know what, I think we are missing something. This wine is very very mature. We are guessing, instead of letting our senses do their job. I have been listening to you all, and thought I must be wrong, but I think this is the most fantastic wine I have ever tasted and I think it's a Bordeaux 1961.'

A gasp from everyone. Disbelief, amazement, incredulity that anyone could be so off-course. Some even smirking. But Anthony, with his lower jaw on the table, looking as though he had just seen a ghost, said, 'My God, Simon. How on earth do you know that. It's incredible. You're absolutely right. Oh my God…and can you guess what it is?'

My mind went through a hundred names in two seconds and I said as nonchalantly as I could, 'Possibly Haut Brion or even a Léoville?'

Anthony jumped up and started shouting. 'He's right for heaven's sake.

Absolutely amazing.' And then, 'Oh! No, Simon you've been in the kitchen – you saw the bottles?'

'No, I have not been in the kitchen. I don't even know where the kitchen is.'

Roars of laughter from all and felicitations and I was christened 'Le Nez' on the spot. Anthony tells the story at every Léoville Barton lunch.

CHAPTER XVIII

THE JARDINE ENGINEERING COMPANY

John Keswick retired as chairman of Jardine's in 1974. He stayed on as a director. Henry Keswick returned to Matheson's in London as group chairman and seemed to be vaguely interested in politics. In Hong Kong, David Newbigging became 'senior' managing director – the *Taipan*. Two managing directors were appointed under Newbigging: John Heywood for international affairs and David MacLeod for domestic business. Jeremy Brown, my old boss, remained as managing director, squeezed between the senior MD and the two managing directors. David Edwards was the overall trading director, which included all trading of consumer goods and the Jardine Engineering Company.

We now had lots of MDs. And lots of politics. A bit like investment banks, in which everybody has 'Managing Director' on their business cards to ensure customers feel they are dealing at the right level when attending meetings with them. The cabinet was getting overloaded; too many bosses, too many grand titles and it was becoming difficult to know who was actually leading what. We would know soon enough if things went wrong.

And they were about to.

After two years in London, I was summoned back to Hong Kong to be the managing director of the Jardine Engineering Company (JEC). With all the titles, some of the tension at the top seemed to evaporate but there was still a bit of barbed wire between Newbigging and Henry Keswick. This was a family company and Newbigging was not family. At the Hong Kong end of the business, Newbigging was very keen to make sure we all understood who the real boss was. At meetings it became very clear.

Jardine Engineering was a big step up for me. David Edwards was now my boss and keen to ensure I understood my promotion was due entirely to him and him alone and I should remember that. JEC was one of Jardine's few real in-depth businesses, the largest mechanical and electrical (M&E)

engineering contractor in Hong Kong. We employed over 900 people and we were the leaders in the lifts and air-conditioning business in Hong Kong, representing Schindler lifts and York air-conditioners. We were also the leading plumbing and electrical contractors in town and of course we represented Mather and Platt, introduced by yours truly, for pumps and other products such as fire protection (the old Grinnell's inheritance still working).

JEC were distributors of many products, but also contractors. We bid for projects through tenders and took on the consequent risk, which was different from the rest of the Jardine's trading business. If a main contractor or a building owner went bankrupt, JEC could suffer and, in extremis, not get paid. Credit judgement was a big part of my business. We were often sub-contractors to the main contractor, not the owner of a project, which could considerably increase risk and attract misdirected blame for delays.

Fortunately, our customers were the big property companies in Hong Kong, the biggest of which was Hong Kong Land. The chairman of Hong Kong Land was, under the company's articles of association, automatically the managing director of Jardine Matheson, nominated in perpetuity as such. In this case, David Newbigging.

Paradoxically, Jardine's shareholding in Hong Kong Land was still a miniscule 3 per cent, in spite of which they had total control of everything, including nomination of all senior employees and all the directors of the board of the company.

Hong Kong Land was nevertheless a public company: 97 per cent of the company was owned by non-Jardine Matheson shareholders, a fact which didn't worry Newbigging in the least. Hong Kong Land did what it was told as far as he was concerned.

When I arrived at JEC in 1975, Hong Kong was booming again. The world had recovered from OPEC's oil blackmail, but they had learned a lesson: that the OPEC cartel would ensure the oil price was now going upwards for a very long time. The world accepted it and had learned to live with it. The good old days of US$3 a barrel were gone forever. A new height has been US$120 per barrel. And economics would take priority over the environment. We would drift back to coal.

The local Chinese companies in Hong Kong were pushing up government revenues at land auctions, but strangely Newbigging began selling Jardine's and Hong Kong Land's property. The joke among the Chinese was that 'If Jardine's are selling, it's time to buy.' Newbigging created major headlines by selling Jardine's properties in Hong Kong's mid-level district to Alan Bond, an Australian swagman who eventually ended up in jail.

Australians paying high prices for land in Hong Kong set the market roaring. Local Chinese property companies were buying into this rising market. One of them, later to become a giant, was Cheung Kong, a company controlled by the former plastic flower merchant, Li Ka Shing, known universally as K.S. Li.

After going in the wrong direction for two years, Hong Kong Land and Jardine's realised perhaps that they had made a mistake and it was time to outbid the local boys and start buying again.

Newbigging used to call me into his office on some evenings and probe me on local property companies. I was certainly the man at Jardine's with the best relationships with the local property boys. I was dealing with them on a daily basis with my JEC hat on.

One evening he asked me if I could arrange a lunch with K.S. Li. I was surprised that Newbigging did not seem to know him. It was arranged and we had a good lunch, jocular but without depth. The lunch was devoid of any meaningful discussion.

At this time the government brought to the auction table a strategic piece of land in central Hong Kong on which it was planned to house the Hong Kong stock exchange among other things; it was to be known as Exchange Square.

All eyes were on the auction (sealed bids), and this time Hong Kong Land would show the local boys what they were capable of. A massive bid went in from Hong Kong Land, in excess of HK$4 billion.

The managing director of Hong Kong Land, serving under Newbigging's chairmanship, was now Trevor Bedford, a very experienced old China hand previously employed by the Hong Kong government. He had replaced the retired Vernon Roberts who had left Hong Kong, taking his dreaded wife Bonnie, of wallpaper fame, with him.

The result of the bid?

Hong Kong Land won with the highest price ever paid for land in Hong Kong's history, but they left HK$2 billion on the table. Meaning they had bid $2 billion more than the second highest bidder. The locals were in hysterics. Matheson's in London, now chaired by Henry Keswick, was apoplectic. Henry Keswick blamed Newbigging. Newbigging blamed Bedford. Newbigging claimed that Henry had agreed the bid and round and round it went. But the knives were out and Newbigging began a long walk on a tight rope.

At this time Hong Kong's largest infrastructure project, the Mass Transit underground railway system (MTR), was being planned. The principal bidders for this project, after the elimination of some early runners, was a UK consortium led by Metro-Cammell railways and a Japanese consortium, comprising principally Mitsui, the Mitsubishi group, and Kawasaki. It was a massive project with potentially huge rewards for the winner.

JEC represented the Mitsubishi corporation for power generation equipment, such as boilers and turbine engines, as a consequence of which I had a very special relationship with them. I suggested to Newbigging that we should represent them for the MTR project and it should be a full Jardine Matheson group effort. This project was going to be a contractor's dream.

To increase my authority in front of the Japanese, whom I already knew well, David Edwards decided, as a main board director, that he should accompany me on the visit to Japan to attempt to secure the franchise.

I would brief him on the way to Japan on our plan.

This briefing did not happen, as Edwards was knocking back vodka tonics as soon as we were on board Japan Airways and he was not in listening mode during the journey.

I would brief him over dinner.

It never happened because we ended up nightclubbing. I went to bed around midnight but was awakened by a knock on my bedroom door at around 3am and there was Edwards swaying in front of me, with vodka dripping out of his eye sockets.

We arrived at 9am the next morning in the very grand Mitsubishi boardroom, confronted by about twelve directors of the Japanese consortium, waiting for Mr Edwards to explain to them that with Jardine Matheson as their representatives they would have the best chance of securing this huge contract. There would be a considerable amount of local 'politics' involved and Jardine's, the Princely Hong, would be the best people to handle the government etc. etc.

At the crucial moment in the Mitsubishi boardroom, in front of these twelve Japanese directors, Edwards was unable to find his voice and had a coughing fit. He recovered for a moment and passed the buck to me. I stepped into his silence and explained that a core element of Jardine Matheson was their local mechanical and electrical contracting business; JEC would provide all the credibility that would be needed for vital local on-the-ground support and under the auspices of the great Jardine Matheson, this would be their sure way to win the contract.

The senior Mitsubishi Electric director was a Mr Yufu. I knew him well and he was a great friend. Yufu came out in total support and three hours later, Jardine Engineering Company became the representative of the Japanese consortium for the Hong Kong Mass Transit railway project. We returned to Hong Kong as heroes.

The work began and it was two years of hard slog. I spent many hours with the project consultants, Freeman Fox, a British company. As such, they were very familiar with Metro-Cammell, our competitors, but had little understanding of the Japanese systems and ways of doing business. There was lots of work to be done with Freeman Fox, but they were good listeners and I got on very well with them.

At the top of the board of the MTR Corporation was the chairman, Norman Thompson, with his right-hand man and managing director, Tony Ridley. Ridley was very straight and fair in everything. Thompson on the other hand was cagey and massively pro-British and could see a knighthood on the horizon if Metro-Cammell, run by a Mr Tony Sampson, won the contract.

The main contract was the 'rolling stock', effectively the trains and carriages, after which there were a number of other smaller contracts to be awarded for air-conditioning in the stations, escalators and lifts and so on and of course all the civil work. The closed bids were submitted and the day came for the announcement of the main contract, the rolling stock.

Hong Kong was on tenterhooks.

The announcement was to be on a Monday, following a meeting of the project committee. The committee had a number of government officials and some senior citizens on it, including Y.K. Pao, Hong Kong's senior and best-known businessman.

Two days before the meeting of the committee, one of the senior directors of Freeman Fox asked me to see him outside the office in a bar. Over a drink he told me that Norman Thompson had allowed the Brits to reduce their price in order to beat the Japanese offer, which he had revealed to them.

I practically died on the spot.

I called Yufu and explained what I had heard from the Freeman Fox director (under sworn secrecy). Yufu asked me to seek a meeting with Norman Thompson immediately and to tell him that the Japanese were withdrawing their bid with immediate effect and very publicly. I said he needed to send me someone from Japan to accompany me and make Thompson understand that we were 100 per cent serious. I requested an urgent meeting with Thompson but said I could not tell him what it was about unless I met him face to face. He told me, with reluctance, to come to his flat on Sunday morning.

I arrived with Kei Okano, Yufu's man, to be confronted by a very irritated but wary Thompson with Tony Ridley sitting beside him.

I told him point blank that I had heard that he had passed our price for the project to Metro-Cammell, who in response had cut their bid; we were now withdrawing from the tender immediately and would be making it public. He was screaming with anger and said we could not do it. I repeated with emphasis that we *were* doing it. He demanded to know the source of my information but I refused and Kei was hugely impressed; we became friends for life. Thompson said it was all illegal and we could not now withdraw our offer. I gave him a short, very direct letter to confirm that we *could* and we *were* legally doing so.

The next day, Metro-Cammell, nevertheless, were awarded the rolling stock contract but there was only one bidder: Metro-Cammell; the smell was nauseating. Y.K. Pao resigned from the committee when he heard that the Japanese had withdrawn. He knew why we had done it. Thompson was awarded a knighthood by the British government.

Colonialisation is not a give, but a take. Paradoxically, some good would eventually come out of it for me personally as it sealed a life-long relationship between myself and Yufu and Mitsubishi.

Trevor Bedford, the managing director of Hong Kong Land and I were good friends, not just because it was in my interest to be his friend as he was the boss of my biggest customer, but because he was a good man and I liked him. We laughed our heads off together, played squash twice a week and found we shared a particular attitude to life. Bedford was planning a trek to Annapurna in Nepal and asked if Jeffa and I would like to come along. The party ended up including Newbigging, his lovely wife Carolyn and two friends and their wives from the Olayan group in Saudi Arabia, Azziz Silyan and Gilbert Gargour – two very good fellow travellers.

The trip got off to a bad start. The party initially flew to Bangkok. I missed the flight but caught up with the team that night in the Oriental Hotel. The hotel was owned by the Italhai group, who had sold 25 per cent of it to Hong Kong Land. The main restaurant, the Normandy Grill on the top floor, was very elegant and they insisted on jacket and tie at dinner. We had all agreed to meet there at 8pm. All arrived in mandatory jacket and tie, except Newbigging, who arrived in an open-neck T-shirt.

The maître d' explained the rules. Newbigging explained who he was. The maître d' held his ground and explained the rules again. Newbigging flipped and insisted on seeing the general manager of the hotel. He was a Frenchman that Jeffa and I had known in the old days when we lived in Thailand. More indignation and loud protests from Newbigging, to our embarrassment and that of everybody in the full restaurant, but the general manager held his ground. The answer was no deal without coat and tie. We ended up in the garden of the hotel at a buffet. The food was good but the taste was not.

The next day we flew to Kathmandu.

The climb up Annapurna was wonderful and tremendous fun but quite hard work. We had a great guide and managed to get to 21,000 feet, the base camp for the climb to the summit. It was a fantastic experience. I lost 20kg and felt fitter than I had done in years.

I would often march ahead, enjoying myself hugely. I would leave notes for the rest of the group to find, held down on the path with an empty beer bottle 'Not long now and there's a café at the top – the beer is good. I'm waiting for you there!' I would write, encouraging them. And then, the next note would read:

'Café is closed.
I've drunk all the beer.
Keep Going!'

It cemented the relationship between Newbigging and Bedford, and in fact it did improve mine with Newbigging. He is a good man when he is not in the public arena and Carolyn, his wife, is a saint. All in all an unforgettable trip and totally different to Everest, which is like trekking up an underground escalator at rush hour, as I learned a few years later.

CHAPTER XIX

POLITICS

One of the big players in Hong Kong was Hutchison Whampoa. They were very similar in structure to Jardine's: property owners, a ship-repair business, retail outlets such as supermarkets and pharmaceutical stores, consumer goods agencies, wines and spirits stores and an engineering business very similar and a competitor to JEC. They also had a container terminal in the port of Hong Kong as well as ships. They were Jardine's main direct competitor. They also had a number of other ventures outside of Hong Kong and were particularly active in Indonesia.

In 1973 they ran into trouble through their company in Indonesia. Hutchison were leasing construction and farming equipment on a very large scale. The Indonesian economy was in a nosedive and Hutchison was facing bankruptcy because of bad debts in their leasing business. The company was hugely indebted to the Hong Kong and Shanghai bank (HSBC). They were effectively bust.

The bank let Hutchison off the hook and exchanged their debt for a 33 per cent share in the company and appointed a man called Bill Wylie as the CEO. Hutchison slowly crawled back to life over time. The bank controlled the company.

In 1979 HSBC sold their 33 per cent stake in Hutchison to Li Ka Shing (K.S. Li) for about £60 million. The managing director of the bank, Michael Sandberg, did the deal with reference to no one. It was a very personal deal. Too personal.

There were lots of rumours of insider trading. John Broyer, who was a senior executive of the bank and also chairman of the *South China Morning Post* in which the bank had a 49 per cent interest, was accused of leaking the information to the editor. Chinese newspapers accused Li Ka Shing of leaking the information to friends. Vickers da Costa, a stock-broking company very close to him put a number of its private clients into Hutchison shares before the announcement.

All the Hongs were furious. All declared they would have paid more to get hold of Hutchison had they been offered a chance to bid. Swire's, Jardine's, Y.K Pao, Inchcape, and Wheelock Marden were all potential buyers, but they didn't get a look in. Hutchison offered tremendous property potential with its land bank, which was K.S. Li's primary focus. There was an insider trading tribunal. It concluded that K.S. Li and indeed the bank had nothing to answer for. Case dismissed.

Bill Wylie stayed at the helm although Li was the controlling shareholder and chairman. Wylie had two right-hand men, John Richardson and Jonathan Hubbard-Ford; these three together with the finance director David White ran the business.

With the release of the debt the company grew rapidly and was soon back with the leaders at position three, behind B and S (now known as Swire's), and Jardine's.

K.S. Li looked after the property side and the other four ran the rest of the businesses. The company grew fast and the executives were earning big money. Wylie declared in a television interview that he was receiving over a million US dollars a year (unheard of in those days). He was also on a profit-sharing arrangement, but it brought him trouble.

According to K.S. Li, Wylie transferred assets from one subsidiary company to another and revalued them at the same time, declared a profit and took a commission. K.S. was furious. A row followed and Wylie was fired and fled to Australia, never to be seen in Hong Kong again. John Richardson became the CEO. The trio of Richardson, Hubbard-Ford and White did well with the company. They extended the container port operations, the retail outlets and the trading business, which was a list of product distribution franchises in direct competition with Jardine Matheson. Hong Kong was growing fast at this time. The Chinese could come in freely from the mainland and annual tourism was in the millions. But Jardine's remained larger and more prosperous than Hutchison on all fronts, for the time being.

I continued to prod Newbigging about increasing our interest in Hong Kong Land. He continued to explain it was not necessary as we already controlled it. I also continued to build JEC with zero support from the head company as Edwards was preoccupied with other things.

We represented Dupont from the USA for explosives, used essentially in the construction industry. Our main competitor was China Engineering, who looked after ICI explosives.

One day the government decided they would auction a piece of land to build an explosives company on Stonecutters Island, close to Hong Kong. It was going to be a gold mine. I approached Edwards to ensure full support and suggested to Dupont that we should do a joint venture with them. They were delighted. Nothing like a bit of local know-how for them.

Edwards came back to me a week later and said he had discussed it with Newbigging, who had no interest, and I should advise Dupont accordingly.

I did, but it was very embarrassing.

They were disappointed but made the bid alone and won. ICI were out of the business and Dupont had a virtual monopoly. But sadly not with JEC.

I didn't see Newbigging for a month or so after the Dupont affair and when I did, at a cocktail party, I said what a huge miss it was and how surprised I was that he had no interest. He swore he knew nothing about it and Edwards had never mentioned it. That was the end of the explosives business for Jardine's.

One of my main businesses was supplying equipment to Hongkong Electric who sourced electricity to Hong Kong Island exclusively. JEC was the agent for the Mitsubishi group of companies and our business with them was mainly the supply of equipment for the power stations: turbines, boilers and other electrical accessories.

The Kowloon power plant, China Light and Power, owned by the Kadoorie family, was furnished with equipment from GEC in the UK. They procured their oil from Exxon, and Shell supplied oil to Hongkong Electric. These two power companies were not in competition. They had individual territorial rights. Monopolies. One for Hong Kong Island and one for Kowloon. These arrangements had been running for many years without interruption.

Edwards came to see me one day, very excited, to tell me that Hong Kong Land was going to make a bid for 30 per cent of Hongkong Electric. This was exciting news and would firm up our relationship with the electric company, which was already a real money spinner for JEC. Two weeks later it was done and Hong Kong Land controlled Hongkong Electric.

The electricity companies operated with government licences allowing them to make a return of 16 per cent on their assets, which included the power plants and all other assets such as cars and pictures on the walls in their offices. If they made a return of more than 16 per cent, the excess went into a reserve fund; if they made less than 16 per cent, they could dig into the reserve fund. If the fund was below a certain amount, they could increase the price of electricity. This was the best business in the world. Impossible to lose money.

The great incentive given to the electricity companies was to ensure that when new power plants were to be built at a cost in excess of £2 billion, the companies did not lose their nerve with the approaching dreaded date of 1997, when theoretically the Brits would hand Hong Kong back to China.

This, of course, we all believed would never happen. 1997 was nearly twenty years away and certainly nothing to worry about at that time, so the electricity companies enjoyed mouth-watering profits through their schemes of arrangement.

Newbigging became the chairman of Hongkong Electric, through his chairmanship of Hong Kong Land and this in turn, was going to be good for my business.

CHAPTER XX
JARDINE'S IN TOYLAND

I continued to meet Edwards, as my boss, periodically once every three months. Four times a year. I was supposed to go through the business and the accounts with him once a month. But he had formed a new company called Jardine Industries and it was absorbing most of his time. Its prime occupation was selling toys made in Taiwan to the USA. The fact that he had no time for me was no problem at all and anyway I saw him often, socially.

JEC had no independent capital. We had a permanent money supply from Jardine Matheson and twenty-eight people in my accounts department to keep an eye on it. They reported directly to Jardine's finance director Bill Downey, not to me. But I paid for them.

The one figure that caught my eye in the accounts was the interest I was paying to Jardine's for their perpetual loan. No less than 11 per cent. JEC was making too much money and would be paying too much tax. That needed sorting.

One day, in an evening session with Newbigging, he was complaining that I had lost a particular construction contract with Hong Kong Land. I explained that I could not win every contract with Hong Kong Land if it had to be at the lowest price, or JEC would go bankrupt. He was at pains to point out, for the thousandth time, that we 'owned' Hong Kong Land, that we controlled Hong Kong Land, and all their contracts should be awarded to us.

I was at equal pains to remind him that Hong Kong Land was a public company in which we only owned 3 per cent – Trevor Bedford had pointed this out to me very clearly – and that if we wanted to win contracts, we would have to cease taking them for granted and be the lowest bidder, at least some of the time. I suggested it would perhaps be a good idea for Jardine's to increase their shareholding in the Land company to 25 per cent, which would provide at least some entitlement to steal from the other shareholders. We were up to our necks in related party transactions. End of conversation! Newbigging told me that I misunderstood the situation completely.

Edwards, in the meantime, seemed to be having some problems with his new show: Jardine Industries. He had taken the lift business, a joint venture with the Schindler lift company, away from JEC and restructured it as a joint venture with Jardine Industries, reporting directly to him instead of me.

I explained to him that this was a lousy idea because the lift and air-conditioning businesses under JEC catered to the same customers; the information flow, plus the pricing of our joint contracts, enhanced our relationships with our customers. In addition I had a relationship with the architects which Schindler, and certainly Edwards, did not have. His prime reason for doing this was to boost the profits of the Jardine Industries group. Was I missing something? I somehow began to feel that Edwards saw me as a threat. He seemed to be putting up roadblocks for JEC, and all this coming so soon after the Dupont fiasco.

The reality was that he was building a fortress of businesses around himself which he thought would increase the perception of his value to the company. He was now the global trading director, with the biggest portfolio of companies within Jardine's. He was also front runner to be the successor to Newbigging as the next *Taipan* as Newbigging was still on that tightrope. And yet something was not quite right that he needed to constantly reinforce Jardine Industries' standing in the group.

At the monthly meetings, chaired by Newbigging, all the department heads met with the directors to report on their respective businesses. Edwards would constantly tell us how successful Jardine Industries was, with profits rising in leaps and bounds and it was the fastest growing business in the group.

The facts were different.

The toys had been rejected in America for failing to meet safety standards. Edwards was of the view that those standards would eventually change and he would then have a clear run. In the meantime he had created a subsidiary company in the States to which he 'sold' the toys and was building unsellable inventory in an American warehouse, all the time recording sales and profits which were totally fictitious. He had dug a hole big enough to bury Jardine's and made it worse by concealing it.

His American subsidiary company was financed with a secret loan from the First National City Bank of America. A loan guaranteed by a Jardine director's signature: his, but unknown to the Jardine's finance director. This loan of £35 million enabled the American-based subsidiary to purchase the goods sold to it by its parent, Jardine Industries. Jardine Industries' revenues were increasing every month as a result – on paper. Eventually the bubble burst with a very big bang. There was blood all over the carpet. The headlines were huge. One magazine cover had a picture of Newbigging in a room with toys all over the floor. The headline was 'Newbigging in Toyland'. Edwards disappeared.

I did not realise he had been 'allowed to leave' until my next visit to London when I passed through Matheson's. Henry Keswick was in his office, watching a cricket match on the television when I was ushered in. He said he was very sorry about David Edwards, who he knew was a great friend of mine. He explained what had happened and said that they had no choice but to let him go. He asked me about the Hong Kong marketplace and which Chinese companies were coming up the ladder. I told him K.S. Li was the guy to watch.

He scoffed and said, 'Oh Simon, he'll be bankrupt within a year.'

Meanwhile another man had come to Hong Kong from nowhere, under the name of George Tan. He had formed a company called Carrian.

Carrian's wealth was rumoured to come from illicit corrupt funds in Indonesia, or drugs and God knows what in Malaysia. Nobody seemed to know much about George Tan except that he had unlimited funds. He started to buy out companies and bought property at a rate that had the local property companies in a panic. He became friends with Trevor Bedford and a year later he bought shares in Hongkong Electric on a large scale and became essentially joint owners with Hong Kong Land. He did a number of property deals with Hong Kong Land who were becoming much too independent for the likes of Jardine's.

Certainly that was the feeling in London.

After Edward's departure, I had begun reporting to David MacLeod, a very dreary fellow without the slightest interest in what we were doing. He had once told me when I was sitting next to him on an airplane bound for Tokyo, that his main interest in life was photography and he couldn't wait to retire from Jardine's, go back to England and spend his life in pursuit of his hobby. Very inspiring stuff for me, his subordinate.

He was also in charge of Jardine's shipping operations which were going steadily south. In fact, not so steadily. He was regarded as a serious intellectual because he was rumoured to have got a double first at Cambridge. This was never verified because nobody knew what a double first at Cambridge was.

I was made acting trading director following Edward's departure. Sadly, not on his salary. But there was a wave of freedom that came with it. I asked Newbigging if I could go on the Stanford Executive Program for eight weeks. He generously said 'yes' and that the firm would sponsor me. At last, I had arrived at university at the ripe old age of thirty-nine. I couldn't wait to get away from Jardine's politics and MacLeod.

Stanford Business School is on a par with the Harvard Business School but warmer in winter. Participants are sponsored by their companies and are all senior executives. Then, it cost US$50,000 for the course. It was superb in every way from the first day. Not least, the weather. The professors were inspirational. The dialogue in class was stimulating. Most of the students were business leaders, including David Simon, later to become head of BP in the UK.

I built a particular friendship with Alister Smith-Laing. He was working with Boustead's in Malaysia. They were in the rubber business but also traders and distributors of consumer goods. They had the franchise for Hennessy brandy, as did Jardine's in Hong Kong. 'Keinatato filo' as the Greeks say: 'Common are the things in friendship.' Alister and I had something in common, with much more to come.

In our case studies of where companies had gone wrong: one of the most insightful lessons we learnt was that our own companies had committed many of the same errors we were examining. Apparently, 40 per cent of executives who attend the Stanford Senior Executive Program resign when they return to their companies. This seemed particularly ominous to me.

I scored a few points with my fellow students by swinging by my feet from the chandelier in the mess hall while chucking bottles of wine across the room that I picked up from the table as I sailed through the air. Somebody leaked this to The Times in London and I got a bit of publicity!

I also caused a minor hit when I balanced a full open magnum of champagne on my head and bent down without touching the bottle with my hands and picked up a handkerchief in my teeth from the floor and stood up again without spilling a drop. I had a ten-dollar bet with each of my fellow students, who were betting against me. I won $1,900. I hosted a mammoth dinner and imported a Laurel and Hardy film as entertainment. No risk of shooting here, but still, I was never one to pass up the opportunity to get a laugh and my audience and fellow students were good people. I enjoyed myself hugely and learnt a great deal.

CHAPTER XXI
ADIOS JARDINE MATHESON

In a conversation with John Heywood some months earlier, he had told me that at a previous full board meeting, John Keswick had suddenly said, 'When is Simon Murray going to be a director of this company?' Good old JK!

All the directors had looked at Newbigging, who had passed the ball to Edwards.

'He reports to you David, what do you think?' said Newbigging.

Edwards mumbled something about my need for a bit more experience and perhaps I was still a bit young blah blah blah, and the subject died away. I think at this time Edwards knew his demise was near after the antics at Jardine Industries and he was not going to promote a potential successor to himself. It might have hastened his exit.

Then one day in late 1979, I was informed that Newbigging wanted to see me. Reason unknown.

I entered the office. His face was frosty white with half-controlled anger. He said, 'I have heard that you have said that you will resign from this company if you are not a director by the time you are forty. Is that true?'

I was sandbagged. Straight out of the blue.

I said, 'Yes, it is true. But I said it fourteen years ago when I first joined the company in Thailand, so this is old news and I'm amazed its only just got to you.'

Newbigging did not find this funny at all and started raising his voice. Why hadn't he heard it from me? Why did he hear it on the grapevine? He had sent me to Stanford Business School, and this was my appreciation? And then on and on about absurd things such as 'Why had I bought a piece of land on Lantau Island. Did I not realise I was competing with Hong Kong Land?' He ended by saying, 'You will be a director of this company, when I say so, and that will be when I think you are ready.'

I said, 'I have been acting trading director for well over a year since Edwards left and nobody has said anything negative about my performance.

I am coming up for forty and history shows that very few make it to director at Jardine's after that age.'

He went on to say again that I would be a director when he felt it to be the right moment and I replied, 'If I come to see you next June, will you be in a position to tell me whether or not I am going to be a director? Because I don't want to hang around if I am not going to make it to the board.'

He said, 'If I have made up my mind by then, I will be able to tell you.'

It was my moment to leave the room, which I did, and it was the moment I decided to leave the company.

My most frequent lunches, when I did not have a business lunch, were with two of my greatest friends, Mike Stapleton and Alan Johnson-Hill, and they would constantly urge me to leave and start my own business. They could not believe I was doing a full director's job on an annual salary of £4,000.

The more I thought about it, the more I felt I had to get out. Jardine's did not give me the feeling at all that I was riding a good horse. They were losing out to the local Chinese companies on the property side and property is a better asset in Hong Kong than cases of whisky sitting in the cellar in Japan and Jardine's single biggest business in Japan was the White Horse whisky franchise.

At one time, I had pressed Henry Keswick to buy out some of our principals like White Horse Whisky, Christian Dior and Dunhill. Sooner or later mainland China would open up and we had no guarantees of agreements for distribution rights in China, nor would we be given those rights automatically when China's door did open. Much too much potential there.

Henry's answer was, 'Simon, we make more money through the distribution here in Asia than they do owning the entire business, so why buy them?'

He was wrong. It was a massive opportunity missed. Many of the brands were facing tough times and it would have been easy for us to buy them. Some years later they started to buy each other and large groups like LVMH and Richemont acquired many of the brands. Jardine's distribution agreements went out the window and 35 per cent of global sales of luxury goods and brands would be sold in China. Jardine's got nothing.

While considering my resignation from Jardine's, I had to weigh up the risks, particularly to my family's welfare. Currently I received a miniscule salary, but Jardine's paid my housing costs and my children's education. So I was safe. Was the risk worthwhile?

'We only live twice.' I had already had one life in the Legion but I was now contemplating a third life: life after Jardine's.

On a Sunday morning in mid-December of that year, I went to see Newbigging at his house in Sheko. He thought I was coming over for a pre-Christmas drink.

I told him I wanted to resign.

He looked as though I had hit him with a baseball bat. But he kept his cool and said that as we were all going away for the Christmas holidays, why didn't I think it over during that time and we could discuss it in January.

Later that month, Jeffa and I were in the United States for the holidays and I told my old friend Piers Brooke, who was head of an American bank in Hong Kong, that I was leaving the Princely Hong. He rang Simon Keswick in London, who then told Henry Keswick, who rang Newbigging and asked what the hell was going on. Why is Simon Murray leaving? Newbigging claimed I had forced him into a corner, which I suppose I had. He was also angry because he thought I had gone behind his back to the Keswicks, which I had not.

The return to Hong Kong was going to be tough.

I wrote a letter of resignation to Newbigging. It was one of the nicest letters I had ever written to anyone explaining why I was leaving to run my own business and emphasised how much I had enjoyed working in this wonderful company over fourteen years and how grateful I was for the opportunity to work there, and I meant it.

The next day I was summoned to Newbigging's office with alarm bells ringing!

As I entered his office, he opened up in a voice choking with anger. 'You said you were going to come and see me in June this year,' he said. For a moment, I was transported back to my eighteen-year-old self, hauled up for some misdemeanour in front of the ship's captain when I had joined the Merchant Navy: Newbigging looked strangely like 'Captain Bligh' of the St Arvans.

'No! I did not,' I replied. 'What I said was, if I came to see you in June, would you be able to tell me *when* I would move from acting director to being a normal director and *you* said, "If I have made up my mind at that time, I will be able to tell you." For me that was two "ifs" too many. I made up my mind to leave there and then, on the spot, when I left your office that day.'

His response was to throw me more reminders on what the company had done for me and basically to tell me I was an ungrateful little shit. I offered to repay the cost of Stanford, which he kept harping on about. The meeting ended with a threatening 'You will be hearing from us', and I left.

The letter came two days later.

It ordered me to leave the company *and* Hong Kong in two weeks' time. My housing loan with HSBC could no longer be guaranteed by them and I must also vacate my accommodation within two weeks. This, after fourteen years of service to the company. I had a housing loan, as did all senior executives, which enabled us to buy a property back in Europe. With this loan I had bought a house in France.

This was a huge blow straight to the solar plexus.

The letter went on to remind me that the provident fund arrangement, which entitled me to a lump sum at any time I left the firm after ten years' service, had been replaced by a pension fund. My pension fund would be payable at the age of sixty-five and would be £5,000 per annum with no increase.

If I preferred to revert to the provident fund arrangement, I could take my contribution only (not the company's contribution), which amounted to £7,000, and the pension would be cancelled immediately.

After fourteen years, my own contribution to the provident fund would be returned to me, and that was that; the alternative offer was that I could leave now with nothing and I would receive £5,000 a year at the age of sixty-five, with a 'guarantee' that it would never be increased. I chose to take my £7,000. My *own* money and my *only* money.

Never to be forgotten.

It was normal for a departing senior executive to be hosted at a farewell drinks party. No such party for me. In addition, I was invited to see the directors one by one to say farewell. I received the list of directors to whom I was to report to say goodbye. It was short. There were twelve directors, but only three agreed to see me: Bobby Kwok, our token Chinese director; Ray Moore, our legal director, who asked me what the hell was going on –

'What have you done??' he asked – and John Heywood. David MacLeod, my direct boss, declined to say goodbye. All the others stayed under cover for fear of risking disapproval.

I had always considered Heywood a friend. My appointment with him was at 3pm one afternoon. I arrived to be told he was in a meeting with Newbigging and could I wait. I waited for two hours and then left. He could easily have said to Newbigging, 'I've got Murray waiting outside my office to say goodbye, why don't I just nip outside and send him on his way.' He didn't.

The Princely Hong was infested with sycophants and the politics at the top made the US Congress look like a children's playground. Power, free of opposition, breeds arrogance and belief in one's own pre-eminence, one-way vision, self-righteousness and an inability to accept that you might be wrong from time to time. On top of that, if you are surrounded by sycophants who tell you only what they think you want to hear, it can swell an ego to bursting point and result in monumental errors of judgement.

In many ways Newbigging was a good man; honest and straight-forward, but my resignation was seen by him as defiance, rebellion and treachery. He would also be given a bad mark by the Keswicks, though I say it myself, for losing a good man. His ego was damaged.

Hong Kong is a small place and the news was round the market in minutes. One newspaper had a headline: 'The Legion moves out. *Vive la liberté.*'

I was a director of Hong Kong Aircraft Engineering Corporation, a company owned jointly by Swire's and Jardine's. MacLeod removed me from the board and at the next meeting somebody said, 'Simon has resigned from Jardine's' and another director said, 'Yes, and have you heard how they're treating him?'

It was the talk of the town.

～⌇～

These were dark days for me. Suddenly, with a wife and three children to look after, I was out of a home, out of a job, with £7,000 to my name. I was worried and getting close to panic. But then, three people, to whom I will be forever indebted, emerged from nowhere.

John Mackenzie, boss of the Chartered Bank, asked me to lunch. I knew him well and his wife Jane had been a friend of ours for years. John said he had heard I had left the Hong and was about to start my own business and asked how he could help. I was absolutely overwhelmed, explained the position in full and good old Chartered Bank lent me £20,000 on the spot without any collateral. Thank you, the late John Mackenzie.

Willy Purves, at that time number two at HSBC, summoned me to the bank. He was holding a letter when I entered his office which he said he had just received from Newbigging. 'You've had your hands in the till haven't you?' he said, with a grin on his face. I told him the whole story. He showed me the letter from Newbigging, which effectively implied I had been fired with two weeks' notice, would be leaving Hong Kong immediately and that they could no longer guarantee my housing loan or anything else for that matter.

Willy called an underling into his office and asked him to find out the amount of interest I was paying on my loan. The man re-appeared a few moments later and said 10 per cent. Willy smiled and said, 'Well I think we can do better than that can't we? What about 4 per cent?' The other guy smiled and said, 'Why not?'

And it was done.

Another moment engraved on my memory forever. Thank you, Willy Purves, the best chairman HSBC ever had.

As for Newbigging, my conclusion was that he liked me and was actually pretty devastated that I was leaving. I suppose I will never know. But when somebody who you like and have a high regard for leaves the team of which you are the leader, you feel the loss of value. It can induce sorrow and regret but it can also conjure up feelings of ingratitude, lack of respect and loss of face. This is the sensation of being insulted by a subordinate who you interpret as saying effectively, 'Fuck Off' rather than 'I am fucking off!', which is slightly different.

These negative thoughts compounded together can create anger, and in this case, violent anger. It can smother the more practical and perhaps more intelligent reaction, which is to make the departing soldier a good ambassador, instead of an enemy (Memories of something Bill Mather had once said to me many years before).

MacLeod proceeded to suck up to King Newbigging's anger, by making my life as miserable as possible. The letter of '*Adieu valise,*' (French for 'get your suitcase packed'!), had his name all over it, even though it was actually signed by Newbigging.

I would look back on this later and recognise it as two people egging themselves on down a path of vitriolic behaviour, but MacLeod was the real villain. Newbigging was just dumb with anger. To hell with them. I was going to build a successful business, doing exactly what I had learned to do at Jardine's.

Another fork in the road and I took it.

And the third person was John Keswick, the grandee of Jardine Matheson and former chairman of the Jardine empire. He came out to Hong Kong and invited me to his apartment in the Mid-Levels. On my arrival, there was a bottle of champagne already in the ice bucket. He said, 'Simon, I know why you're leaving and I don't blame you at all. Jardine's loss and Newbigging's fault.' He wished me good luck and said he knew I would do well. Good old Sir John, an unforgettable friend.

In the Foreign Legion, we called it l'*esprit de Corps*. It is the driving force in an organisation that provides loyalty and builds friendship. It occurs more often in family-owned companies more than in some faceless corporate company. My loyalty was to the Keswicks but they were in London and the Hong Kong 'minders' created no inspiration and no loyalty from me.

John Keswick died a few years later. His wife, the lovely Claire, sent me a note inviting me to his memorial service. I was in Indonesia and flew on the night flight to London for the service and then straight back to Indonesia the same day. There are not many people in this world for whom I would have done that.

CHAPTER XXII

STARTING FROM SCRATCH

My first move was to seek advice from my ex-school friend Tim Gallee, now a prominent lawyer in Hong Kong, to see if I could sue Jardine's. He said their letter was outrageous, on top of which there was no way they could instruct me to leave Hong Kong. On the money side they owed me their contribution to the provident fund, as I had passed the ten-year mark. He nevertheless advised me against suing them, as they would drag it out for years and bleed me to death in the process.

I had to raise some capital to start a trading business. I had spent fourteen years trading and I could do it again but I needed a company and some capital.

I bought a dormant shelf company from Deloitte's called Davenham Investments. Deloitte's were fantastically helpful in all things related to formally registering the company, about which I knew nothing.

I decided I needed enough capital to last me for three years and if I didn't have positive cashflow by then, I was in the wrong business. I needed a minimum of £100,000. That was about twenty-five times my income at Jardine's, but before anything, I needed a roof over my family's head. My friends rallied around, all feeling terribly positive about my future and pledged their support. It gave me a good feeling.

My friends Stapes and Johnson-Hill came in as investors.

I was having lunch in the Hilton Hotel with Michael Green one day and he asked me all about it and what was I going to do. I told him. He said he would put in £40,000. By the time I got back from lunch there was a cheque from him to me for this amount on the desk in the office I was renting on short lease.

Michael Green was one of my dearest friends and also one of my competitors when I had been at JEC. He ran a family company called Arnold. They were mechanical and engineering traders. JEC was primarily an equipment trading company as well as being contractors. I had horrified some of my colleagues at JEC by purchasing machinery from Arnold's, whom they saw as competitors. But in some cases, Arnold had equipment that was superior to ours, and less expensive, and buying from them enhanced our success as contractors. It was difficult for some of the JEC directors to follow.

Michael's was one of the nicest gestures I have ever received in my life. I was overwhelmed and a huge blast of energy crashed into my blood stream. If I had this kind of support, we were going to the moon. The dark clouds vanished.

I had told potential investors that they had to pay a 100 per cent premium, so for every dollar they subscribed, 50 cents went to me. I was the one doing the work.

Jane Merrill's father, Fred, sent me a cheque for £55,000 and the Belgium Bank offered me a mortgage for any property I wanted to buy.

I had become good friends with Fred Merrill whilst at Stanford. He was the chairman of American Express. He had invited me to the Bohemian Grove, a very upmarket private club that held a big camping event for a month every year in the redwood forests north of San Francisco. About 2,000 people were invited over a period of eight weeks. Guests included presidents from different countries and famous actors and politicians. Various members of the Grove had their own camps of about fifteen people. Fred introduced me to Henry Kissinger and George Bush senior, as though I had been his friend for life. We had invitations to breakfast sometimes from other camps. I found myself sitting over a campfire one morning next to James Stewart. No photographs allowed. No autographs and always remain calm and reserved, were the rules of the club.

I wanted to say, 'Jimmy Stewart for Christ's sake, oh my God!' but I kept my cool and casually asked him to pass the toast.

I also met Neil Armstrong, the first man on the moon.

We sometimes lay casually by the lakeside in the sun and listened to talks by famous people. Lying around on the grass, one could spot familiar faces chewing a piece of grass or puffing idly on a cigarette. There was Helmut Schmidt, Chancellor of West Germany and over there, isn't that Ronald Reagan? And so on... and then it was Al Haig giving a lecture and telling us where all the Russian tanks were located and how many there were, and then a lecture on how to make a plutonium bomb and Neil Armstrong telling us about his trip to the moon, and on it went. An unforgettable experience, for which I will always be beholden to the late Fred Merrill.

Henry Kissinger remains a life-long friend and eventually joined my advisory board.

I went to Japan one day after the new company was formed and called on Yufu to say goodbye. I told him everything that had happened. He and Kei Okano took me out to lunch. Yufu said I was the only one at Jardine's over the years who had really worked for them. Jardine's had just accepted 5 per cent commission as the Mitsubishi agent on everything that Mitsubishi sold in Hong Kong, mainly to Hongkong Electric, without ever lifting a finger in support, until Simon Murray came along.

That support had been badly needed one day when Hongkong Electric invited Hitachi to bid on one of their contracts which had been with Mitsubishi for the previous fifteen years.

The chairman of Mitsubishi, Mr Toshi, came to see me and told me of their disappointment that Hitachi had been invited to bid against them and that given it was now going to be a tendered deal, they would have to reduce our commission to 3 per cent; I of course agreed.

I then went to see Newbigging about it and he, the chairman of Hongkong Electric no less, was unaware that Hitachi had been invited to tender. He made it worse by summoning Mr Toshi, who was still in town, and telling him that Jardine's refused to accept the reduction in the commission. Attending this meeting in Newbigging's office were Mr Toshi, two of his men, myself and MacLeod. Much 'face' was on the table.

The Mitsubishi chairman said that Mr Murray, the managing director of JEC, had already agreed to 3 per cent, and that was it as far as he was concerned.

Newbigging said, 'Murray doesn't have the authority to reduce the commission.'

To which Toshi said, 'We have always dealt with Mr Murray and made all the decisions with him.'

Newbigging said he would call the Mitsubishi president there and then, in response to which, Toshi, to my amazement and joy, invited him to do so.

'There's the telephone, Mr Newbigging; go ahead. Call him.'

For a moment I thought we had lost everything, but Newbigging squeezed out of the trap by saying he hadn't got time and we were virtually thrown out of his office.

Once outside, Toshi started saying how worried he was about me, and would I get fired? He then told me they had made more money than expected on the previous contract with Hongkong Electric and he would pay additional funds to JEC out of that, as compensation for the reduction in the commission on the coming tender. I assured him it was not necessary. But what a gesture!

Memories of the Nihon Bed Company.

Several months later, Downey, the finance director, reported a whack of money coming in from Mitsubishi. MacLeod rang me and asked what it was for. I told him it was compensation for the reduction in commission on the last contract for Hongkong Electric, which Mitsubishi had eventually won against Hitachi.

Now here I was saying goodbye to these wonderful people in Japan. Yufu said they had never forgotten my efforts for the MTR project and after lunch he went into a huddle with Kei. They were scribbling on a piece of paper and talking in Japanese.

Finally, Yufu looked at me and said, 'Simon, here's what we propose. We will pay you US$2 million over six years as a retainer, and on top of that we will pay you a commission on any business you can secure for us.'

What could I say?

I said, 'Thank you.'

And I meant it.

Davenham Investments was in business. It wasn't just the money, but I was the agent for Mitsubishi: that was a huge credibility banner over my front door.

Next problem was where to live. I knew all the architects in town and one of them, Francis Wong, said he knew of a lovely little house on the island of Lamma that was for sale. It was on a hilltop with a 180-degree sea view, overlooking the ferry pier. The daily journey to Central was to be by ferry.

The house was a total ruin, but Francis, my friend, said he could do it up and I could pay him later. The house was owned by a Taiwanese family and had not been lived in for ten years. It took two months to locate the family and talk to each member, one of whom lived in the States, for them to agree a price. £40,000. Those were the days.

Living on Lamma would not all be roses. Jeffa's textile business became difficult because of logistics: her retail outlet was in Stanley. And Christie, our latest and youngest daughter had to go to school each day by fishing boat. But what an experience!

Newbigging, out of the blue, asked me to come to his office one day. He was as usual in a foul mood and started haranguing me for telling everybody about the terms of my departure.

'It's confidential' he said, 'and you've been talking to everybody in town. It's in the bloody newspapers and all over the place.'

'David, it may be confidential as far as you're concerned, and I don't blame you wanting to keep it confidential, but as far as I am concerned, it is not confidential. It's a bloody outrage and I have told everybody I know on the planet and everybody agrees with me. And for your information I bumped into Simon and Henry Keswick two nights ago on the steps of the Mandarin and they said if I ever want to come back, I would be welcome, when you have gone.' This was true! 'Throwing me out of my house with two weeks' notice after fourteen years and trying to make it look as though you have fired me for some crime or other with that letter to the bank! You have no idea how badly this reflects on you, but I can tell you, if you're interested.'

It suddenly seemed to dawn on him that this was all bouncing back on him. The remark about the Keswicks turned him white.

He said, 'Okay! OKAY! So how long do you need to stay in the house?'

I said, 'I need six months and I am not leaving Hong Kong.'

'All right. You can have it, but not a day longer.'

And I was gone.

Within a month I had raised £200,000.

I bought a flat at the top of Elizabeth House in Causeway Bay for £30,000, which was to be my office. The Banque Belge gave me a mortgage to buy the house on Lamma. I had annual income from Mitsubishi before I had even started.

My wonderful secretary Cynthia, who had been with me through the JEC days, said she wanted to come with me. I made it clear that I couldn't afford to pay her the same amount as at Jardine's. She said she would come anyway. Lifetime loyalty. Later I sent her son Adrian to Bedford, my old school. It was the least I could do.

I had recently been working with a Norwegian company called Kongsberg. They made gas turbines to be used as standby generators in the event of power failure. Their representative was Jarle Nielson. Davenham Investments became Kongsberg's agent for Hong Kong and Jarle joined us. We formed a subsidiary called Davenham Engineering, in case people thought we were an investment bank! And we now had a genuine engineer on the staff: Jarle.

Soon we had become agents for a number of companies, including my old friends H.H. Robertson from Thailand days. Some were willing to pay retainers as well as a commission. Some had been represented by Jardine Matheson and now moved across to Davenham.

Did that ever make me happy!

We were now in a trade war with Jardine's. Their war with me was led by the inept David MacLeod, so we had an indirect advantage.

CHAPTER XXIII

COAL

When I had been running JEC in the mid 1970s, I had a close relationship with Hongkong Electric, with whom I had many equipment supply contracts. I also knew the China Light and Power people well, the general manager of which had become a good friend, although we did no business. His name was Bill Stones, and he had been brought in by the Kadoorie family as general manager from GEC in the UK.

One day over lunch back in 1977, while I was still running JEC, he had casually said that the next generation of power plants, which would be completed in 1982, would be dual fired, coal and oil. This was because of the OPEC oil price hike in 1972 practically bringing the Western world's economy to its knees. Hence the switch to coal for the future power plants in Hong Kong. The environment was less of an issue in those days. Economics came first. Bill said to me, 'Simon, if you want to make some money, get into coal.'

I had gone to see Shell, whom I knew well because of our joint interest in the business of Hongkong Electric. The manager of Shell's Hong Kong operations was a guy called John Lawrence. I also knew Shell had coal mines in the Caribbean. I informed Lawrence that there was going to be a substantial demand for coal in Asia in a few years and could we, Jardine's (at that time!), represent them.

He asked me, 'Where?' and I said, 'If I tell you where, you will say "Oh we already know about that."'

'No! No! Simon, we are not like that, but you must tell me because London will have to approve it and I need to know if they already know about it. So, where is this demand for coal going to be from?'

I said, 'Hong Kong.'

'What!' he cried in amazement. 'How do you know this?'

'Market intelligence,' I said, with a grin on my face.

He was blown away and then said he would have to check with head office in London and would get back to me in a couple of weeks.

Two weeks later, he came back with the news that Shell London were aware of the future demand for coal in Hong Kong and he was sorry they would be unable to work with Jardine's this time (perhaps forgetting that Jardine's controlled Hongkong Electric through Hong Kong Land). I said, 'If Shell London knew about this, how come you, their managing director in Hong Kong, did not know about it? It's total bollocks Lawrence, you have just been back to tell them the news you got from me and grabbed the credit. Stuff it. Thanks for nothing.'

And I went to BP.

JEC handled marine oil distribution for BP in Hong Kong, so I had a contact. BP had a coal mine in South Africa. It was the Ermelo coal mine which they owned jointly with the French oil company Total, and Asia was Total's business as far as coal distribution was concerned. BP told me the regional headquarters for Total was Japan and I would have to discuss it with them. Total Japan introduced me to Claude Bouilly, who operated out of Paris and was the commercial director for coal.

This reminded me of my old contracting days in Thailand, running around trying to find the man who made the decisions: owners, architects, contractors, subcontractors, project managers, and the rest.

I went to Paris and finally met Claude Bouilly. He introduced me to his chairman, Louis Deny, who had been chairman in years gone by of Total's Algerian operations. We got on well. We had a verbal accord and Jardine Engineering became Total's agent for Ermelo coal in Hong Kong.

But by the time the first shipment was ready to roll late in 1982, I had already left Jardine's two years earlier. The cargo was destined for China Light and it was the first shipment of coal to Hong Kong since the Second World War. Total had continued to work with me personally after I left Jardine's earlier in 1980, and Jardine's had been left far behind in all this. Shell began shipping coal to Hongkong Electric soon after the arrival of the Ermelo coal for China Light and Power. I introduced Ermelo coal to Hongkong Electric. It had better characteristics than Shell's coal: lower sulphur and higher calorific value. All this unknown to Jardine's, in spite of the fact that Newbigging was still the chairman of Hongkong Electric. Hongkong Electric management wanted to switch from Shell to Ermelo. It eventually reached the ears of MacLeod.

On hearing the news, Jardine's flipped. They sent Robert Friend to see me. He was an old buddy of mine from Thailand days, now working for MacLeod. The message from MacLeod was that when I made the agreement with Total, I was working for Jardine's and therefore Jardine's was still the official agent. If I wanted to do business with Hongkong Electric, or anybody else for that matter, I would have to give them 50 per cent of my commission. I told Robert the agreement was verbal; there was nothing in writing and therefore I had nothing to give them. My response would not have won for me the English Literature prize at Bedford School.

Claude Bouilly supported me completely.

Jardine's went to the French Consul General's office and asked them to intervene and emphasised that Jardine Matheson controlled Hongkong Electric and Simon Murray was a maggot running a tiny office out of a flat in Wan Chai. Were they making themselves clear?

Total at this time was a state-controlled company; 73 per cent government owned with a good degree of bureaucracy, as one would expect from a French nationalised company. They decided to send a team of five to Hong Kong to investigate what they should do. They did not include Bouilly in the team. The team's objective was to determine whether on the one hand should they go with Jardine Matheson, the Princely Hong, or should they continue with Simon Murray, who had found them in the first place and had actually done some business for them. The Consul General seemed to be suggesting Jardine's was the way forward.

They arrived and went to see Jardine's and were wined and dined at the top of the Connaught Centre, the highest building in Hong Kong by a factor of three. They were invited to look out of the windows down onto Hong Kong and Jardine's were able to point out the buildings they owned through Hong Kong Land. 60 per cent of central Hong Kong. They were left in little doubt about who ran the town and with whom they should be doing business in Hong Kong.

The next day they were due to visit me. My office was too small to seat them, so I arranged the meeting to be over lunch in a private room in a hotel. Not the Mandarin. The leader of the Total team was a Monsieur Alain Dandrieux.

When they arrived, I felt they had already made up their minds as to who would be their agent and it wasn't me. They bombarded me with questions, mostly technical: sulphur content, calorific values, government's attitude regarding pollution, storage etc. etc. One plus point for me was that the discussion was all in French. The French prefer people to speak French. They were intrigued by my relationship with Hongkong Electric and they were slightly taken aback when I could show them that I knew the people at Hongkong Electric far better than the Jardine's guys did; and of course, I mentioned that the only business Total had done in Hong Kong so far, through me, was with China Light and Power. China Light was far bigger than Hongkong Electric and they would be very reluctant to buy their fuel through Jardine's, who indirectly controlled the other power company! Every time any of them asked me a question that stalled me, and thought that they had scored a point, they would glance at Dandrieux for approval. He said nothing. Nothing, the whole way through the lunch.

It was time to conclude the meeting and everybody looked at Dandrieux, the chairman. He spoke for the first time. Very slowly.

'Monsieur Murray, do you mind if I ask you something personal?'

'No, not at all,' from me.

'I have heard that you were in the French Foreign Legion. Is this true?'

'Yes. It's true.'

'When was that and where did you serve?'

'I joined at the beginning of 1960 and spent five years in Algeria.'

'What regiment were you in?'

'The 2nd REP,' (the 2nd Parachute Regiment).

There was a very long pause from Dandrieux. The silence was palpable.

Then he said, very slowly, 'I was in Algeria at that time, in the regular army Parachute Regiment and I remember in 1961, April, I think it was, I was ambushed with my company in a steep-sided gorge at El Kantara. I was a second lieutenant at the time and the Fellagha had us surrounded with machine guns. I thought it was the end. And then your regiment came and got us out.'

He paused and looked at me. It was my turn.

'I remember it well', I said. 'It wasn't April, it was 25 March. I remember it particularly because it was my birthday. We had been out on operations in the mountains for eight days and were making our way to our trucks, 3km away, which would take us to our base camp. We had finished our water and our food but we didn't care because we were on our way home. Suddenly there were helicopters everywhere and we were picked up and dropped at El Kantara. We lost twenty men in the first two hours and many more wounded, but we got you out over two days.'

Dandrieux smiled. And as he slammed his hand down on the table, he said, 'Gentlemen, I think I know who's going to be our agent.'

And it was done.

Vive La France. Vive La Légion!

MacLeod continued to refuse to let Total do business with Hongkong Electric because of my involvement, so Shell prospered and held the business. But even without Shell, we were soon doing a million tons a year for Total on long term contracts with China Light.

CHAPTER XXIV

DAVENHAM

In the late 1970s, everybody was running. It was the new sport. James Fixx had produced a book called *The Complete Book of Running*, and the running revolution began. It was deemed as the way to long life. The subject at lunches was no longer only about the stock market but now also about running shoes. First it was Brooks shoes, then Reebok, Adidas, New Balance and Puma and then Saloman and Nike. We were constantly buying new running shoes instead of stocks and shares, reporting our findings and questioning each other on results and also on each other's mileage per week. All very competitive. And then James Fixx died of a heart attack at the age of fifty-two, ironically while running and, as Peter Ustinov joked, we all slowed down a bit.

Jeffa and I did the second London Marathon in 1982. Our combined age was eighty-four and we completed it in under four hours and raised £15,000 for the Little Sisters of the Poor. Not bad!

Davenham prospered. And we had some interesting moments.

Total recommended Davenham to a large French state-owned aluminium company called Pechiney, who were looking for an agent for China. Total asked me if I could meet with the chairman on his forthcoming trip to Hong Kong. It was arranged.

By this time, I owned a speed boat in which I would drive every morning from Lamma to the Aberdeen Harbour, in the southern part of Hong Kong, and then I would run eight miles over the hills to my office. In the office there was a bathroom for me to have a shower after which I would go into my private office where I kept my clothes, I would change, and the day would begin.

On the occasion of the visit by the chairman of Pechiney, I was running over the hills when it dawned on me that I was running forty minutes late for the appointment

Panic.

I arrived at the office and tapped gently on the door. Cynthia opened it, but I held it tightly so that it was only an inch ajar and whispered, 'Has he arrived?'

She whispered back, 'Yes, I've put him in your office and closed the door and told him you have been in a traffic jam.'

Good thinking.

I jumped into the shower.

Normally after a run I would drink a glass of fizzy water. On this occasion there were two champagne glasses beside the basin, left from a drink with a friend the previous evening. I filled one with sparkling water, not appreciating that its appearance to someone looking at me would be that it was a glass of champagne.

I put a towel around my waist and went into the reception area. As I was debating how I was going into my office to get dressed, with my visitor sitting there, I casually put a black cheroot in my mouth and lit up and did some thinking.

Cynthia offered go into my office and get the clothes.

And I thought, that would look terrific in front of Monsieur Pechiney, taking my clothes out of a cupboard: 'These are Mr Murray's socks and these are his underpants and this is his shirt' and so on... 'and he is semi-naked outside in reception drinking champagne (forty-five minutes late)... and by the way he wasn't in a traffic jam, he was on his morning run and he will be with you in a moment!'

No! That would not do.

Seconds were ticking very fast. And then to hell with it and I crashed in, holding a glass of champagne (from his angle), smoking a black cheroot, wearing a towel around my waist and dripping water.

His eyes were about a foot out of their sockets.

I shook hands and welcomed him to Hong Kong.

'First time?'

It was.

He must have thought this is how things are done in Hong Kong and this was just routine stuff. We chatted for an hour and he said he would think about the representation in China and let me know. I think he left Hong Kong in a hurry and, strangely enough, I never heard from him again.

One day a Swedish man came to see me and said he had been sent by someone in the trade department of the Hong Kong government. His company made coffins. Very refined coffins out of hard papier-mâché, with the interior of the coffins dressed with velvet and outside, beautiful imitation wood and gold handles. He showed me photographs.

The Hong Kong government had explained to him that 90 per cent of people who died in Hong Kong were cremated. They buried their relatives in hollowed-out oak tree trunks, imported from New Zealand and other places. The bigger the tree trunk, the more prestigious the burial was deemed to be. Face was always important in Hong Kong. Who would want to be buried in a non-distinguished apple tree?

Traditionally the government organised all cremations and paid for them. The larger the tree trunk, the more expensive the cremation because it took longer to burn. By sending this guy to me, the government thought I could persuade people in Hong Kong to buy these very fancy-looking, but much cheaper coffins, which would enable the prestige of the burial not to be lost and the government would save money because they would burn more quickly than the heavy oak trees.

I became his agent on the spot and he said he would send me a sample coffin shortly. He did and I leaned it against the wall in the reception area of my office. It took up a substantial amount of space, but I was flattered that the Hong Kong government had thrust this honour upon me. I was broadening our base of operations.

My friend from Stanford, Alister Smith-Laing, wrote one day to say he was coming to Hong Kong. I invited him to come and stay on Lamma. Three days before he arrived, I had to fly to London, but I said he was welcome to stay in my house and he did.

He wrote to me sometime later to say how much he had enjoyed it and added that he had gone through our visitors' book and noticed that when Jeffa and I had been living in London in 1973, a Smith-Laing had visited us. My Aunt June had come to dinner one night and had brought her sister, another aunt called Marie, whom I had not seen since I was five years old at the end of the war. Marie's married name was Smith-Laing and it was in the visitors' book. Alister said in his letter that there were very few Smith-Laings in the London telephone directory and she must be some sort of relation of his. I sent a message to Aunt June to ask if she knew anything about Marie's husband and she said he had been in the Fleet Air Arm during the war and had lost an arm. I told Alister, who then asked his father whether he had any knowledge about this man with only one arm, and the reply came back that it was his father's brother, and he had run away with a girl called Marie years before, joined the Fleet Air Arm and had never been seen since.

So Alister turned out to be my cousin.

Alister was a director of a company called Boustead's, operating in Singapore and Malaysia. They were big in the rubber business but also distributors of many products and well-known brands such as Hennessy brandy. A sort of mini-Jardine's, but they had been around a long time. Through Alister, I met his chairman, Allan Charton, and we got on well. To cut the story short, they wanted a foothold in Hong Kong and I sold them 33 per cent of Davenham.

£250,000 in the kitty.

I also started a headhunting business with David Norman, who had fallen out with his boss at Russell Reynolds, the biggest headhunting company on the planet; he was starting his own business, with a partner called Michael Broadbent.

Norman was having a drink with me the following day having had a row with his boss the previous evening and we clicked. He asked me if I would like to start 'Norman Broadbent' with him in Hong Kong. I recruited Simon Swallow from Jardine's to run it and Davenham was in the headhunting business.

Around this time, the Hong Kong and Shanghai Bank had decided to build a new headquarters on the site of their existing building. This piece of land, essentially the centre of Hong Kong in front of which was Statue Square, could easily be judged as the most expensive piece of real estate in the world. Certainly the airspace above the land was the most valuable on the planet.

Given this fact, Michael Sandberg, the chairman of the bank, had told the architect, Norman Foster, to design a building which would justify the value of the air space. Unlimited costs. The budget was US$5 billion.

Davenham Engineering scored well on the building. We got the standby electric power supply with Kongsberg gas turbines. Then, through an H.H. Robertson subsidiary, Cupples, we were awarded the contract for the glass curtain wall enveloping the entire building, plus the raised flooring inside the building, exactly the same as was installed by H.H. Robertson in the twin towers in New York. The building was the most modern and technologically advanced in the world at that time. It looked like a pile of containers on top of each other, forty-seven stories high, with pipes going in every direction. Something like an oil refinery. The containers were supplied by the Mitsubishi corporation (friends of ours) and thanks to Jarle, we got the central waste disposal unit supplied by Centralsug from Sweden, for whom we also acted as agents.

Centralsug behaved badly. As the building progressed, the bank feared the costs were running wild and they put pressure on Norman Foster to cut back. Foster approached many of the companies who had been awarded contracts not by a tender process but through negotiation and made them reduce their prices. One of these was Centralsug.

They came to see me in the office one day and explained that they had to lower their price for the project and would therefore have to reduce my commission from 1.5 per cent to 1 per cent. I objected, saying my commission was a percentage, so that if they reduced their price, the amount I was paid would automatically be less as well, as a percentage of a lower amount. They said they would discuss it with their boss in Sweden and come back to me.

Three weeks later the boss and his cohorts came to Hong Kong to visit the bank and also to visit Davenham, their agent, who had secured the contract for them. We went through the discussion again with me giving the same argument regarding the percentage commission. The boss said, 'Mr Murray, it's either 1 per cent or nothing at all.'

Jarle and Cynthia held their respective breath.

There was a long pause and I thought hard about it and then I heard myself saying, 'In that case, if you will not pay me the 1.5 per cent due, I would prefer to take nothing and I will not forget it.'

They left my office. Jarle was lost for words.

I received a letter from a Mr Sam Cummings from Monaco.

He said he had read my book *Legionnaire* in which he had seen that on numerous occasions when we had clashed with the rebels in Algeria, we had found they were using English weapons. I had always found this slightly embarrassing. Cummings went on to explain in his letter that he was an arms dealer and he had indeed sold the guns to the Arabs. He had bought them from dealers in Egypt and they were the guns left behind after the abortive bid by the French and British to take back the Suez Canal from Nasser, after he had nationalised it in 1956.

The Americans had been very unsupportive of the British/French aggression and threatened to end financial support for the UK. This was eleven years after the Second World War and the UK was effectively broke and very dependent on American generosity. Harold Macmillan was at the treasury and informed the Prime Minister at the time, Anthony Eden, that if the Americans cut off loans we would be bust. The Russians had supported Nasser's takeover of the Canal and Eisenhower, the American President, was of the view that if the Brits and French did not withdraw immediately, we faced the real threat of nuclear war. The Brits and French fled Egypt in a hurry and left half their kit behind, including thousands of guns. Anthony Eden resigned.

Sam Cummings bought all the guns left behind and sold them throughout the world, including of course, to the Fellagha rebels who we were fighting when I was a legionnaire in Algeria. I had read a book written by Anthony Sampson called *The Arms Bazaar* about arms dealers, which listed Cummings as the largest seller of small arms in the world. Cummings said in his letter that he had enjoyed my book and he would be delighted to have dinner with me next time I visited Europe.

Two months later I invited Cummings to join me for dinner at Alfred Hecht's flat. He looked like a young, plump, happy schoolboy. Nothing could be further than one's image of an arms dealer. He said that he was aware that before 1949, when the communists took over under Mao, the Chinese National Army had used Mauser rifles from Germany. After Mao's victory over Chiang Kai-shek in 1949, they had switched to Russian guns and all the Mausers were still in storage and he could buy them for $10 each. He could then convert them into sporting rifles and sell them in the States. The market for sporting rifles in the States was $2 billion a year. He would come and see me in Hong Kong to discuss it further.

Three months later, he arrived.

In the meantime, I had been chatting to my friend Bob Miller in Hong Kong about this. Bob Miller was one of the shareholders of Duty Free Shoppers, a hugely successful global business that operated duty free shops at airports around the world. Less well known was the fact that he had been a quartermaster in the American army in Vietnam and he knew the workings of the PX where the US army did their shopping and he really understood retailing. He also, as a side-line, had a small-arms manufacturing business in Hong Kong and manufactured pistols for the Hong Kong police force. He was very excited at the prospect of meeting Sam Cummings.

Cummings arrived and he was ready for business. He had even prepared brochures with an impressive sporting rifle on the cover. I put the brochures on the coffee table in my office. All that remained to be done was to negotiate with the Chinese. This was Sam's role. He went to China and came back two weeks later. It was done. The Chinese would get back to us as soon as they were ready.

Sam called to inform us a month later that the Chinese had ratted on us and had started selling the guns through a Swiss arms dealer at a higher price than they had agreed to accept from us. Sadly, it was the end of the gun business for Bob and me. However, in the intervening month, business had continued as usual. One day, there was a visitor in my office whom I left sitting for ten minutes while I went out to make an important telephone call. When I got back, he was waving Sam's brochure at me and laughing as he said, 'Simon, you've really got a vertical business here haven't you? On the one hand you're selling guns and on the other you're selling coffins,' pointing at the coffin leaning against the wall.

I saw instantly what he meant and how funny it must have seemed. I made Al Capone seem like a novice.

'Yes,' I said. 'And when the coffin business slows, we push hard with the gun sales. It works very well!'

One day I took a call from David Norman. 'Simon. We have an assignment from N.M. Rothschild's. They are looking for a project finance director for Asia – any thoughts? David Newbigging has apparently left Jardine's and has put his hat in the ring. What do you think?'

'I think they could do better.'

'That's what we thought. What about *you*? With all that MTR experience.'

'I have my own company.'

'They would be interested in buying into it.'

And so it began.

My friend Alister Smith-Laing had told me Allan Charton was moving on from Boustead's and a new guy had arrived, for whom Alister had no time. I asked Alister if Boustead's would sell their shares in Davenham; he thought 'Yes' and added, 'Simon, buy them back, I am leaving Boustead's and the new bloke is a nightmare.' Three days later the new Boustead man arrived in Hong Kong and I asked him if he would like to sell his shares back to me. The deal was done in fifteen minutes. I then sold 49 per cent of the company to Rothschild's for US$500,000. The Rothschild name was good for credibility and the cash was good too.

Three months later, the Singapore government announced that they too were building a mass transport railway system, following the huge success of the Hong Kong project.

They appointed Freeman Fox, the same British consultants that had built the Hong Kong MTR. The same team. I knew them all. This time there was no Norman Thompson in the way. Metro-Cammell were the favourites. But Singapore was no longer a British colony!

I went to Japan to see if we could be appointed as the agents for the same Japanese consortium that had worked on the Hong Kong MTR project. Thanks to great support from my old friend Yufu, and to be fair, it was no harm having Rothschild's name as our partner, we were appointed as the Japanese consortium's agent.

Rothschild had introduced their contact man as Johnny Louden, one of three managing directors of Rothschild. He was a great addition to our team. I made him our chairman and Michael Green came on to the board. We were beginning to look quite serious.

We won the contract. US$350 million. In those days, that was serious money.

The Japanese paid Davenham a commission annually for eleven years. Every time the Singapore mass transit company ordered anything for their railway:

a new carriage, air-conditioning replacement or the general expansion of the system, the Japanese, without any request from us, sent a commission.

They were the best.

Rothschild's were over the moon. I should have charged them more for their Davenham shares. Dupont sold its dynamite business to Dyno, a Norwegian company, and we were appointed as their distributor in Hong Kong. We got to Stonecutters Island the long way round. All thanks to Jarle. So maybe my explosives training would come in useful after all. Something I had discussed with Middleditch so many years before.

And then there was the Bickerton bike story.

Bickerton had developed a 'foldaway bicycle'. Davenham became their agent for Hong Kong. This was going to be a huge success for weekend boat trips. Everybody with a boat would buy a Bickerton or two.

We had a good writeup in the local press and then Hong Kong Television invited us to do a demonstration on the evening news channel. After the news on the American presidential election, which Reagan won by a landslide, 'the Bickerton Bike'. Jeremy Harbord, who had joined Davenham six months earlier, practised day and night for a week, so that he could assemble the bike in two minutes.

The great day came and the television show was on. The scene was at the top of the Peak above Hong Kong and the camera zoomed in on Harbord assembling the bike, with the commentator saying all sorts of things about this incredible piece of kit. Two minutes later the camera was following Harbord charging down Old Peak Road at full speed followed by the commentator in hysterics about how wonderful it all was and getting more and more excited.

And then, disaster. The pedal fell off. Harbord lost control and drove the bike into the flood ditch at the side of the road and disappeared. Legs and wheels in the air. Shrieks from Harbord and the end of the Bickerton Bike story for Hong Kong and nearly the end of Harbord.

No bikes were sold.

So we had some ups and downs. As they say, interesting times.

CHAPTER XXV
THE HANDOVER

In the early 1980s, companies in Hong Kong were becoming nervous about 1997, but something else was happening. Chinese local property companies began flexing their muscles. Li Ka Shing (K.S. Li) had accumulated 12 per cent of Hong Kong Land stock. Larger than that held by the Keswicks.

This presented Jardine's think tank with real problems. They decided to merge the two companies, Hong Kong Land and Jardine's, to create a joint company with a combined market capitalisation that would be too big for predators. Jardine's began selling their own property assets to Hong Kong Land and bought shares in the Land company with the proceeds; Hong Kong Land borrowed money and bought shares in Jardine's.

In some ways, it may have been good for Jardine's ego, but it was in no way good for their minority shareholders. Jardine's were selling valuable and high yielding properties in return for a Hong Kong Land dividend, which itself was squeezed by interest rates of around 11 per cent and a declining cashflow through purchasing Jardine's properties. The arithmetic did not make sense and minority shareholders were expressing unhappiness. One of them was K.S. Li.

He demanded that Jardine's buy his 12 per cent share in the Land company. Newbigging refused. When K.S. threatened retaliation, Newbigging effectively shrugged his shoulders and told K.S. that he didn't give a damn; according to K.S., who recounted this to me some years later, Newbigging said he wouldn't lose any sleep over it and would 'sleep like a baby'.

K.S. never forgot it.

Jardine Matheson and Hong Kong Land now owned 27 per cent of each other and egos were back at their correct levels, but they were mired in debt to some HK$38 billion, carrying an interest of 10 per cent which, together with the loss of the high yielding properties they had sold to the Land company, made a large dent in their accounts.

Against this was the low yield dividend from the Hong Kong Land company, which itself was suffering from heavy interest rates on its substantially increased debt. Neither side benefitted and minority shareholders simply could not follow the strategy. All this to prevent the Land company and Jardine's from being taken over, which perhaps would have been the best thing in terms of increasing shareholder value for both companies.

Newbigging was blamed for the decline in the Princely Hong's welfare and London determined to get rid of him and they did. They levied various sins against him, one of which was Jardine's sponsorship of Chris Bonington's ascent of Mount Kongur, which had happened some years earlier, to mark Jardine Matheson's 150th anniversary.

Newbigging had formed a small group of Jardine seniors, including himself, to join Bonington and his team for the first part of the climb to the base camp at 18,000 feet. This was paid for by the company, without reference to Matheson's.

The boys in London felt they had enough ammunition to force Newbigging's resignation, also for neglecting especially as he had neglected to see the threat of K.S. Li's accumulation of 12 per cent of the Land company.

Simon Keswick, Henry's younger brother, was posted to Hong Kong to replace Newbigging as senior managing director. Newbigging disappeared. Literally, gone. There was no public announcement. Nobody really understood what had happened.

After a short while, Simon Keswick started making some changes. A new managing director, an American, Brian Powers, was appointed. A man with an investment banking background. MacLeod was eased out, not to Matheson's in London as was the normal exit route of retiring directors, but to his home in Norfolk – where doubtless he could focus on his photography!

Other directors including Heywood found early retirement. He started his own company manufacturing rivets. Trevor Bedford found the exit with twenty-four hours' notice and left Hong Kong under a cloud. It seemed he had borrowed money from George Tan of Carrian, 'interest free'.

I had done a lot of research on Hongkong Electric and tried to get Total to buy Hong Kong Land's shareholding. Bedford had told me confidentially that they were sellers. But Total baulked at the slowly approaching dreaded date of 1997.

Meanwhile the heavy business brigade in Hong Kong had been pressing the UK government to appoint a new governor on the retirement of David Wilson in 1992. They wanted a politician, not someone from the Foreign Office, which was traditional. The Foreign Office had shown itself as being inept in the face of the up-and-coming handover. The business elite wanted a tough negotiator. We were not going to hand over to China just like that. This was going to be a 'negotiation'. After all, Hong Kong Island was British in perpetuity under the agreement with China; it was only the New Territories that were due to be handed back in 1997, under the lease terms.

Whether Hong Kong could survive on its own without the New Territories was the real question. The whimpering British Foreign Office said 'No', but the people of Hong Kong said 'Yes'. A huge infrastructure programme was rolled out: bridges to Lantau, which made the Golden Gate bridge in San Francisco look like a rope bridge; Plans to build a new airport to be reclaimed from the sea off the coast of Lantau; more underground tunnels across to the Kowloon side and a new governor called Chris Patten. A politician. Chris Patten was well supported by the British Prime Minister, John Major.

As 1997 grew closer, one issue that was constantly flagged was the subject of British passports for the people of Hong Kong. When the British had given independence to its colonies in the past, they had been generous in handing out British passports. Time had changed attitudes over the years and anti-immigration sentiment was growing in the United Kingdom. Nevertheless, Britain had a duty to fulfil towards its ex-colony. This was the first time a colony was not being given its independence, but rather it was being handed over to another government, and a pretty hostile one at that.

I formed a group called 'Honour Hong Kong' with Algy Cluff and David Tang, the vision and aim of which was to get the UK to give as many people of Hong Kong British passports as was politically acceptable. Chris Patten gave us his full support. He was active in every way as the new Governor. He introduced new laws and had a democratic way of doing things, previously unseen in British-run Hong Kong. I liked him and more importantly, so did the people of Hong Kong. I discussed the passport issue with him and he understood. We could not simply walk out on Hong Kong. There was a need to leave with 'honour' after 150 years.

After Tiananmen Square in 1989, when the alarm bells had really started ringing, I had gone to London and had an interview with the then Prime Minister, Margaret Thatcher, at No. 10, to discuss the delicate subject of passports. She was supportive but politically she felt there were limits. I explained to her that the people of Hong Kong would not want to come to the UK for multiple reasons. I included myself, although I had a British passport. We loved Hong Kong. It was passports to *stay* that we wanted, not to *leave* Hong Kong.

If the Chinese behaved badly after the handover, a British passport would enable us to leave and that would make China tread with great care when the time came. The business community in Hong Kong was mixed in its reaction. Many wanted to be seen supporting the future arrival of China. They were scared of China; they feared their economic empires would be nationalised. They were in 'suck' mode and it was very unattractive to watch.

There was some justification for their viewpoint, in that they believed Hong Kong Island could not survive without the New Territories under its control. They had laid this thought on Thatcher. She eventually realised she could not fight Chinese leader Deng Xiaoping for both Hong Kong Island and the New Territories to remain British in perpetuity. There was no way that Deng was going to hand over Chinese territory to a foreign government. When Deng made this clear to Thatcher on her visit to China in 1984, she finally gave way.

Mrs Thatcher mentioned this to me when I saw her, and although she was not totally convinced, I had to accept the business sector had a point. This was a strong card in China's hand; even if we were building a new airport in Hong Kong territory, Hong Kong could probably not survive without the New Territories. It was tempting to look at Singapore that had performed well since they had separated from Malaysia in 1965, which many had thought not possible.

Thatcher's Foreign Secretary, Geoffrey Howe, was very unsupportive of her regarding Hong Kong and other things and indeed treacherous. He resigned with a very derogatory speech in the House of Commons against her.

Michael Heseltine, the President of the Board of Trade, also betrayed Margaret Thatcher and was not a friend of Hong Kong. Both were back-stabbers of Mrs Thatcher.

There were endless discussions over the months and years, with Chris Patten leading the British side after Thatcher's downfall. He was constantly undermined by the British Foreign Office; British businessmen in Hong Kong started to slide away from him.

The Chinese were giving Patten a tough time in their press as well. They described him as the 'biggest whore in a thousand years'.

Shakespeare would have loved it.

Meanwhile Hong Kong people were leaving in droves, for America, Canada, Australia and elsewhere. We were losing our best and only a British passport in their back pocket would persuade them to stay. Doctors, lawyers, architects, dentists, engineers, and ministers were leaving. The administrative sector of our society was about to disappear. We were facing a disaster.

Deng had come up with a potential solution in the early 1980s: 'One country two systems'. The people of Hong Kong could continue to live under the current rule of law and constitution for another fifty years beyond 1997, and the New Territories would remain part of Hong Kong for that period.

It was a good compromise and suited China for all sorts of economic reasons.

There was a lot of talk about democracy. The Chinese agreed we could vote for our own leader, to be called Chief Executive, not Governor. After more wrangling it was agreed that there would be a body made up of representatives across society which would be the Electoral Committee and would vote in the Chief Executive. This Electoral Committee would be made up of 1,200 appointees, who must be citizens of Hong Kong and must be Chinese. Twelve hundred people out of a population of about six million was hardly a democratic vote, but it was a step in the right direction. The truth was that the British had failed Hong Kong regarding democracy. They could have given this 'right' to Hong Kong years before, instead of appointing the Governor over the years without any input from the people.

In years gone by, the right to vote for the Governor had been requested frequently. As long ago as 1895 an 'elected' member of the Hong Kong Legislative Council, a Mr Whitehead, had written to the British government, suggesting that Hong Kong, given its status and importance to the British Exchequer, should be given the same degree of democracy enjoyed by many other colonies at that time. Even in remote states such as British Honduras the locals had the rights to vote for their own governor.

Whitehead as an 'elected' member, was in the permanent minority of the Council, subordinate to the members 'appointed' by the Governor. Even though he had the support for his Petition signed by 97 per cent of Hong Kong's business sector, the government ignored it.

On another occasion, some of the government Appointees voted in support of Whitehead's demands, which prompted the Governor to put his foot down at such insubordination at the beginning of the next meeting, by saying:

'Gentlemen, you are at liberty to speak and vote as you like; but if holding official positions, you oppose the Government, it will be the duty of the Government to inquire whether it is for its advantage that you should continue to hold these positions'.

Always the Foreign Office had fought against it, fearing China would freak out. The reality was that China had on many occasions been far too occupied with their own problems, such as war with Russia and indeed their own civil war, to have got involved. Why shouldn't Hong Kong elect their own governor rather than having one thrust upon them from London? It might even have been in China's own interest, with a far greater ability to influence a 'local.'

My personal view was that we should have voted for a 'mayor' of Hong Kong. Every city in China has a mayor and it would reduce tension with the centre. In a corporation there is often tension between the chairman and the chief executive. Who is the real boss? Creating a 'Chief Executive' in Hong Kong would lead to misunderstandings of this sort in the future. Whereas if we had a mayor, like all the other cities in China, we would have a greater chance of being left to get on with local management.

Cynthia, my wonderful secretary, said she had applied to leave with her family for Canada. I did not have the heart to dissuade her, although I probably could have done so with the promise of a British passport.

There was still another thirteen years to go to reach 1997, when suddenly there was a run on the Hong Kong dollar. Its value against the US dollar dropped 50 per cent in a week from HK$4.50 down to HK$9.

Jeffa – the first woman to fly solo around the world in a helicopter

Keeping cool in Antarctica

JANE SHILLING
Knickers to that: how a nation fell out of love with the thong **3**

MICROWAVE MAN
On meeting the ghost of love, one last time... **11**

ARTS
B-side myself: the appalling state of pop cover versions **13**

THE TIMES
FRIDAY

28.11.03

QUITE OLD, VERY RICH, REALLY COLD

CAN MILLIONAIRE BUSINESSMAN SIMON MURRAY MAKE IT TO THE SOUTH POLE? INTERVIEW BY GINNY DOUGARY PAGES 4-6

Old and cold but not very rich

Not as smooth as everybody thinks

Abseiling down the Shard – thank God for Legion training

The Deutsche Bank head offices in Frankfurt

On Everest

Hong Kong, business 24 hours a day, 7 days a week

An unwelcome return to Algeria

Looking for lions in Africa

With Jeffa

Total panic ensued. There were queues a mile long along Queens Road Central to the HSBC bank with people wanting to withdraw their money. I had cash in the Chartered Bank and called the bank to change my HK dollars into US dollars and very grudgingly, after I mentioned my connection to John Mackenzie, they obliged.

The next day the Hong Dollar was at $10 to the US dollar and heading for $11.

Two days later the Finance Secretary, John Bembridge, announced the government had pegged the HK dollar to the US dollar at 7.8, guaranteed by the Hong Kong government.

In three days I had lost 13 per cent of the value of my cash.

There was life turning on a sixpence again. All the short players like Soros and the rest were screwed. And so was I. Or so I thought.

I was in my office one evening in March 1984 when I received a telephone call from my friend Phillip Tose. He was a stockbroker with Vickers de Costa and very close to K.S. Li (Li Ka Shing).

He started off, 'Murray, you know those three guys who run Hutchison for K.S., John Richardson, Hubbard-Ford and White? Well they've been up to no good and the old man is going to fire them and he's looking for someone to come and run Hutchison... and I was wondering if you've got any ideas on someone who could do that?'

I gave a great guffaw of laughter and said jokingly, 'The only person in Hong Kong who could run Hutchison, is *me*.'

'That's exactly what *we* thought, Murray. The old man wants to see you tonight for a drink.'

'I was joking for Christ's sake.'

'The old man knows you well, Murray, from your JEC days and he's checked you out with people like Willy Purves at the bank and they all say you are the man for the job. Just come and have one drink tonight, for God's sake.'

'I can't ', I said. 'I'm on the six o'clock ferry to Lamma and I've got things to do tonight.'

'All right,' said Tose. 'Tomorrow morning then.'

'No, it's Saturday and I'm playing golf with Jerry Soames.'

'Murray, for fuck's sake, just come for one bloody drink tonight.'

Pause...

'All right I'll come.'

I arrived at K.S.'s office. He was sitting on a sofa with his hatchet man, George Magnus, beside him and Phillip Tose, looking amused, in an armchair.

As I walked into the room, a big wave from K.S.

'Simon, we want you to come and run Hutchison, managing director, what you think?'

'Well K.S.,' I said. 'I'm hugely honoured and would love to, but Rothschild own half my company and they have said they will never sell.'

'Simon, everything for sale, just a question of price. I buy the company, Simon, you tell them.'

'But K.S., they have told me they will never sell.'

'Simon, you call them. How much they want?'

'I don't know, K.S. We have never discussed it.'

'Simon, I give them US$4 million (US$10 million today) for the company. You tell them and then you become managing director of Hutchison. Call them now, Simon. There's the telephone.'

This was dream country. Davenham was three years old and here was somebody offering us US$4 million for the company and me the job as managing director of one of the largest companies in Hong Kong.

I got up slowly and dialled Rothschild's in London. It was about 10am London time. I asked to be put through to Michael Richardson, most senior of the three managing directors. Without thinking, I had dialled the number on the speaker phone, so the others in the room could hear the conversation.

'Michael, you're not going to believe this but K.S. Li has just offered to buy our company for US$4 million.'

'Oh my God, that's wonderful,' he said. 'Are you serious?'

Before I could say anything, K.S. shouted out, 'You see Simon, he's a seller.'

Everybody roared with laughter.

Company sold.

CHAPTER XXVI
LI KA SHING

Li Ka Shing, known as K.S. Li, is an inspirational business leader. He was born in 1928 in Guangdong Province. The family were forced to flee to Hong Kong in 1940 as refugees. After his father's death, Li left school and worked long hours in a plastics factory to support his family. He started his own plastics company in the 1950s and began a real estate investment company shortly after. He developed new businesses and became one of Asia's most renowned and respected businessmen. His is the ultimate rags to riches success story.

George Magnus called me with details. I was to start on 1 August and I would receive a salary of US$400,000 plus a house and an annual bonus.

'Agreed.'

Davenham was to be merged into a Hutchison subsidiary, Hutchison Boag. Hutchison's business was similar in many ways to that of Jardine's: major retail businesses with supermarkets, pharmaceutical outlets, wines and spirits stores, property development, a growing container port business, a trading business and an engineering business. In addition they had shipping interests and insurance, as did Jardine's; lots of parallel businesses and plenty of competition between the two companies. Hutchison were even the agents for Nike running shoes. I switched from New Balance to Nike immediately.

At this moment in time, my mother died. I had not seen her in ages. I flew to France to attend the funeral. A solemn affair, in a crematorium in the small village of Tremolat in the Dordogne area. K.S. Li had taken the trouble to send some flowers. I was very touched.

My mother and Leo had divorced some years before and she had lived alone in the Dordogne with my half-sister, Caroline. Leo came to the service. It was good to see him again after so many years. My brother surprised me with a no show.

Before the service began, I wandered into the garden of the crematorium. My mother and I had somehow never been close. I felt very sad for her. To have a son with whom she was never at one must have weighed heavily on her. I felt the tears coming and I cried as I have never cried in my entire life. I would never really know my mother and she was now gone forever, so we were never going to make it.

After the funeral I took a train to Paris. I waited for a taxi for an hour at the station in Paris in a long queue of returning holiday makers. The rain poured down in buckets and when I finally got to the front, the taxi driver refused to get out of the taxi to open the boot. He was shouting at me to stick my suitcase in the back seat and I was shouting at him that there was insufficient room for me and the suitcase. I threatened to take the next taxi, which would mean he would have to drive round to the back of the queue and wait thirty minutes until he was at the front again. By this time universal discontent filled the air and the balance of opinion was in my favour. The driver got out, opened the boot, slammed it shut and got back in his seat and aggressively demanded to know my destination.

I said, 'The Windsor Hotel.'

'Moi, je connais pas L'Hotel Windsor. Je ne suis pas le guide de Paris. Je suis le chauffeur du taxi. C'est tout!' he shouted.

I told him to just start driving, Nom de Dieu, and I would direct him to the hotel.

Finally, silence, and we drove off.

I was looking at the back of his neck and then at his profile and then at his face in the mirror, and I had the distinct impression that I had seen him somewhere before. Perhaps I had been in this cab the year before when I was in France. As we continued, the feeling that I had seen him before increased.

And then... Bang!

I realised it was none other than Sergeant Reiper, the very same man who had stuck a loaded and cocked pistol in my head at two o'clock in the morning, twenty-six years ago when I was on guard duty in Algeria. And here he was driving my taxi at seven in the morning in Paris.

Unbelievable! Impossible!

I slapped him on the shoulder and said, 'Stop the cab! 2nd Parachute

Regiment, Foreign Legion, Philippeville, 1962. You were there!'

He slammed on the brakes so hard I nearly went through the front window.

I said, 'You son of a bitch, you put me in the slammer for fifteen days for being drunk on guard duty.'

He turned around and stared at me. His face dead-pan. And after a long pause, he simply said, 'You deserved it.'

I just collapsed laughing and he finally joined in. These Legion sergeants don't change. We drove to the hotel. He refused to let me pay, carried my suitcase in and walked straight through the lobby into the bar. There was a solitary bar boy drying glasses and Reiper yelled, 'A bottle of Ricard, two glasses, water and ice, *et dépêche-toi!*'

We killed the bottle and had lunch.

That was the last time I saw him. But I suppose he will turn up again. The Legion is a very extended club, and no better *esprit de corps* to be found anywhere on the planet.

I returned to Hong Kong. K.S. asked me to come to the Hutchison boardroom to attend their board meeting at 3pm on a Friday. I sat outside the boardroom for twenty minutes and then was asked to enter. 'Gentlemen,' said K.S. as I entered, 'This is Simon Murray, our new managing director. Simon, come and sit here,' ushering me into the seat next to him. There were about fourteen directors in the room, of whom I knew about six, including John Richardson and Hubbard-Ford who looked as though they had just fallen from the top of a sixty-storey building. I learned later that they had no idea this was coming. Nor did any of the other directors except George Magnus. K.S. made a short introduction with a few words about me and then declared the meeting over.

Several directors, although notably not Richardson or Hubbard-Ford, came over and shook hands and said 'Congratulations'. And then the room was empty. I was left sitting in an empty boardroom. I left after fifteen minutes and went home.

The following Monday the news of my appointment was announced. It was covered in the global press. Murray becomes the new managing director of Hutchison. Most of it was complimentary. There was a very nice article in The Economist, with lots of comments on K.S. Li and indeed Rothschild's, and the odd word or two about yours truly.

I arrived at Hutchison's office on the top floor of Hutchison House the next morning. The receptionists did not know who I was. Neither Richardson nor Hubbard-Ford were in the office. I asked to see the human resources director.

He had not yet arrived.

What a welcome! I waited in reception. Finally, the HR man strolled in with his hands in his pockets. A receptionist pointed him to where I was sitting.

'I'm Simon Murray', I said. 'Your new managing director.'

He looked shell-shocked and said he was Ben Hui and that nobody had told him I was coming and he knew nothing about it. I asked him if there was an office for me. He showed me to what had obviously been my predecessor Richardson's office, but he had cleaned it out. No telephones, no books, no pictures, no secretary, no nothing. It was an empty box. I looked at Hui and said, 'You'd better get this into shape pretty quickly and above all I want a telephone in here and a copy of the annual report and a list of all department and divisional heads with their telephone numbers in one hour.' He ran off like a frightened rabbit.

K.S. Li's office was in a separate building at the other end of Central and I wandered over. He was there and introduced me to Bill Shurniak, whom, he explained, he had just hired from the Bank of Canada and who was going to be my finance director. He had just arrived in Hong Kong. Bill had a good pedigree and I was relieved to have him on board with his office next to mine at Hutchison House. Somebody to talk to! He was a real number-cruncher: just what I needed.

The various divisions of Hutchison were spread around the town. The port operations were obviously in the port, the trading division under John Bartley was in Central, the supermarket headquarters were in Kowloon and so on. I had a busy two weeks travelling to the different divisions.

I went to see the head of each department and spent a few days with each of them, learning the ins and outs of their business, running the numbers, feeling for their problems and meeting their troops. There were so many different operations including a quarrying operation. Good for Davenham's explosives business.

K.S. Li's holding company was called Cheung Kong and it was the vehicle that had purchased the 33 per cent of Hutchison from the bank. There were some clearly visible signs of potential conflicts of interest, particularly on the property development side.

All land in Hong Kong is owned by the government and periodically they auction sites for development, to the highest bidder. The land sites are auctioned in lots big enough to secure bids of not less than US$100 million and often much larger. This means that only the big players can participate. Not so different from communist China where all land is owned by the government. The 'big players' used to meet periodically before an auction just to make sure everybody knew what was going on. It's called a 'cartel' in polite society.

The Hong Kong government annually runs very high surpluses, in spite of a low corporate tax rate of 16 per cent, because of the profits from land sales, among other things. 30 per cent of the population lives on two bucks a day. The gap between the haves and have nots is amongst the widest in the world. In addition, Hong Kong needs no defence budget like most other countries. It's China's territory.

Hong Kong is rich, but that wealth is very unevenly spread.

I didn't care in those days, but I do now I'm older.

CHAPTER XXVII

HUTCHISON WHAMPOA

K.S. Li was fantastic to work with and we hit it off immediately. Perhaps because we were both born in the Year of the Dragon. He was twelve years older than me.

It was clear to me that his interest in Hutchison continued to be focused on the property development side. Everything else he would leave to me, as he had done previously with my predecessors since Wylie's appointment at Hutchison by the bank.

25 per cent of Hutchison's profits came from property. They had great tracts of land for re-development and we were building 10,000 apartments a year in what was one of the most expensive cities in the world. On top of which we had substantial properties for rental. The container business was another money-spinner run by a very seasoned and experienced team under John Meredith.

It was a critical time for the expansion of the port when I arrived. The government was auctioning space in the water for a new berth, exactly the way they auctioned land for development. In this case they were auctioning water for terminal six. I was chairman of all Hutchison's subsidiary companies automatically, as group MD of the holding company. Our container company, known as Hong Kong International Terminals (HIT), was the only bidder for the terminal on offer. We got the rights to build it for a fee of HK$600 million.

My first big deal.

To have an understanding of what that meant, three years later terminal seven was up for grabs. Roughly the same size as terminal six. There were eight bidders. We got it for HK$4 billion.

That illustrates how the Hong Kong economy was growing at that time. Today, as I write this, Hutchison controls 23 per cent of all the world's container terminals, including Felixstowe, where I arrived so many years ago on the St *Arvans* on my way to Buenos Aires. Felixstowe was our first overseas acquisition and I felt great satisfaction in negotiating with P&O to acquire it, under very different circumstances from those of my first visit with my potato knife in hand, thirty years previously.

My relationship with K.S. was one of harmony. He made me feel trusted and he wanted my opinion on everything. We often saw things differently, but he was a good listener and respected my views even if he did not agree with them. He said many times, 'Simon, we only do things when we both agree.' There were no surprises. It was all rather different from the way things worked at Jardine's.

Once, when we were alone, he bemoaned the fact that one of my great friends was David Tang and what a terrible person he was. And why did I have such a man as my friend? David Tang's grandfather had owned the Kowloon bus company and was a multi-millionaire and also had a knighthood. He was extremely well known in Hong Kong's business world for both these reasons. When David's father was born, his father – Sir Tang, as he was known, had him checked out by a feng shui man, who declared that he would grow up to be an evil person. As a result, Sir Tang kept the boy as a prisoner in the house until he was eighteen. The boy asked for some money and said he would go to England and never return. He was given the money and left.

David Tang himself was brought up in England, attended a public school and went on to study law. Tang's grandfather divorced his wife (a concubine), and left her in a tiny flat in Kowloon with virtually nothing; she lived as a pauper. One day she was told by a friend that under Hong Kong (English) law, she could sue her ex-husband for millions. She was guided to the biggest law firm in Hong Kong, Johnson, Stokes and Masters (JSM), who took on her case and asked her to write an affidavit, which she did. Nobody at JSM could understand it, and they decided to send it to her grandson, David Tang, at his law firm in London. Tang translated the document and signed it. It was sent to his grandfather, who, when he saw his grandson's signature on the document, declared to all and sundry that his ex-wife and now his own grandson were plotting together to steal his money. He told everybody in Hong Kong who cared to listen. This included K.S. Li.

K.S. did not know the truth of what had really happened and Tang's grandfather had long since passed away. David Tang had told me the whole story in great detail.

Li went on, 'Simon, David Tang, very bad man; tried to get his grandfather's money by suing him. Simon, in Chinese family, we don't sue each other. Never happen. Only in American family can sue. And Simon, everybody says this man now your friend?'

'K.S., yes, he is my friend. He is not your enemy. I would never have a friend who was your enemy. But K.S., I make my own friends by choice, not by chance. You cannot tell me who I choose as my friends unless you have something personally against them. You do not even know David Tang.' And then I told him the true story of David Tang and his grandfather who had been so tough on his own son because of the prophecies of the feng shui man. I left K.S.'s office after that with him in a sombre mood.

Later, I discovered from the accountant Canning Fok that K.S. had called in his three senior staff and his two sons and told them what a great guy Simon Murray was and 'He choose his own friends,' as though that was an amazing thing for someone to do.

⌐⌐⌐

Early on, K.S. explained that he had a full reservoir of cash in the company, which of course I could see for myself, and asked if I had any ideas where we should invest it. I was of the opinion that the marriage of Jardine's and Hong Kong Land had been very expensive for both companies. Jardine's because they effectively had to acquire control of a huge company by market capitalisation, in which they only held 3 per cent of the equity, and the Land company because it was a leveraged property company and was acquiring shares in a perhaps over-valued conglomerate, Jardine's.

My suggestion to K.S. was that they were gasping to sell assets to straighten out their combined debt position. Jardine's were allergic to debt and always had been. In addition, Trevor Bedford had previously told me the Land company had considered selling their interest in Hongkong Electric; perhaps Jardine's would agree to this, and Hongkong Electric would be a great acquisition for us. Also I knew the company backwards.

K.S. was amazed. 'Simon. They will never sell Hongkong Electric.'

I said, 'Well, why don't I go and ask them?'

'Simon, they never sell.'

'K.S., you once said to me, "Everything for sale, only the price is the question."'

Ten minutes later, I called Simon Keswick at Jardine's headquarters at the top of the Connaught Centre, the tallest building in Hong Kong, owned unsurprisingly by Hong Kong Land, and asked if I could come and see him right there and then. When I got to his office, he was very pleasant and we chatted for a while and then I posed the question of Hongkong Electric. He was totally negative. Indeed, affronted, that I would even suggest it.

'No Simon!' he barked. 'Hongkong Electric is the most valuable asset we have and we will never sell it. So that is that. Tell your boss it is not for sale.'

I told K.S. and he said, 'You see Simon. They never sell.'

The next day K.S. was screaming down the telephone for me to come immediately to his office.

'Simon, Simon Keswick is coming to my office now. He say he want to sell Hongkong Electric. Come quickly Simon. Come now.'

I was over to his office at the speed of light (186,000 miles per second).

It took thirty minutes and the deal was done. We acquired control, 37 per cent, of Hongkong Electric, for £300 million. The largest deal ever done in Hong Kong's history.

I later asked Simon Keswick why he had not agreed to sell the night before. His reply was that he wanted to see K.S. alone, because he knew I would show off and be very tough on the price in front of my boss! I did show off and was very tough because I knew he was desperate to sell. K.S. was over the moon and declared I should become the new chairman of Hongkong Electric immediately. I protested and said I was already working day and night trying to get a grip on the complexity of Hutchison's business. But he would not budge.

My first visitor, who called to congratulate me on my appointment as chairman of the electricity company, was none other than Lawrence of Shell. He bought a bottle of champagne which he insisted on opening and made a toast. I said thank you and then added, 'Lawrence, I have to say only this. I don't know for how long I will be the chairman of Hongkong Electric. It could be one year or ten; but I do know this. So long as I am in this chair, we will not take coal from Shell even if you give it to us free of charge. From now on the business goes to Total. I'm sorry. Thank you for the champagne.'

He may have chosen to forget that he had tried to do the dirty on me all those years before, but I never would. I have not spoken a single word to him from that day to this. Nor he to me. And that was thirty-five years ago.

The next few years were busy at Hutchison.

An early story concerned our one-time friends Centralsug, the very same people who ratted on our commission for getting them into the Hong Kong bank building with their central waste disposal system.

Hutchison had just embarked on a huge project of 14,000 apartments and I was discussing it with our property manager. He was very excited about this company Centralsug who could build centralised waste disposal systems and I told him it was fine with me. He authorised the architects to work with them and they were included in the design. At the last minute, I told K.S. about my row with them and how they had been treacherous over our commission on the bank job.

He said, 'What! These people bad to Simon. We cancel. We cancel now. Cannot do business with people who cannot be trusted, Simon. You tell them "No".'

I told our property manager that we could not go forward with the contract. He was to tell them it was not his fault, but the new CEO (me) had vetoed the deal and his name was Simon Murray, who had said Centralsug were not to be trusted.

They are probably planning my death as I write. But it is a good example of why K.S. and I got on so well: we held in highest regard the importance of honesty and integrity in our dealings with each other.

We negotiated to buy Husky Oil in Canada. It was K.S. Li's idea to get into the oil business, but my job to spend six months flying backwards and forwards between Hong Kong and Calgary trying to get the deal done. Endless meetings with twenty lawyers around the table negotiating a contract. I was advised by Stikeman Elliott, a prominent law firm with a lawyer called Frank Sixt at my side all the time. He was brilliant.

The market capitalisation of Husky, a public company, was around C$1 billion. The deal was made complicated by the Canadian government foreign investment regulations, which determined all natural resources should be 50 per cent owned by Canadians. We managed to get a Canadian passport for Victor Li, K.S.'s eldest son, and the deal was going to be done 57 per cent/43 per cent Hutchison and the Li family.

Yet more endless meetings followed with the Canadian authorities in

Ontario and then the pricing. K.S. had told me he would not pay one cent over C$11 a share. The Husky team, led by Art Price and Bob Blair, had made it clear they would not sell below C$12 a share.

I was flying to and from Calgary, a thirteen-hour flight on the dreaded Canadian airline that made a British Airways flight seem like a trip through heaven in comparison. Finally, we could go no further on the price differential. K.S. rang me from Hong Kong and said, 'Simon, not one cent over C$11 per share. If they cannot accept, come back now. Forget it.' This was after four months of negotiation. Canning Fok, who was an accountant and essentially my numbers man for the deal, appointed by K.S. to ensure I didn't go too high on the price, looked knackered and said forlornly with his voice full of despair, 'Come on Simon, let's go home.' I sent him home and said I had some business to do in the UK on the way back and would come the following day. Husky had a private plane and I sat down for a farewell drink with Bob and Art.

'We want to do this deal,' I began, 'and so do you and I know K.S. does as well. We are separated by C$1 per share. You have an office in Hong Kong on Pedder Street, on the opposite side of the road to K.S.'s office. If you fly to Hong Kong tonight via Tokyo, I will fly east and you will be in Hong Kong before me and I think I can get K.S. into a final meeting with you and maybe we can make this work.'

They agreed and flew westwards in their private plane that night. I flew east. I went to see K.S. as soon as I got to Hong Kong. I could see he was disappointed but he had put it behind him.

'Anyway, Simon, you work very hard on this and do a good job, but this time cannot win. You say goodbye to Bob and Art from me and maybe we meet again sometime.'

My turn to erupt. 'Oh no K.S., I'm not going to say goodbye for you. You must do that yourself. They have an office on the other side of the road and I know they have flown back from Calgary and they are there now. I think they will discuss the project with other people here in Hong Kong and the very least you can do is say goodbye to them yourself, after all this time.'

He was slightly shocked at my tone but he understood.

'Okay! Okay! We go together to say goodbye.'

Across the road we went. Thirty minutes later the deal was done at

C$11.80 and I became the joint chairman of Canada's largest fully integrated independent oil company. A long way from selling Avery Hardoll petrol pumps in Thailand. The oil price was US$12 a barrel at that time and it peaked over the next thirty-five years at US$120, until Husky's market value hit the moon. Ten minutes later, back in K.S.'s office, his secretary Ezra came in with two glasses of cognac on a silver tray. K.S. passed me one and took one himself.

'Simon, I'm very happy. You've done a very nice job. Thank you.'

<hr />

Sometime later, K.S. showed concern about the future when we were discussing 1997 and he asked me to find an investment to place spare money into the UK for safe keeping. Guided by investment bankers, we searched the UK for a safe investment and finally our attention alighted on Pearson. Pearson was a box full of wonderful assets. They owned The Economist, Madame Tussauds, Royal Doulton, Wedgwood, Chessington Zoo, Château Latour, the Financial Times, Longman publishing company and a host of other great brand names. My attention was particularly drawn to Château Latour.

We started creeping up on the stock, buying cautiously so as not to spur the share price. We had to go public when we got to 5 per cent and London went bonkers with the news. Some unknown company called Hutchison in Hong Kong was buying Pearson's. The sheer audacity of it. Who the hell was this guy Li Ka Shing? We got a bashing for it and some old stories resurfaced to the delight of some mischief-makers.

In 1984 K.S. Li had been judged 'culpable' of insider trading in Hong Kong. It was not illegal at the time but it was rewarded with a public slap across the wrist and obviously produced embarrassing, negative publicity. Normally a committee of three or four people would be formed by the Finance Secretary, in this case Piers Jacobs, to judge whether or not an accused was 'culpable' of insider trading. The word 'guilty' was avoided.

In the case of K.S. Li, he was found 'culpable'. I had just arrived on board at Hutchison when the verdict was given. After our first board meeting, K.S. was discussing the issue and was toying with the idea of an appeal to the Supreme Court in London, to overrule the 'culpable' verdict. His men around him, led by George Magnus, were all urging him to appeal. 'It was absolutely outrageous,' they declared, and the Supreme Court would most certainly overrule the conclusion reached by this ridiculous local committee.

He asked me my view and contrary to the advice being heaped upon him by his staff, I told him to forget it. The publicity the incident had received in Hong Kong was relatively mild; a few paragraphs in the *South China Morning Post* (in which Hutchison had a 25 per cent stake), and virtually nothing in the Chinese press. Insider trading after all was not uncommon in Hong Kong. In fact, on the contrary, it was common.

If, on the other hand he took it to the Supreme Court and he lost on appeal, it would hit the international press and particularly the press in London, like an earthquake.

I was new on the block. He chose to listen to the advice of his sycophantic howling dogs and took it to the Supreme Court. It became headline news in London. He lost the appeal and it was suddenly front-page news globally. He was after all one of the richest men on the planet. Insider trading: so this is how it's done is it? Not good news at all. He screamed at his underlings who had advised him to go to the Supreme Court and perversely, I gained extra marks as he shouted at them, 'Only Simon get it right. You all wrong...' Magnus and I had crossed swords. Not for the last time.

All this was dragged up again when the Pearson investment came to light. The Chinese often have difficulty with English names as indeed we do with Chinese names and sometimes they simply will not stay in our heads. It is like reading a Russian novel and somebody might ask you the name of the hero when you've finished it. You have seen the name written all the way through the book and recognised it every time it came up (something like Vanderliakov), but unless you read out loud, it does not stay in your memory and you are unable to repeat it.

Such was the case with K.S. He could never remember the name 'Pearson'. We even had a board member of one of our companies with the name Pearson, and K.S. could never remember it. He used to whisper across to me at meetings, 'Simon, what the name of that man on the right at the end of the table?'

'Pearson, K.S.' For that was indeed his name.

'Ah yes. Thank you.'

And as we continued our investment in Pearson, he used to ring me first thing in the morning.

'Simon, how we doing with that company?'

'Pearson, K.S.?'

'Yeah... the Pearson case.'

'We've got about 3 per cent K.S. So far it's cost us about £40 million.'

Pearson was controlled by the Cowdrey family into which Lord Blakenham had married; he was now the chairman. I explained to K.S. that it would be practical for us to have 20 per cent of the company in order that we could equity account the profits. Less than that and we could only bring in the dividend, over which we would have no say. Or we could make an outright bid for the whole company. If we did, they would probably fight us and bring in a big partner to bid against us. Lots of publicity.

K.S. had no appetite for a fight in the UK, even though we had the financial resources, primarily because he felt in some ways beholden to them vis à vis China. He wanted to be welcome. I thought I could perhaps persuade Lord Blakenham to allow us to settle with 20 per cent and no more, and I went to see him. By this time we were at 5 per cent and had announced it.

Blakenham was still getting over the fact that we had already got to 5 per cent without him realising it.

He was friendly but firm. It would not be 'friendly' if we went beyond our current holding; he could live with the 5 per cent but no more.

A few months later it was time for a General Election in the UK. We now had a considerable amount of money invested in the UK, with Felixstowe, Pearson and our own office in the West End; K.S. felt it wise to support whichever party was going to win. I was questioned on this and predicted a win for the Conservatives, so we made a contribution to their war chest.

Next, with help from my friend Algy Cluff, we received an invitation to lunch at 10 Downing Street after Mrs Thatcher had been elected Prime Minister. There were about twenty people around the dining room table and when we got to the coffee, Mrs Thatcher spoke and there was a hush. K.S. was sitting directly opposite her, the only non-Brit in the room. I was down at the other end of the table. The guests were heads of major companies in the UK. Mrs Thatcher began by saying, 'Now, I like to have these lunches two or three times a year, because I want to hear your views on how we are doing running the country, and to hear what you think we should be doing more of and what we should be doing less of. So please feel free to express your opinions. I really want to hear what you think.'

Total silence.

Mrs T.: 'Now come along, somebody start the ball rolling.'

And to my utter amazement K.S. dived in.

'Mrs Thatcher, I like to say, I think you're doing a very nice job. Already got rid of the unions and UK looking very good. We already making investments in UK and already invested £100 million.'

'Oh Mr Li, that's wonderful; and what's the name of the company you've invested in?' asked Mrs T.

Long pause from K.S. Then he shouted down the table to me, 'Simon. What the name of that company?'

'Pearson, K.S.'

There were roars of laughter from everybody, including K.S, although I don't think he will ever know why!

As time went by so the handover to China slowly crept nearer. And then, in 1989, the people of China rose up against the authorities in total rebellion against the ever-growing corruption. The rebellion was mostly sponsored by the young, particularly students, centred in Beijing in Tiananmen Square, but there was also chaos in many of the other big cities. Every day the protestors grew in number. The world watched in great excitement. All supporting them.

One person in China whom I knew reasonably well, was Zhao Ziyang, China's premier. He had visited our container terminal on one occasion. We regarded him as our 'friend' in China. He was destined to be Deng Xiaoping's successor. He was also the third vice-premier and general secretary of the Communist Party. He publicly showed some sympathy towards the students.

Mistake.

He was levered from office and never seen again.

There was a process known in Roman times as *damnatio memoriae* – condemnation of memory – and it is practised in China when the Party feels betrayed. Maximum shame is brought to bear on your family, which is airbrushed from history. He was never again seen in public. He died thirty years later in 2019 and is buried no one knows where. Dust. Unjust dust.

Eventually Deng had had enough. He ordered the army to clear the streets. The tanks arrived and the world watched in horror as they drove through the crowds in Tiananmen Square. Nobody ever claimed a definitive number dead. Some of the estimates were around 3,000. The world went into mourning. The lights went out on the Eiffel Tower in Paris. The bells tolled throughout the western world.

By coincidence I had invited the Foreign Legion band to come to Hong Kong. They arrived the day of the massacre. They stayed and played in Hong Kong for two weeks. It helped.

4 June 1989 will never be forgotten by the people of Hong Kong nor by the people of China. 1997 was now far too close and the Tiananmen Square incident had revved up a panic like the roar of a wounded tiger.

CHAPTER XXVIII

MOBILE TELEPHONES

In the 1980s, the largest companies around the world on any stock market were the government-controlled telephone companies. Mr Alexander Graham Bell had made them rich with his invention. There were as well, perhaps, security reasons why the governments controlled their telephone operators. The giants were British Telecom, France Télécom, Telecom Italia, Deutsche Telekom and so on. In America the anti-trust rules allowed private telephone companies to develop, such as AT&T and Bell. The manufacturers of telephone equipment were Ericsson, Motorola, Samsung, Nokia and others.

And suddenly the world welcomed the mobile phone. But the big boys resented the arrival. They couldn't believe that they were about to lose 70 per cent of their income over the next two decades. They were managed by bureaucrats who had never needed to think. They just collected revenues from customers who had no say, no choice, not even the means to complain of poor service.

All this was exemplified by British Telecom who had a subsidiary mobile telephone company called Cellnet, in which they had a 50 per cent share. The boss of Cellnet once told me that he had to book an appointment at least two weeks in advance to get to see his chairman, who, incidentally, had zero interest in what he was doing.

In Hong Kong in the mid-1970s while I was still at JEC, the government asked Cable and Wireless, a UK company which had a monopoly of the international telephone business in Hong Kong (and most other ex-British colonies), to do a survey on the estimated demand for mobile telephones in the event that a licence was issued. I received a questionnaire that simply said, if you could buy a mobile telephone for US$5,000 and every call was about 30 cents a minute, would you buy one?

Domestic telephone calls in Hong Kong at that time were free. The telephone company made money on installations, unlike their comrades in

Europe. Cable and Wireless charged about HK$7 a minute for international calls and shared a bit of that with the domestic telephone company.

The response to the Cable and Wireless survey was, unsurprisingly, distinctly negative.

Hutchison, however, just before I arrived, had the foresight to form a joint venture with an enthusiastic Canadian, who had entered the mobile market in Canada, by the name of Rick Siemens. His company was called Distacom and they persuaded Motorola from the USA to join and applied to the Hong Kong government, with Hutchison, for a licence.

Motorola were manufacturers, not operators. It would normally be counter-productive for them to be operators, as it could put them in competition with their own customers. But in Hong Kong, where they had no customers, they thought they could get away with it. This became their first investment, as operators in a minority position in the mobile telephone market.

In spite of Cable and Wireless's negative survey, the Hong Kong government, which had some very forward-thinking civil servants such as Anson Chan, granted the first mobile telephone licence in Hong Kong, and one of the first in the world, to the Hutchison consortium. Jardine Matheson, who had a minority stake in the Hong Kong telephone company of around 5 per cent, missed this one by a mile.

I arrived at Hutchison a week after the licence had been granted and had to give a speech to the news outlets that we were going ahead. In the middle of my speech somebody passed me a piece of paper on which it said, 'Cable and Wireless have just announced they are dropping their prices by HK$2 a minute.'

Nice one and very typical. This was not going to be a free ride.

Within eight months we had 33,000 customers. The hand-held telephone itself was the size of a wine bottle and nearly as heavy. People used to plonk them on the table in restaurants, which provided an air of affluence, and it was not long before plastic imitations were being made that were not real telephones at all but looked good on the table. We sold the genuine article at about US$3,000 a piece. They were certainly not for the masses at this stage.

The installation costs of the base-stations installed on the high rooftops of the buildings around Hong Kong were expensive, as the landowners squeezed us. Costs overall were high and we needed more users. Fortunately, at the same time, over a period of two years, mobile phone manufactures like Motorola and the Scandinavian boys were producing smaller telephones at lower costs.

There was also much development from analogue phones to digital with a constant increase in speed of transmission.

K.S. never warmed to our mobile telephone business and saw the revenue from the sale of the phones as a barometer of the business, which it was not. I urged him to look at the number of minutes the phones were used for as evidence of how the business was doing. I told him once that we should look forward to the day when we could give the telephones away free of charge and just live off the revenue from their calls. I was in the car with him one day when he made a call and then turned his phone off. I asked him why he did that.

'Simon, the person who pays for the call is the receiver of the call. I don't want people call me, because then I need to pay, Simon.' Emphasis on the final 'Simon'.

'I realise that, K.S., but the point is, the convenience that you can receive calls when you are not at home or in your office. That's what you are paying for.'

He was not an enthusiast and his lieutenants followed his lead.

As far as I was concerned, Rick Siemens was a visionary. He persuaded me to buy up all the paging companies in Hong Kong, of which there were six, and gradually we moved all the pagers on to mobile phones.

The business flourished in volume because we had an early start, but a good profit was still illusive.

I eventually bought Rick Siemens' shares but kept him on as managing director of the telephone company. Hutchison now had 80 per cent of the company and we were leading the way in mobile telephones in Hong Kong. I understood the long-term nature of this business and could see Rick's vision but the boys over at Cheung Kong could not; sadly, neither could K.S. They constantly complained about Rick's attitude and questioned why he had such a big office and so on, but I was totally on his side and gave him full support.

One day Rick produced a man called Michael Johnston. He was from South Africa where he claimed he had been a schoolmaster teaching astronomy He was a satellite observer and had become something of an expert on the subject. He proclaimed that we could run telephone services from a satellite, which would be a fraction of the cost of having earthbound base stations. He knew of a company called Pan Satellites that had launched a satellite at the cost of US$40 million and had insured it at Lloyd's. The satellite had gone rogue after launching and was swinging around in space. I was a 'name' at Lloyd's insurance at the time and fairly soon, we were completely *au fait* with the story.

Lloyd's had entered into an agreement by which NASA would send up another satellite with 'arms' on it to try to get the rogue satellite back. It had never been done before and the idea of a satellite with arms was a Canadian invention. NASA would charge Lloyd's US$10 million to get the rogue satellite back from space. Lloyd's agreed and the Canadian satellite with arms was launched.

It was a brilliant success. The rogue satellite was brought back to earth and Lloyd's handed it back to Pan Satellites. Cost to Lloyds – US$10 million instead of US$40 million (insurance claim). Sadly, in the interim, the Pan Satellite company had gone into liquidation and the satellite was sitting in the Hughes manufacturing company in America, 'for sale'.

Michael Johnston had persuaded Rick Siemens that we should buy it. More importantly the China Great Wall Industry Corporation (CGWIC) could launch it for us at a fraction of the price that NASA would charge. All this information was coming to us via Johnston, who was working with a mysterious woman employed by CGWIC. We bought the satellite for US$8 million after Hughes had repaired it.

At this time, there were only two western companies that could launch satellites, NASA and Arianne which was a French satellite company based in French Guiana, guarded incidentally by a regiment of the French Foreign Legion.

CGWIC had launched many satellites for China, but never for a foreign entity. We had numerous discussions with them, via this woman, and they were finally okay that Hong Kong was part of China, and for this launch we would be considered as domestic. It would cost us US$20 million.

Then to deal with the Americans.

I finally convinced Hughes that if China could launch their satellites at a much lower cost than their own people or the French, then they would sell more satellites. Then I had endless meetings with the Trade Department in America, the CIA, my friend Henry Kissinger, the embassy people in Hong Kong; finally we got the okay. There was one condition: we had to take twenty-five marines to be with the satellite the whole way through the journey.

The French, as part of CoCom (The Coordinating Committee for Multilateral Export Controls), then got involved and also objected. More visits to the French Consul General in Hong Kong. A bit about the Foreign Legion and 'honneur et fidélité' and we were once again through the gate.

The week before the launch I went in to tell K.S. what was happening. He had followed the narrative since the beginning but had shown very little interest and certainly no excitement.

'K.S., we are launching the satellite next week from Chengdu, so I hope you'll be ready for that.'

He looked up from his desk and said, 'Who's coming from the Hong Kong government?'

I said, 'No one's coming from the Hong Kong government. I haven't asked anybody. It's nothing to do with the Hong Kong government.'

And he said, 'Well Simon, I don't think I need to come then.'

'Just a second K.S. You should be asking me who's coming from the Chinese government, not the Hong Kong government', my voice rising slightly higher than I meant it to.

'Who's coming from the Chinese government?'

'Well! Li Peng is coming and they'll be…'

'What! Li Peng's coming… I'm coming, Simon… I'm coming.'

We flew to the Great Wall launching site.

I had seen American satellite launches on television, but this was different. We were not locked down in trenches 400 yards from the launch pad. This was far from what was anticipated. Spectators were all over the surrounding hills eating picnics as though we were about to watch a football match. In the middle was this colossal rocket on the launch pad which was so near you felt you could simply climb on board. No security, except for our marines sitting on the back of trucks at a distance of 500 yards. The whole thing was so relaxed. I expected a guy to come out with a box of Bryant and May matches, light the fuse at the bottom of the rocket and up she would sail. We were eventually ushered into an underground room full of screens and gadgets and 'bingo', up she went, with screams and clapping and cheers and a roar of engines like the start of a Formula One race.

K.S. was overjoyed. On the way home we chatted away and I learned that he had never been to Beijing or Shanghai. He had only been to Shenzhen. He was staggered that I had first come to China in 1970. He hadn't realised I knew so many people in China. I was equally flabbergasted that he had never been north of Canton. Based on his conversations over previous lunches with foreign visitors, I had assumed that he practically owned China. I remarked that as we had made no investments in China, the Chinese might feel that the reason was because we didn't trust them.

'No,' he said.' I don't want to do business in China, Simon, because if it goes wrong we will fight them and that will be very bad for our relationship.'

'Yes', I replied, 'I can understand that, but I still think that they think that we don't trust them. Other Hong Kong companies have invested in China. Even Jardine's has invested there.'

He took it on board.

CHAPTER XXIX

REUNIONS

I arrived, as one does eventually, at the ripe old age of fifty.

While I was away on a trip to Turkey, Jeffa got busy and organised, unbeknownst to me, a huge black-tie party to celebrate my fiftieth birthday. There were no less than 300 people, in a marquee tent with a fantastic band, in the grounds of our house in Somerset, with friends that I had known all my life, including a table full of *des amis de France*.

When we were all seated, Jeffa stood up in her beautiful yellow dress to welcome everybody and said, 'We are not all here yet. Some of you will have read Simon's book, *Legionnaire*, and will have read in the epilogue about his rendezvous at midnight on New Year's Eve in 1965 with two of his old Legion chums, Eduardo de Soto and Daniel Vignaga, at the statue of the Manneken Pis in Brussels, after they had left the Legion. The arrangement had been made in the Algerian mountains at three o'clock in the morning three years before they left and was never discussed again. They all left the Legion at different times, at least a year apart, and they had not seen or heard from each other since those days in Algeria.

'Everybody told Simon not to go to go to Brussels believing his friends would not be there. They had not discussed the idea again nor seen each other since Legion days. He went anyway and I went with him. We waited in a little café opposite the statue of the Manneken Pis. The rendezvous was for midnight. We were the only two in the bistro and it was pouring with rain and the bells of Brussels' churches rang into the night as the New Year arrived. Very romantic for Simon and I who had just become engaged to be married.

'But no sign of his friends.

'At 1:30am it was clear that they were not coming and we were about to go back to our hotel, when down the road and through the rain, a voice yelled "Johnny!"

'It was Soto. He had hitch-hiked all the way from Barcelona.

'It was the most wonderful moment. On a par with the meeting of Stanley and Livingstone. We stayed for three more hours waiting for Vignaga but he didn't make it. Simon kept in touch with Soto for a few years and they would meet up in Paris every year and then one day Soto disappeared and Simon has not seen or heard from him since.

'The good news is that both Soto and Vignaga are alive and well and, are here with us tonight...'

At this moment the door opened and in marched three legionnaires in full dress uniforms with rifles, and behind them Soto and Vignaga in black tie, with hair now grey. It was jet black when I had last seen them. General Loridon came in behind them in full dress uniform, medals and all. He had been a lieutenant with us so many years before. At full volume Edith Piaff was singing 'Non je ne regrette rien', which she had dedicated to the Legion.

Jeffa had been amazing: without telling me, she had asked General Loridon, with whom I had kept in touch, to see if he could find Soto and Vignaga. He had found then through Interpol, one in Geneva and one in Madrid.

There was not a dry eye in the house. A reunion like no other. A surprise like no other. At 3am, the party still raging, I discretely took Vignaga and Soto into my library. We turned to Vignaga and asked him why he had not made it to the Manneken Pis. He agreed to tell us on the condition we swore not to tell a soul. And being true to my word, I will never disclose that reason which he gave us. The whole party: Jeffa's thoughtfulness and planning, Vignaga and Soto's arrival with General Loridon and our conversations in the library, are moments which will live with me forever.

~~~

The satellite launch was a success and we formed a company together with CITIC (CITIC Group Corporation Ltd., formerly the China International Trust Investment Corporation, is a state-owned investment company of the People›s Republic of China, established by Rong Yiren in 1979) and Cable and Wireless, called Asiasat. I alternated annually with Wang Jun, the head of CITIC, as chairman. The joint venture prospered not in the least for the reason that we discovered we could run television services off the satellite, which we had not known originally.

We started Star TV and covered a vast territory over tracts of China, India and the Middle East and we formed a joint venture with BBC Overseas. It was not a financial success because of the lack of advertising revenue. We forced some of the merchant banks, who were constantly approaching us with deals, to assist, or they wouldn't get to see K.S. Tough? Yes, but one's got to make a living. However, advertising merchant banking services over southern India did not yield any recognisable benefits to the bankers and they eventually gave up.

We did use it for mobile telephone connectivity.

We put K.S.'s younger son, Richard, in charge of it and he eventually sold it to Rupert Murdoch for US$400 million and started another satellite TV station, called NOW, to be run by Michael Johnston.

When I told K.S. that we had sold it for $400 million, he assumed I was talking Hong Kong dollars and nearly died when I told him it was US dollars. Richard rightly got the credit for it, and his father's reward to him personally was US$400 million. But he could afford it, so why not? it was his money.

Prior to this, through an introduction from Henry Kissinger I had flown to Denver and spent the day with Warren Buffett, one of the most successful businessmen in the world. Just before my departure, K.S. had asked me if I would take Richard along for the experience. To spend the entire day with Warren Buffett was indeed a fascinating experience. He ran his empire from a small office, aided by two elderly ladies and that seemed to be it. I received a lot of Warren Buffett business philosophy during the day. Never to be forgotten.

He was the largest shareholder in ATV and we discussed the possibility of working with them through our own Star TV business; he was very amenable and said he would get back to me on it. When we returned to Hong Kong, Richard contacted ATV, without waiting for Buffett's go ahead, and told them Buffett had authorised him to discuss programme acquisition and other matters, which he had not. I heard later that Buffett was furious that Richard had used his name before he himself had discussed it with his own people and that was that. He never wanted to hear from us again. A potentially wonderful relationship had been blown out of the water.

And later again a repeat. Rupert Murdoch was going through a difficult patch with his company and I was approached through an intermediary to meet with him. Richard and I were still in the States, so we met with Murdoch at News Corporation in New York. Murdoch, with a lawyer in tow, told us the situation with his company and said the door was open if we would like to invest. He gave us the numbers in detail. I had told Richard to say nothing but listen. With our new television company, our satellite business, our substantial holding in the South China Morning Post, there were plenty of areas of potential cooperation. I liked him as well. It is always helpful to have good chemistry. He suggested a private placement to us for a percentage of his business at a discount. The timing was good.

Richard returned to Hong Kong before I did and gave a very negative report on Rupert to his father; K.S. told me he was not interested in taking it forward when I got back. That was that.

Over the next year News Corp's share price trebled. We had sold them Star TV and the South China Morning Post for a massive sum, so the meeting paid off but it could have yielded much greater rewards if we had bought into News Corp.

Hutchison and the Hong Kong Shanghai Bank owned collectively, but separately, 70 per cent of the South China Morning Post, the main local English newspaper in Hong Kong. I was on the board. They often published negative reports on the major local corporations, such as HSBC, Swire's and indeed Hutchison. K.S. finally sued them. When I told him he was suing me, we both agreed it was time for me to exit the Post's board.

The sale to Murdoch was timely.

CHAPTER XXX
HELICOPTERS AND GOODBYES

K.S. had a habit of calling me when I was on holiday in Europe with an urgent request that I return to Hong Kong for multiple reasons and frequently I would get a helicopter to come and collect me from the depths of the French countryside in the Dordogne, where we had bought some property (Jardine housing loan!).

On one of my rides, I asked the pilot if his was a profitable business. He said it was. I then asked him how many helicopters his company had. The answer was six. Would he make more money if he had another helicopter? Yes! And if I bought a helicopter and let him run it, would he come and pick me up and fly me anywhere at any time? Yes! 'Okay, I'll buy a helicopter and you can manage it. Done.'

I bought a second-hand Robinson R44 helicopter through Quentin Smith who ran a helicopter company at Denham and who also gave flying lessons. I set out to become a helicopter pilot. It took me a year because I had so little time to train. I used to come in from Hong Kong, drive to Denham, have a lesson from Quentin for an hour and then rush to London for the business of the day. Q., as we called Quentin, was a terrific pilot, but it was going to take time because of the long intervals between lessons.

I told Jeffa that she should have a few lessons as well and do what Q. called the 'wives' course, so that in the event I had a heart attack at the wheel, she would at least have the ability to get us down. While I was in Hong Kong, she went to the airport at Denham every day for a month and ended up with forty-five hours of flying in her logbook and a brand-new, fully-fledged licence. It was another eight months before I finally got mine.

The next thing I knew, she was planning to fly the Robinson around the world with Q. to become the first woman to circumvent the globe in a helicopter. But Jeffa was not recognised by *The Guinness Book of Records* as the first woman around the world because she had a male co-pilot with her.

Three years later she went again and did fly around the world solo, accompanied by our friend Colin Bodil who was flying solo in a microlight alongside her, and also breaking a world record. This time Guinness took it on board. But I don't think that *The Guinness Book of Records* was Jeffa's motivation: she loved flying and she was talented at it. From then on Colin and she were constantly plotting their next flight and frequently working with charities to raise funds for them through their exploits.

~~⌒~~

Meanwhile back at the coal face, Hutchison had managed to get a mobile telephone licence for the UK. We were debating what the brand name should be. Hutchison Telephone sounded very dull. I gave the task to Ogilvy and Mather and they made a presentation. They left the brand name until the end of their presentation; they finally lifted a curtain, rather like a magician finishing a trick, and there was the word 'ORANGE'.

Magnus and Canning from Cheung Kong, whom I had invited to the presentation, didn't like it and didn't grasp it. But Rick and I loved it and Orange it was going to be. Apple was by this time roaring around the world and now an orange was to follow. And it did.

~~⌒~~

We opened telephone operations in India. Again, K.S. was not really interested. He said he, like most Chinese, had a negative view on India. We had already formed a joint venture with an Indian partner and at K.S.'s insistence, we sold our shares back to him for US$26,000, which is what we had invested.

We eventually became very big in the mobile telephone business. Orange was a world leader. The container business flourished, and so did our retailing which we had now spread to Singapore, Taiwan and the UK.

We had also gone into China and acquired the container port of Shanghai. I had previously bought the Hilton Hotel, located on the Hong Kong side, from Cheung Kong and we already owned the Sheraton in Kowloon. So we were also in the hotel business. My days at Harry Wicking were turning out to be useful. We acquired the Sheraton Hotel in Shanghai, to which I invited David Copperfield for the opening. He was terrific. Practically made the bloody hotel disappear!

But as in all businesses, there were politics. The boys at Cheung Kong were jealous of my independence and indeed my great relationship with K.S. and would not miss a chance to dilute it. Sadly, this jealousy wove its way into the spirit of K.S.'s eldest son, Victor. He saw himself as the logical successor at Cheung Kong and Hutchison and why not? But I worked for his father and was honoured to do so. K.S.'s son Richard started his own business with an insurance company and he asked me to be a director of it. I accepted and we got on well but the same could not be said regarding my relationship with Victor.

We bought the Expo site in Canada after the exhibition in 1986. I had tried to bring in a local partner, Bell Canada, but they reneged at the last minute and we went in with a small local partner to give it a Canadian flavour; plus, of course, we now had our own Canadian, Victor Li. So he could be useful.

It cost us C\$300 million and we flooded it with apartments and did well. K.S. in one of his many generous moments let some of us invest alongside.

Memories of the tales of the late Sir William Mather in Paris after the French Expo in 1889, when he had bought the steel-framed buildings that had housed the exhibition and shipped them back to Manchester.

And then there was an incident that had occurred earlier and throws some light on my so-called 'colleague', George Magnus.

Some years earlier, K.S.'s mother had died and Canning Fok came to see me after the funeral and said that under Chinese tradition, there would be another ceremony exactly three months after she had died and I should definitely be there. He had been told this by one of the older directors. All directors should be there. Compulsory attendance.

The day arrived. In the morning, I was at a budget meeting of ParknShop, our supermarket business, at Shatin on the Kowloon side of town. The ceremony for K.S.'s mother was to take place at her old house on the Hong Kong side and was about an hour's drive from the head office of ParknShop. It was due to start at 3pm.

In the middle of the budget discussion, a secretary came in to say that George Magnus, who was attending the meeting, was wanted on the telephone. He came back five minutes later to say he was wanted back at the office, grabbed his papers and rushed out like a man late for an appointment with the emperor.

The time was 11am. Canning and I looked at each other for a moment and both raised our eyes towards the ceiling. Typical Magnus. Canning had no time for him either.

Later I was sitting in my office at my desk, back on the Hong Kong side, at around 2pm, when Canning walked in. His face was dark as thunder and he looked quite ill.

'The feng shui man brought the ceremony forward to 12:30pm, so we missed it. That telephone call to Magnus was to tell him, and he deliberately didn't share the message with us,' he groaned.

I was ready to puke.

This guy Magnus was supposed to be the deputy chairman of the company. I said to Canning, 'I'm going to resign. I am not working in a company with a creep like this as our deputy chairman. It makes me sick.'

Canning went off back to the Cheung Kong office. Unbeknownst to me, he told Ezra, K.S.'s secretary, that I was going to resign. Half an hour later K.S. was yelling down the phone, 'Simon, no problem you couldn't make it this morning. Feng shui man change it. Simon, not your fault, no need to worry Simon. No problem Simon. Don't worry. I know you working very hard on budget meeting. No problem...'

I cut him off and said, 'K.S., I'm sorry, but I will not work with people like George Magnus, who received a telephone call saying the time had changed and didn't tell us; deliberately, so that Canning and I would miss the ceremony, but he would be there. Sorry K.S., I cannot work with people like this.'

He continued telling me not to worry and all was fine and he would deal with Magnus.

Later, Canning told me that K.S. was screaming at Magnus across the office and saying, 'If this is how you treat people in the office, what are you like with people outside the office?'

Magnus rang me later and started to make excuses. I told him to 'fuck off' and slammed the phone down on him.

The next day K.S. asked me to go to his office. I walked over and Magnus was waiting at the lift as I stepped out. He must have known I was coming over and was spewing out excuses for his behaviour the previous day as we walked to K.S.'s office. He followed me into the office. K.S. was on the telephone and waved me to sit down on the sofa while he finished his call. Magnus sat beside me, pretending he was in discussion with me. I wasn't listening. K.S. came over and looked at him and said, 'Yes, George, what you want?'

Magnus said he was with me. K.S. freaked out and started shouting, 'Not you, George. It's Simon I want to speak to. Simon. Please George. You got nothing? Then please go, George. NOW! PLEASE!'

George sloped out, trying to make it look like a trivial routine matter. The door was wide open. Everybody heard the whole encounter. He had been castrated in public and he deserved it. K.S. was very anxious that I was not going to resign and I assured him all was okay.

Eventually he felt all was back to normal. But it pushed my thoughts towards the exit.

I stayed for a total of ten years. Ten great years and the company grew to about five times the size of Jardine Matheson, which gave me some satisfaction. Then I told K.S. I wanted to move on. He pleaded with me to stay, but I said working for him was one thing but now the boys were growing up and they would take over and want to appoint their own people. He brushed it aside.

But I was insistent that I wanted to leave and it filtered into the market. I sought advice from Robert Kuok, an old friend originally introduced by Charles Letts, once the king of the sugar trade, now the owner of Shangri-La hotels. He had been a good friend for years, although I did not see him often. Robert was a multi-billionaire with shipping and trading interests as well as the wonderful worldwide network of Shangri-La hotels. He had originally bought the Trader Vic's hotel in San Francisco. Robert probably understood China better than anyone in Hong Kong and had superlative intelligence on the country.

I decided to go and see him about the relationship with K.S.'s two sons who were constantly getting between myself and their father. K.S. always sided with me in our growing number of disputes, but would that last? Robert was very sanguine but felt at the end of the day, as we all know, 'Blood is thicker than many other things.' I went to see the old man and told him that his sons were waiting to stand at the wheel. K.S. was approaching sixty-four and pressed upon me that he would never retire, and there was no way I should feel that it was time to leave.

I brought it up every few months for another year and he finally realised I meant it.

I was approached by Deutsche Bank with an offer to become executive chairman of their Asia-Pacific operations. I hadn't been into a bank in years, but they went on and on and they had done some deep research, it transpired.

I finally accepted.

A Singapore newspaper printed on its front page 'Murray to join Deutsche Bank'. It had leaked out through the bank from its headquarters in Singapore. I told K.S. and he at last accepted that it was going to happen. He called a group of us together.

'Simon going to leave. Richard to be new managing director of Hutchison. Victor become managing director of Cheung Kong. Canning become director of Hutchison. And Simon you stay as non-executive of Cheung Kong and Hutchison.'

All done.

Later that day Richard came to see me. He said he had told his father he didn't want to be the MD of Hutchison if he had to take Canning along, because everybody would assume Canning was there to be his overseer. His father had replied, 'It's with Canning in tow or you don't get the job.' He refused again. Canning became CEO.

Canning was a good accountant and he would be an excellent watch dog for the old man. And that is exactly what he became.

Meanwhile, I had reached another fork in the road and was about to embark on a new adventure as a banker.

CHAPTER XXXI

THE FUTURE IS BRIGHT

Three months after I left Hutchison, Rick Siemens left as well. He couldn't stand working for Canning. He had formed a company using the old name Distacom and asked if I would like to invest and join the board. I did both. Deutsche Bank had no objections to my joining outside boards. It could lead to new clients.

Distacom, led by Rick, was a great success. We invested in a Japanese telephone company and did well out of it and we started a mobile company in Madagascar which we later sold for a very good return. Temasek of Singapore, where we had an old relationship, bought shares in Distacom and joined the board. We linked up with our ex-partner in India, who had bought back their shares for a song because K.S. had not been interested in telephones at the time, and we formed Mumbai Telephone and another company in southern India.

One day, K.S. called me in and I found myself in a room full of his executives. He complained that I had sold our investment in India to Rick Siemens while we were both still in the company. I explained what had really happened and reminded him he had told me he had no interest in the Indian market, which is why I had reluctantly returned Hutchison's shareholding to our Indian partner. He refused to accept this and Canning and Magnus supported his memory of events.

'Simon, I never tell you to sell the shares back to our partner. Canning, George, you hear me say that to Simon?'

'No. No. No. We never heard you tell Simon to sell those shares.'

Then Richard, K.S.'s son, suddenly interrupted and said, 'Yes you did, father. I was in the room when you said it.'

Good old Richard. I was grateful for his support and I admired him for standing up to his father and his cronies. He had given me a Porsche as a farewell present when I left Hutchison. He was generous and he was plucky. His tenacity and good business sense would pay off later too.

When things had calmed down, I told K.S. that Rick and I had invested long after we had both left Hutchison but if he wanted to come back in, I could probably offer him 40 per cent. He answered yes. The mobile telephone business was running fast throughout the world by this time and even the big old kings of yore like BT and AT&T in the States had come bounding in years after the starting bell had rung.

Rick and I discussed it with our Indian friend. The capital costs were rising as we expanded the business and we needed cash. We sold 40 per cent to Hutchison and they more or less took over the Mumbai business. Distacom expanded in other areas too, including operations in Hong Kong which we named 'Sunday', and later sold to Richard Li for US$65 million. We eventually sold out our shares in Mumbai for US$124 million and Hutchison took it over with Essar as their new partners. We sold all our interest for a gain of about US$700 million. But we were early. My shareholding was quite small. Too small. But Rick Siemens was a hero and Distacom was a total win.

Years later Vodafone bought out Hutchison in India at a valuation of US$19 billion. Yes, that's billion: not a misprint. I was the one who persuaded Essar to allow the deal to happen. And Orange was sold to Mannesmann in Germany for US$30 billion. All the mumblings of discontent by K.S. Li and his cohorts in the early days had paradoxically resulted in incredible rewards for the company.

Essar stayed in the Indian operation with a 40 per cent interest and later, John Bond, the chairman of Vodafone, had asked me if I could help bring the acquisition of Hutchison's shareholding in the company in India to a close. This needed Essar's blessing. Essar were initially against doing business with Vodafone and very unhappy with Hutchison for getting them involved.

I was not a director of Vodafone at the time, but I knew the Essar controlling family well as they had been clients of Deutsche Bank, so I went to see them. Ravi Ruia, the boss of Essar, agreed to come to a lunch that I arranged with Bond in London. At that time, he had never met Bond and he had a very poor view of Vodafone as a partner. He was seething over the fact that Hutchison had approached them without coming to Essar first. It was a cordial lunch, over which Bond agreed several points about which Ravi was concerned and the deal was done. Essar finally accepted the transaction between Hutchison and Vodafone, with themselves agreeing to stay in with their 40 per cent minority position.

I later suggested to Ravi that Essar should include a 'put option' to sell their shares to Vodafone in the future in case things went wrong in the relationship. Always be prepared for another fork in the road! The 'put option' was ultimately agreed at US$5 billion for their 40 per cent. They did not pay me for this advice, nor did I ask them to.

After the deal was done Bond asked me to join the Vodafone board. It was a three-year marriage and there were some good times. I played a leading role in their investment in Qatar. I knew Sheikha Moza. I had actually presented her with her honorary degree at Imperial College, where I was the chairman of the advisory board, and got to know her through her advisor, the one and only Tidu Maini.

I also helped Vodafone in their purchase of a government telephone company in Ghana, with the help of my friend Benjamin Ntim, the son of the Minister of Communications. We had been outbid at auction by France Télécom, who were advised by Goldman Sachs. Their offer was $700 million higher than ours. Well done Goldman Sachs! Ben introduced me to the President of Ghana and after an unforgettable lunch he decided it was not all about money and Vodafone's offer was better for multiple reasons, even at a lower price. Later we learned that France Télécom had been trying to get out of the deal, having bid twice as much as us, so ultimately it was a most agreeable outcome for all.

But then the cracks began to show. Vodafone reneged on the agreement with Essar on a number of issues. The chief financial officer of the company was to be appointed by Essar but Vodafone appointed the CFO and refused to budge. The relationship began to slide. The company was to be called Vodafone-Essar. Vodafone dropped the 'Essar' six months after the marriage.

Essar eventually 'put' their shares to Vodafone. We had a rowdy discussion in my office. I was the arbitrator. John Bond walked out of the meeting in a huff. But we got there and had finalised it at a sum of US$5 billion for Essar's 40 per cent, that had been agreed.

Essar also had a substantial energy business in India and Africa. They took their company public in the UK and asked me to be a director. I accepted and then was challenged by John Bond for supporting them against Vodafone. He said it was Essar or Vodafone.

I explained that I had been offered a directorship in Essar's energy business, not the telephone side and there was no conflict of interest. Actually, I would have been a good friend at court for Vodafone. But Bond simply said it was Vodafone or Essar and if it was Essar I would have to resign. I did. I had helped Vodafone directly with their business in Ghana and also Qatar through personal relationships, but Bond was not prepared to recognise this. I was relieved to be out.

Now they understood that there was money in telephones, Hutchison bought a licence in the UK for a mobile telephone service for £4 billion. They called it 3. After lunch one day, I told K.S. that the name 3 wasn't a good idea but he wouldn't agree. I explained the current telephones had 2G technology and eventually as speed increased in the system, it would go to 3G and 4G and even 5G and so on. He didn't understand what I was talking about. They lost millions of pounds in the UK in the first five years of operations. All that they had gained from their previous sales to Mannesmann went out of the window. We mourn.

Richard Li on the other hand made a fortune in telephones.

In the years of steamy excitement about techy stocks, around the millennium, Richard exchanged a tech company stock that he had acquired, for control of Cable and Wireless's business in Hong Kong. It was the deal of the century. Cable and Wireless made 60 per cent of their global profits in Hong Kong and they exchanged the whole thing for what turned out to be a bag of nails. The late Eric Sharp, whom I had known well and had been the chairman of Cable and Wireless before he retired, and also our partner in Asiasat, was a brilliant man but surrounded by goons. He would be turning in his grave.

It happens often. When my friend Arnold Weinstock retired as chairman of GEC, he too was replaced by goons who took the company down a Cresta run. In America, same story; Jack Welsh retired from G.E., whom I had known so well as investors in Davenham, and his successor Immelt led the company on a long, weary, downhill path. Succession is so critical in business but so often it is neglected by partisan directors.

CHAPTER XXXII

ADVENTURES

Life was by no means all business. There were at least ten items still on my bucket list and I had already ticked off climbing two mountains and running a marathon. Some years previously I had done the Everest trek to the Base Camp at 18,000 feet. But it was boring. It was full of tourists, all marching along the same track. I have always advocated taking the path less trodden, and in the case of Everest, it is all too well trodden. Jeffa and I had climbed Annapurna with the team at Jardine's and that – with fewer people – had been much more fun, and a challenge I would more readily recommend than Everest. I had also run the 100km race in Hong Kong, known as the MacLehose Trail. It was actually quite tough: and I say that as an ex-legionnaire and seasoned runner. Don't forget that both Jeffa and I had run the London Marathon back in 1982 when we had had a combined age of 84!

In 1998, a small group from Hong Kong were planning to run the *Marathon des Sables* and asked me to be their patron (a non-participating patron, but helping by raising money). The Marathon des Sables is the 'big daddy' of them all, described by Google as the toughest race on earth. 251km across the Moroccan desert over six days. Effectively six consecutive marathons over six days, and participants must carry their own food and kit. They are given two litres of water every four hours. Take it or leave it but if you ask for water at any time because you have run out, you are disqualified.

It is in your interest to take the two litres, although it weighs when you are running in sand at temperatures of over forty degrees centigrade. At the end, most participants had each consumed 120 litres of water. Twenty litres a day. That is a lot of water.

I had flown to Morocco from London with Q. in the R44 helicopter. It was enormous fun flying across the Mediterranean.

Whilst we were lying in the sand watching the runners struggling past, Q. said, 'I bet you couldn't do that, Simon. Not now. Yes, in the old days when you were a legionnaire but not now, at nearly sixty.'

I replied, 'I bet I could,' and made up my mind to do it the following year.

I went to see Paul Bauer, the founder of the race, when it was over and signed on for the following year. He was delighted.

A year later as I was approaching my sixtieth birthday, I was ready to run it with a friend, Robert Stein, a colleague from Deutsche Bank. We had trained by running roughly fifty miles a week. It was not really enough but we made it. 'Tough' is an understatement. My friend Silas Chou was at the winning post to cheer us in with a bunch of beautiful girls in tow from Hong Kong. It made it all worthwhile.

Then I formed a small group of friends including Riccardo from Italy, Karl Abawatt from Lebanon, Vincent Pang from China, and myself, and we started climbing mountains and going on expeditions. We did a month in Tibet. One mountain a day, then two weeks in the Atlas Mountains in Morocco. Then there were three weeks in the Algerian mountains, with me telling our guide where to go.

An incident occurred in Algeria, which could have made our stay much longer. We were arrested on our last day in a crowded café and taken to the gendarmerie. Heavy questioning followed for over three hours with me in the hot seat speaking French. They had four gendarmes with machine guns watching over us. When we were led into the gendarmerie, one of the gendarmes had stuck a pistol in my head, an experience I had not had since the sergeant Reiper had caught me napping on night-guard duty so many years previously.

They were convinced we were spies. How come I knew the mountains so well? Our guide had told them I knew the mountains better than he did (the little shit). What were we looking for? We would be kept there for six months if I did not confess, declared the head gendarme aggressively.

And so there was nothing else for it but a bit of quick thinking to try and lighten the mood. I told the senior officer doing the interrogation that he looked like Daniel Day-Lewis.

'Who he?' he barked in his Algerian French.

'An important Hollywood film star,' I replied.

There were roars of applause from the machine gunners and a definite change in the prevailing atmosphere.

But the senior was still probing how I knew the mountains so well. In the name of Allah, how could I know the mountains better than the mountain guide? And so I told him that I knew the mountains because I had climbed them before he was born.

He stood up ramming his thumb into his chest shouting, 'I am fifty-one years old!'

'I was here fifty-seven years ago,' I stated in a very quiet voice.

They all looked aghast. 'You were born here?' he asked aggressively.

'La Légion Étrangère,' I said,

There was a long silence. Then they all stood up together and saluted. It was an amazing and wonderful moment. I was very moved. They didn't hate the Legion. They respected it and maybe admired it. Instant friendship! They said the road ahead was dangerous and they would give us an escort for the next 50km over the mountains. Lots of hand shaking followed together with invitations to come back soon.

When I had marched through the hills of Algeria so many years before, I had often wondered whether one day I would come back to these beautiful lands in better circumstances: and here I was. It was another memory I would cherish and never forget.

⌇∽⌇

A year later we climbed Mount Kilimanjaro. All good times and more than half the bucket list already emptied.

And then there was another little adventure in colder climes introduced by my wife. Jeffa and Colin had decided to attempt another gigantic helicopter challenge. A flight around the world from the South to the North Pole. If they made it, they would be the first to do so. It was exciting.

Up until now, getting sponsors for their trips and indeed providing additional cash to fill the 'need' box, had been left to me. BP had financed one of their earlier jaunts, but there was always a cash gap at the end of the fund-raising, waiting to be filled. For this trip, Bell helicopters had agreed to supply the helicopter, but they needed much more money to get things moving and I had to insure the helicopter apart from anything else.

Jeffa had worked her socks off securing sponsorship and support, but they also plotted to get me involved, possibly with the thinking that it could lead to a revival of financial support from me too.

One sunny morning at breakfast at our house in the Dordogne, as we zoomed in on the croissants, Jeffa asked me if I had ever thought of walking to the South Pole. When you have been married for nearly forty years and your wife suddenly suggests you walk to the South Pole, you need to pause before answering. The way forward is to stuff the croissant into your mouth and chew while you start thinking. After a good chew, I said, 'Funnily enough, I haven't given it much thought.'

The first moving picture I had ever seen was *Scott of the Antarctic* with John Mills as the star. It was in 1949, my first year at Bedford. Since then, I don't think I had given more than two seconds thought to the South Pole, if that. And here was my wife suggesting that I should walk there. I didn't even know where it was. Yes, somewhere down south, but the Pole could be anywhere.

'So why are you suggesting this?'

'Because as you know, Colin and I are flying there and we thought it might be fun to meet you at the Pole.'

'Yes, but I don't have a clue how to get there.'

'Well, I've asked Pen Hadow to come and stay and he's been there many times and he's going to tell us about the snow conditions at the Pole.'

'You've asked him to come and stay... here?'

'Yes. He's arriving today.'

'Jesus! Well thank for letting me know.'

'What he does, darling, is he flies people to within sixty miles of the Pole and then he walks them in for the last part, over a period of about six days. You'd love it.'

Later that day I flew the helicopter to Bordeaux and picked up Pen. In the flight back we were chatting away and I was showing him the controls and I said, 'Jeffa, my wife, says you go regularly to the South Pole.'

And he said, 'Well, no! I've never actually been there.'

I held the helicopter steady as we did a bit of a nosedive.

'But you have been to Antarctica, yes?'

'No, I haven't. I've been to the Arctic Circle and have been trying to get to the North Pole for fifteen years, but never made it.'

The rest of the flight home was quiet.

We had lunch and began our journey through three bottles of Léoville Barton. By the time we had finished, Pen and I were going to the South Pole and training began the next day. And we were not flying to within sixty miles and then walking, we were going to walk the whole God-damned way. 780 miles.

The main training comprised harnessing six car tyres and dragging them like a sledge around the countryside for ten miles a day.

For a year I did ferocious training every day. Runs, car tyres, the gym, abdominal exercises and I dropped alcohol completely. Pen took me through the swamps of Dartmoor for a few days in the depths of winter, unbeknownst to me to see if I was made of the right stuff. Temperatures at zero. Swimming across rivers and sleeping on the moors. Abseiling down vertical rock faces and training on how to climb out of crevasses. All in preparation for what was to come.

Pulling the car tyres around the French countryside led to some amusing encounters. Cars would stop and the drivers would ask me in French, 'Lost your car, have you?' and 'When did you get out?' – of the asylum!

And 'Where are you going?'

'I'm training to walk to the South Pole.'

'Well you're going in the wrong direction my friend, it's the other way to the South Pole.'

All the time the drivers and their passengers, splitting themselves with laughter at the sight of this totally mad Englishman dragging car tyres along the highway.

A year later we were ready. A visit to the 'quack' was in order and he told me I would never make it. 'You've got plenty of muscle and you're very fit, but by the time you get halfway you will have lost all your muscle and you will have nothing left. You need to put on at least twenty pounds in weight or you're not going to make it.'

Sobering stuff. I embarked on a wonderful three weeks of shovelling burgers, pasta, apple crumbles and ice cream into my tum without any regrets. It made the whole journey worthwhile.

We flew to Antarctica and camped at Patriot Hills where a company called Antarctic Logistics & Expeditions (ALE) built a camp for Antarctic expeditions every year near the Hercules Inlet. ALE was a logistics company. They were the best.

The boss was Mike Sharp, a fantastic man in whose hands we could be placing our lives. We had a small Dakota aircraft on standby at the camp in case of disaster. But the reality of finding someone in Antarctica from the air is that it's not easy, particularly if they have fallen down a crevasse.

Antarctica is the coldest place in the world and the windiest. Winds in the winter can reach 200mph and temperatures can descend to -82 degrees. Nothing lives in Antarctica, not even bacteria. We soon found our path was not as smooth as we had thought. Massive blocks of ice and frozen waves are strewn across the white plateau. These waves are frozen by the icy katabatic winds which roll down the mountain and gouge out cracks and blocks of ice known as sastrugi. Sometimes we could walk round this sastrugi; at others we had to walk over it hauling our sledges. Our sledges each weighed 155kg, laden with our food, tents, our equipment and above all our fuel for an estimated two and a half months. You cannot drink snow as a thirst-quencher. It freezes the oesophagus and we obviously could not carry water. You get your vital water by boiling the snow, in which you also boil the dried rations. Therefore the fuel supply really is critical and it is also the heaviest burden.

It was a long journey from sea level to 9,300 feet and not without incidents.

One day we finally made a rendezvous with Jeffa and Colin. They had scoured the landscape and eventually could see two little black dots on a vast white board and they landed next to our tent. It was a joyous moment and there was dancing in the snow. They gave us nothing and we refused even a bar of chocolate. Ours was to be a totally unsupported journey. But it was a wonderful moment. As they flew off, I felt a pang of envy, watching them flying off in their warm helicopter whilst we were left with still another six weeks of pulling our sledges in the freezing cold of Antarctica.

And then two days later we learned through our satellite telephone that they had crashed. A disaster. The helicopter a total write-off. Colin with a broken back, Jeffa with a broken arm and smashed ribs. The signal of the crash was picked up by chance in Scotland at three in the morning and ALE were alerted. After four hours they found them and brought them back to

Patriot Hills in a twin Otter. A Russian plane had just landed the day before at Patriot Hills and flew them to a hospital in Santiago.

It was a very close thing. And a huge thank you to the Russian pilots whom I met later. They were great guys. We waited a day to see if they were going to be okay or not, in which case we would abandon our trip and return to Santiago. What a wait that was!

Finally, the news came through that Jeffa was fine and Colin also but he would take longer to recover. Justin flew over from Hong Kong and took Jeffa back home and they all spent New Year with the family. I could relax.

Sort of. Onwards into the snowy blizzards we went, Pen and I. We still had another 600 miles to slog through deepening snow and I had lost my skis and one of the runners on my sledge. That made me the first man to make it to the pole without skis.

We made it in fifty-eight days.

A reporter from The Times was there to meet us, Sara Wheeler. She came rushing up as we arrived and asked me how I felt. I said, 'I don't care if I never see another fucking snowflake in my life.'

She managed to get that quote in the paper, verbatim, as 'The Quote of the Day'.

CHAPTER XXXIII

DEUTSCHE PLUS

Deutsche Bank turned out to be an interesting interval for me. I was interviewed by members of the bank's board known as the *Vorstand*, firstly by a director called Ulrich Cartellieri, who would be my boss, and then by Hilmar Kopper, the chairman of this bank, one of the largest in the world.

Kopper said at our first meeting, 'Simon, there are two groups in this bank. The group that does the work and the other group that takes the credit. If I was you, I'd join the first group. Less competition!'

In the discussion with Cartellieri regarding salary, I said I would be happy with salary and bonus and there was no need for a pension. I had already had my experience with pension schemes with Jardine Matheson. He understood. They paid me very well. Double what I was getting at Hutchison.

I had also been offered a job by Arnold Weinstock at GEC, as his successor. He offered £220,000, and said, 'I can't do more, but I can give you some stock options.' I declined – sadly, because I liked him well, but greed prevailed and I liked the Deutsche Bank role in Asia more. It was my stomping ground.

I was appointed the executive chairman of Asia Pacific. This was actually quite heavy stuff. Deutsche Bank was one of the largest banks in the world. Essentially a commercial bank but like many other commercial banks they looked at the American investment banks with envy and saw that their return on equity was far greater than that of the commercial banks. They eventually bought Morgan Grenfell, a moderate-sized UK investment bank as their point of entry into investment banking. They paid a billion dollars for it, with which they could have bought Morgan Stanley at the time, which might have been a better deal. It was quite clear to me after a few meetings in Frankfurt with the *vorstand* that the directors of this great bank did not have the slightest clue about investment banking.

We had offices in seventeen countries is Asia and I toured them regularly, learning much about these countries which extended my knowledge of the continent ever further. I often met senior government officials and particularly finance ministers, including my old friend Tengku Razaleigh. When we opened our bank in the Philippines, President Ramos came to the opening event and made much of the fact that we were both paratroopers. It was a fun occasion.

The important thing for me of course, was that I met many interesting people who banked with us, and my 'who's who book' continued to get fatter. There were not many doors on which I could not knock in Asia by the time I had finished my four years.

I had hired Geoff Spender, who had been with me at Hutchison. Geoff became my finance director. A very able man with numbers and he had very good pair of eyes. I valued his opinion. And I enjoyed working with Ulrich Cartellieri enormously and when he retired, I felt it was time for me to go too. His successor, Josef Ackerman, was not my 'cuppa' at all.

The Asian finance crisis of 1997 was just the start. It was triggered when the Bank of Thailand de-pegged its currency from the American dollar. The Thai baht dropped like a stone and other Asian currencies followed, with an average fall of 40 per cent across the board in Malaysia, Indonesia, South Korea, the Philippines and the rest. Hong Kong held firm with its dollar still pegged to the US dollar.

Meanwhile Ackerman, an ex-investment banker from Credit Suisse, had progressed and was not just my boss but had succeeded in becoming the head of the bank. He had one ratio fixed on his mind, 'return on equity'. He was besotted by the fact that American investment banks made 25 per cent return on equity and Deutsche Bank only 8 per cent.

The reason was twofold. The American banks were more leveraged than Deutsche Bank and Deutsche Bank was traditionally a commercial bank: less risk but far less upside. In addition they had very limited knowledge of investment banking, which is why they decided that the best way to enter was to purchase Morgan Grenfell. Wrong bank.

Ackerman brought in an ex-Merrill Lynch executive called Edson Mitchell and between himself and Mitchell, they completely changed the character of the bank. They also started the bank down a dark road of mischief-making with money laundering for Russian oligarchs and monkeying with LIBOR

(London Interbank Offered Rate) rates. They dived into the mortgage-backed securities business, trading on their own account in derivatives and other trading games invented by investment banks such as Lehman Brothers, all backed up with collateral debt obligations. All businesses in which Deutsche Bank had no historical experience.

These were businesses which collectively created the seeds of the global financial crisis of 2008. Securitising mortgages, rating them as triple AAA, which they weren't, and selling them off to the unsuspecting punters in the capital markets. Deutsche Bank was later fined billions of dollars and its reputation for being one of the great banks of the world was ruined.

Mitchell died in a plane crash in 2000. He was forty-seven years old. Ackerman rowed the boat alone and brought the bank's reputation to its lowest level since the war. In the Second World War it financed the construction of Auschwitz. I suppose they had no choice with Adolf telling them what to do. But this time they did have a choice.

I may not have seen the Asian financial crash coming but I saw where Ackerman was taking the bank. I decided to start my own business again. This time, I was going into the private equity business.

CHAPTER XXXIV

RIDING THE ROLLERCOASTER OF FUND MANAGEMENT

General Enterprise Management Services is not a very memorable name for a company in the business of fund management, but 'GEMS' is. Thus, I named the new company. We would find GEMS in the ashes of Asia. This was one year after the Asian crisis that had bankrupted thousands and brought Asia to its knees.

I decided to raise a fund of US$300 million. I needed a lot of things. Most importantly, I needed good people. I had to have a plan as to what we were going to invest in and where. I needed to create a story about GEMS that would appeal to investors. This was a first-time fund. We had no track record.

I went to see Jack Welch, head of General Electric in the States. The late Jack Welch was highly regarded as one of the most able managers in America. He had turned GE into one of the most respected companies there. I had first met him when I was running Hutchison and he had stayed to lunch. GE had a finance company and they invested US$25 million in our fund, on the condition that they could also invest in GEMS the management company. I asked him why he was doing it.

He said, 'Simon, GE is a battleship in the harbour. You are a speedboat. You go five times round the harbour before we get out of bed in the morning. You will find us some good investments.'

I liked that. Jack was one of my heroes. It was wonderful to have him involved and it generated huge credibility for GEMS. Michael Dobson at Morgan Grenfell, backed up by Cartellieri, persuaded Deutsche Bank to invest US$14 million for a 10 per cent stake in GEMS. Henry Kissinger invested, and so did N.M. Rothschild. They were joined by Lombard Odier, Dubai Investment Authority and Richemont as well as investors from France, Australia, Italy and Qatar. But the very first investor was K.S. Li. He came up to me at a cocktail party and in front of everybody said, 'Simon, I invest in your new company $10 million.' Another one of my heroes. His son Victor was within earshot and looked as though he had swallowed a fork. We raised our $300 million and GEMS had a capital of about $30 million. It felt good.

The advisory board members included the good and the great. John Craven accepted the position as chairman. Johnny Louden joined us and so did Henry Kissinger; Ron Herman from GEC; Jurgen Schrempe chairman of Daimler Benz; Johann Rupert chairman of Richemont; Ebihara, a managing director of Mitsubishi; Toyo Honda, chairman of Japan Tobacco; Endo-san a director of Mitsui and of course my old and wise friend Michael Green. Others included Harry-Fitzgibbon, Charles Powell, who had been Maggie Thatcher's chief of staff, the former Canadian Prime Minister Brian Mulroney, Ken Courtis, the international economist, Haki Singh from Deutsche Bank, Ananda Krishnan from Malaysia, an old friend from days gone by, at that time selling wallpaper but now a multi-billionaire with interests in oil and telephones. And finally Ronnie Grierson, a man of many hats known universally.

What a fantastic team we had.

In addition to the advisory board, we had a formidable local management team. There was Winston Leung, Kevin Yip, Godfrey Ngai, Angela Wong, Kelly Wong and Jane Mackenzie in London. Jane Mackenzie had married John Mackenzie the managing director of the Chartered bank, who had lent me start-up money for Davenham; that now seemed such a long time ago.

Geoff Spender was the best back-office guardian a company could have and he ensured no bad apples fell under the table. They were a dedicated group and all with a good sense of humour, who could sustain the ups and downs of business.

We would be paid 2 percent per annum on the funds raised and 20 per cent of the profits generated on our investments. I had promised Cartellieri we would never leverage the fund, so we were not going to be able to beat the returns generated by US funds, which were often leveraged up to their eyeballs. We got off to a good start with an investment of US$12 million for a 25 per cent stake in a very techy company in Japan, called Yozan. It went public a year later and we sold half our position for $100 million.

Over the next ten years, we invested over a billion dollars in Asia. We invested in companies like the National Steel Company of Singapore and we built the Trisara Hotel in Thailand and sold out at twice our initial investment. Now it is probably the best hotel in Phuket and maybe in the whole of Thailand.

But it was not all plain sailing and we ran into periodic head winds. In 2001, the Islamic attack on the twin towers of the World Trade Centre in New York sent markets spiralling downwards. In 2008 the global financial crisis didn't help our cause. Every hill climbed has a downside.

Morgan Grenfell, the Deutche Bank-wholly-owned subsidiary, was in the fund management business, supported by the Deutsche Bank army of trusting investors. They had invested in Formula One racing. I had met Bernie Ecclestone, the founder of Formula One, through my friend Lawrence Stroll, who was a big player in racing. I probably knew more about Formula One than the boys in Morgan Grenfell and I liked it as a business. They had five billion viewers worldwide. We gave Morgan Grenfell US$25 million to invest in it and they had an option to increase their shareholding from 12 per cent to 49 per cent by a certain date. They missed the date and Ecclestone sold the shares to another American fund.

When it dawned on Morgan Grenfell that they had missed the boat, they got into a fight with Ecclestone and finally, outraged and in a fit of bad temper, they exchanged their shares, without telling us what they were doing, for shares in a German television company. They declared that they had researched the company and the share price was going to the moon, based on a report by Merrill Lynch! The deal was done before we could register our disapproval and the television company went bust six months later.

I met Ackerman – my old nemesis and still in charge of Deutsche Bank – at breakfast in New York and told him we were going to sue Deutsche for negligence. He didn't give a damn and said they would drag the case out until we went bankrupt. I explained that I had already got a law firm which would take our case on in perpetuity, for a percentage cut, as they were so sure we would win. I even showed him the lawyer's letter confirming this. Ackerman nearly choked on his bacon and eggs but remained nonchalant and feigned disinterest. Eventually, with some support from Cartellieri and

Breuer, we bought out their equity in GEMS for a dollar and they gave us some compensation for the Formula One loss.

'Bigness' is not always an indication of 'best'. When Morgan Grenfell had purchased the shares in Formula One, they had valued the company at $700 million. Four years after they exchanged the shares for the rotten German TV Station, the company was valued at $4 billion and eventually sold shares at a valuation of US$6 billion.

In 2015, I took a step back from GEMS and became non-executive and passed the reins to David Van Oppen. The old team left and took off in different directions and Van Oppen formed a new squad. It was not the same. I drifted away from GEMS and in spirit I was gone.

I had met many Japanese company heads by this time and periodically l had been asked to give interviews to the Japanese press. My knowledge of Japan had widened after our success in the Singapore Mass Transit railway project and I had numerous contacts. One day, in discussion with the chairman of the Development Bank of Japan (DBJ), he raised the question of an investment by the bank in GEMS. The DBJ at this time was government-owned and they were about to be privatised. An investment in GEMS would give them far more freedom than that provided by their current bureaucratic ministers and they were making plans to expand their activities. They were very excited about GEMS in Hong Kong. One of their plans was to buy into GEMS and then float us on the Japanese stock exchange. They valued GEMS at US$100 million and bought 20 per cent of the company. We paid out US$10 million to the shareholders of GEMS as a special dividend and capitalised the balance.

And then 'sod's law' stepped in. There was a massive tsunami in northern Japan, at Fukushima, with the resulting explosion of a nuclear power plant and Japan in freeze. There were huge floods in the north and a tsunami that destroyed villages and killed many people. All privatisations were cancelled and DBJ as far as we were concerned went under the table. The listing on the stock market was buried and forgotten and it was a while before DBJ surfaced. When they did, they were back in their bureaucratic government mode, requiring permission even to go to the loo. Nevertheless, we had benefitted from their share purchase and it gave us credibility to have a huge Japanese bank behind us. Even if it was a government body.

Fund management is not an easy business. There are many ups and downs along the way. But overall, GFMS generated a return of around 12 per cent per annum. Not fantastic but with interest rates averaging 6 per cent it was acceptable. Investors in GEMS the management company made on average two and a half times their money. And, most importantly, it was fun.

CHAPTER XXXV

IT'S WHO YOU KNOW

A funny thing happened one day. A previous life came back for a visit. When I was working in Hong Kong, the British Chamber of Commerce rang me and asked if one of their people could come and see me. I thought it was going to be a trade talk. Could we perhaps buy more from the UK?

It wasn't.

The man introduced himself and then opened up with, 'How's Paul?'

A long pause from me and then suddenly my thoughts: was this possible?

'Are you talking about "Paul" Paulson?' I asked, amazed.

'Yes' he said.

'Christ! So you're from 'the firm'?'

'Yes' again.

'Well I haven't seen Paul for a while but I think he's fine.'

'The firm' never lets go, as they had indicated when I had last seen them nearly twenty years earlier. They wanted a little 'favour' at first and from there it went on for ten years. It wasn't James Bond stuff; and there was little need for either my fists or my pistol, but I was in a unique position to help them… and why not? I did my duty. Having served France, why not provide a helping hand to Great Britain? I was happy to have obliged.

I kept riding along as the 'universal' independent director in companies that I respected and in which I often held shares. All independent non-executive directors of companies should have shares. It keeps them focused and reminds them that they are supposed to be working for *all* the shareholders, including themselves. Life became easier, without daily operational requirements. There were more days for climbing hills, even though at a slower pace, but the outside directorships kept me in the loop and connected.

GEMS had invested in China National Offshore Oil Company (CNOOC) and they asked me to join the board. I also spent time on the board of the largest steel company in Europe, Usinor Sacilor. My old and very dear friends Silas Chou and Lawrence Stroll insisted I become a director of Tommy Hilfiger. And the late and great Jean-Louis Dumas asked me to join the board of Hermès. Later, Johann Rupert invited me to join the Richemont board. They were great years with Richemont. My old friend Jürgen Schrempp was also on the board there and it really was a group who became good friends. The boss, Johann Rupert, blended us into an excellent *équipe*.

I was an advisor to the board of Lightbridge, a nuclear fuel company in the States and also to Rothschild's under Evelyn de Rothschild. I was on the board of Edward Cheng's property company in Hong Kong. Edward Cheng was an old intern of mine at Hutchison in days of yore. I became a director of Vivendi, the company which founded the Suez Canal but which was now in everything from book publishing to owning Universal Films in the United States. They never offered me a part in a movie! How disappointing! (that hope had been the real reason for my accepting a place on the board).

I spent twenty years on the board of the shipping company OOCL, originally the company founded by C.Y. Tung, at one time the largest shipping company in the world. The Tungs were great friends over many years. Back in the mid-eighties, they nearly went bankrupt but were rescued by mainland China. All the creditors accepted a refinancing deal except Jardine's, who were owed the paltry sum of US$2 million, out of a total debt of about $800 million. C.H. Tung, the son of C.Y. Tung, later to become the first Chief Executive of Hong Kong after the handover in 1997, was talking to me one day about their situation and I said I would see if I could persuade Simon Keswick to get in line with all the other creditors for an extended payback arrangement. If Simon did not agree, it could pull down the whole company. If one creditor breaks ranks, then all the others could come charging in.

I went to see Simon on Tung's behalf to explain that if Jardine's did not fall in line with the other creditors, then the deal would fall through and he would be the guy who forced the collapse of one of the most famous shipping companies in the world, and that would be Jardine's legacy. After a while he came around and the company was saved.

I joined the OOCL Board at C.H.'s invitation. We sold the company twenty years later to a mainland Chinese company, COSCO, for US$6 billion. Cosco had been our partners back in the Hutchison days at HIT. I had sold them 10 per cent after we had made the drastic overbid for terminal seven.

I stayed on boards that I enjoyed, where there was lots of dialogue and different views from wise men.

And then there was Glencore – the largest commodities trading company in the world of which I became chairman for three years. It all came about because of a one-to-one conversation with Ivan Glasenberg in Klosters. One evening, my friend Nat Rothschild came to my apartment and said, 'Ivan Glasenberg wants you to be chairman of Glencore. He's here in Klosters and wants to meet you tomorrow.'

'I'm leaving tomorrow,' I responded.

Nat picked up the phone and rang Ivan. 'He'll drive you to the airport,' he said. It was a one-hour drive and in that time the deal was done. I had met him in South Africa many moons previously and indeed bought coal from his company. I liked him. The market had Lord Browne as the front runner for this post, but Ivan and his managers turned him down when they had met him. Browne said he had rejected the offer because he had concerns about Glencore's corporate governance. This was bollocks but fine with me.

More proof that the world just keeps going around.

Another coincidence which I cannot let pass occurred in 2020.

Out of the blue I received an email from a captain in the British Army who was based in the Sudan at the time. He said he had just finished reading my book, *Legionnaire*, in which he had read about my trip to South America on the St *Arvans*. I had replaced the galley boy, Martin Fisher who had gone sick, and then three years later I had met him by chance in Algeria. And now nearly sixty years later an email from Johnny, who was Martin Fisher's son. He told me his father had passed away, but when he returned from the Sudan, we had a great dinner together in London.

What a world.

CHAPTER XXXVI

LESSONS LEARNT

A recent event that would be an appropriate moment to end this tale would be the story of the flag.

I went to the offices of Edmond de Rothschild in London one day, to discuss some business. Their office was at No. 4 Carlton Gardens. No. 4 Carlton Gardens was the office where I had been interviewed by MI6 after my service in the Foreign Legion some fifty-five years earlier. I had been interviewed by John Briance, who had informed me, *en passant*, that this had been the headquarters of General de Gaulle, who had commanded the Free French forces during the Second World War. I now stood in front of Richard Briance and told him about the interview of so long ago. He said, 'John Briance was my father.' When I told him about de Gaulle, he became hugely excited.

'We've only been in this building for six weeks,' he said, 'but when we arrived, we found an old French flag rolled up in the cellar. It's still there, I think.'

We went down to the cellar and there was this huge, rolled-up, dust-covered French flag with a cross of Lorraine in the middle. It was clearly de Gaulle's flag. De Gaulle had put the cross of Lorraine on his flag in response to the Nazi swastika on the German flag. At the end of the war, de Gaulle had left in a hurry to get back to Paris for the victory parade down the Champs-Élysées. It was not surprising that he left a couple of things behind.

I knew immediately that I had to get this flag back to France. A legionnaire bringing de Gaulle's flag back to France would wipe away all the ill-feeling created by the *putsch* against de Gaulle in 1961 which still lingered in many hearts and older minds. The Legion had never really been forgiven for the *putsch* and would always be blamed by those that did not understand that the Legion was *used*. The Legion did not instigate the coup d'état.

Briance said he would have to check with his chairlady in Switzerland, Arianne de Rothschild, before he could release the flag. But then Briance suddenly left Rothschild's and a new man took over called Eric Coutts. Coutts could smell publicity for Rothschild's in all this and he started to fob me off. He said that he had had the flag tested and it could not have been made at the time because synthetic fibre had not been invented until long after the war. I gave him a bit of history to dispel his information.

Before the war, Dupont had invented Dacron and ICI, in the UK, were producing Terylene cloth: both were synthetic. ICI built a factory in the same state in which Dupont operated in the United States and were producing essentially the same cloth, but with a different name, Dacron. The 'antitrust' boys in the US got active and so Dupont and ICI went off and built a factory in Germany and called it New York/London. Thus was born NY-LON. I explained to the ignorant Coutts that synthetic fibre *was* used before the war. Coutts, however, kept up the fight and refused to hand over the flag.

I went to Switzerland and through the introduction of a good friend, managed to fix an appointment with Arianne de Rothschild one evening at 7pm in her office. When I arrived, everybody had gone except the security officer. I was shown into Arianne's office and she offered me a glass of red. She was absolutely charming. Over the next hour, I told her the story about the *putsch* in 1961 and my involvement and why it would mean so much if I could return the flag to France. She agreed and said she would instruct Coutts to give it to me.

But Coutts continued to resist, saying the flag had to be given to the de Gaulle Foundation, of which he was a member, and all sorts of rubbish. Eventually Arianne got involved again at my request and told him to hand it over at 11am on a particular Friday. Very precise.

Coutts rang the French Embassy and said he could give it to them the day before this. Fortunately, the Embassy thought I already had the flag and called me and ordered me to bring it to the Embassy immediately. I said I was going to Kazakhstan the following day and would come and see them when I got back. This was a blatant lie, but necessary under the circumstances.

The next day I was supposed to meet Coutts at his office and receive the flag. I thought Coutts would warn the Embassy and that they would send someone over to get it, so I decided to ask my good friend Field Marshal Lord Guthrie to come with me. I warned him that there might be an 'incident' and we might have to fight for it. He loved the prospects of a fight for the French flag against the French Embassy.

When we got there, Coutts had obviously given instructions for a very frigid welcome indeed. Everybody was thoroughly rude and aggressive. We suspected that Coutts was hiding upstairs in the lavatory as he failed to show. His secretary walked up with a dirty plastic dustbin bag and said, 'This is for you.' She handed me the plastic rubbish bag as though she was giving me my rejected unwashed laundry and then turned and walked out without another word. The flag was in the rubbish bag.

We left and took a photograph of Charles and I holding this huge flag in front of the entrance to No.4. Three days later the photograph was spread across the centre pages of Le Figaro in France, with the whole story of the return to France of de Gaulle's flag by a legionnaire: a full-page article by my friend Étienne de Montety, a senior journalist of the most important newspaper in France. I asked Arianne to join us in Paris, and we presented the flag to the President of the Senate in front of 300 people. It was a magnificent and most memorable occasion, with the Legion band doing the honours.

It was also a time for reflection and I thought again on my time in the Foreign Legion. It had founded l'esprit de corps in me, which has stayed with me all my life, and directed all my actions and my decisions. Words like 'honour' and 'fidelity' sound old fashioned in today's vocabulary and yet they are the very bedrocks of life. Our reputation is our most valuable asset and yet so easy to lose with one bad decision or action.

When Soto and Vignaga surprised me on my fiftieth birthday, they stayed on for a day after the party. They planted a tree in the garden of our home which has flourished ever since. They also gave me a book of Legion photos and said that we lived in different worlds and they would not see me again unless I was in trouble. I asked them how they would know if and when I was in trouble. They answered, 'We will.'

I have not seen them for thirty years and though I would love to, I am trying to stay out of trouble. I know they will honour their word. Integrity, fidelity and honour. They are qualities which will last a lifetime.

In 2020 Jeffa and I spent two months at our house in the country in Somerset. In spite of the fact that there was a global pandemic raging, it was very relaxing. My eightieth birthday arrived and Jeffa's followed three months later. We celebrated fifty-four years of marriage. But it ain't over by a long way. A Chinese feng shui man once told me, as he gazed at the palms of my hands, he could get me to 105. After that he said, I would be on my own.

We walked and swam and read books. Our grandchildren came to stay. We now have six: Nicola, Joanna, Sienna, Domingo, Talitha and Carla. Was this what retirement feels like? Maybe it is not so bad. It has provided some time for reflection. Time to philosophise.

I am the direct descendent of three rich and powerful families and yet I started out with nothing. My circumstances had been decided long before I was born. We are not 'born free' as proclaimed by Jean-Jacques Rousseau, in the opening line of his book *The Social Contract*: 'Man is born free, but everywhere he finds himself enchained.' He was wrong. Rousseau was wrong about many things! The path we tread from birth is predestined by the circumstances in which we find ourselves when we arrive on the planet. When I was born, I found myself in an air-raid shelter having the life blown out of me.

If you are born in Boston and your father is a multi-millionaire your path is predestined. You will go to Princeton, join the family firm, become president of the company, retire, play golf and die. If you are born in a Caracas slum, the trajectory of your life's path is predetermined. And if you are born in Africa and half your village has got AIDS, your path from birth is, sadly, on a steep downward slope and there is not much you can do about it.

Our first challenge in life must be to get off the path on which we are born, find some space and in that space we may find ourselves. If we find ourselves and get to know who we are, we have begun to understand the meaning of freedom. It is the freedom of the spirit which provides the energy needed for the 'walk-through' of life. We should have the confidence to do as Uri Geller says: 'When you come to a fork in the road, take it.'

If this sounds a little out of keeping with my usual light-hearted approach to life, try this instead: Life is a fun fair and we should visit the fair regularly and try all the rides, not just sit all day on the carousel. Many never get off, and just go round and round. Have courage! Try the ghost train – don't be afraid to be afraid – it is just a phase and it will pass.

Once, when I was in Marrakesh at the Hermès Villa after completing the Marathon des Sables, I was almost killed by a falling horse. The groom had told me that the horse was unrideable, completely mad. It felt like a challenge to me. I saddled up and mounted the horse. It was like a bucking bronco but I finally managed to get the animal under control. We made to leave the grounds for a trek when a motorbike roared past on the nearby road and startled the creature. It reared up again and fell backwards onto its backside. As it rolled over to right itself, it rolled over me, lying flat on my back and unconscious where it had thrown me. It broke my leg in three places. I had survived a year in the Merchant Navy, five years in the Foreign Legion, forty years in the Asian business world as well as some of the natural world's most hostile environments and yet I very nearly met my end thanks to a great hunk of horse. Another time I was chased by a leopard and discovered first-hand just how fast they can move. They move *very* fast! My advantage: a quick brain. I couldn't talk my way out of that one but I certainly had to think quickly.

Get off the ghost train and onto the big dipper. It is the most exciting ride of all. The view from the top is exhilarating.

Climb the mountains of life. There are many. Take risks. From time to time you will have to come down into the valleys in order to get up the next mountain. Keep climbing. We know that variety is the spice of life. Get out into the sunshine of life.

Learn and lead by example. Live by your principles. We have been told all this before, but we tend to forget it in our busy lives. Do things that will take your breath away. These experiences will give you stories to tell, like abseiling down the Shard, which I did shortly before it opened in 2013. It was terrifying, but I did it.

Make good friends. In Sydney Smith's words: 'Life is to be fortified by many friendships' and I have made many, many good friends. Friends who you can trust with your life and for whom you would do the same. Friends like Soto and Vignaga who travelled a continent to make a rendezvous; friends like John MacKenzie and his wife Jane, K.S. Li, Michael Green, Willy Purves, Stanley Weiss, Alan Johnson-Hill, Michael Stapleton, Benjamin Ntim and all the others who know who they are. People who will put not only their faith but their money into supporting you and your endeavours. My publisher has refused permission to put in any more names, which he says will double the size of the book and the printing costs.

Yes, life is serious, but try not to take it too seriously. The best passport through life is a good sense of humour.

And remember, above all, nobody will shoot you if you make them laugh.

Horace Carpe Diem. From Horace's Odes –

> What time the gods have fixed for us to go.
> The best astrologer can't calculate a thing like that,
> So let's just face our fate.
> Are there more winters marked for you and me?
> Or is the present one which tires the sea
> With constant crashing on the cliffs, our last?
> Who can say? Our lives flit by so fast.
> Be wise and mix the wine.
> More time had passed as I've been speaking.
> Yes it hurries on.
> Don't hope or fear
> But seize today – you must
> And treat tomorrow with complete mistrust

END

ACKNOWLEDGEMENTS

My thanks to Margareta Pagano for all her encouragement particularly in the early stages of the book and for getting the show on the road. To Lucie Skilton, my editor, who really understood me and what I wanted to say. Her contributions have been wonderful. To John Godfray for jogging my memory on key events and dates. To the team at Unicorn for keeping the wheels on the ground and getting this done.